BIBLE STC
FOR
CLASSROOM AND A

THE NEW TESTAMENT

Jack G. Priestley
Principal, Westhill College, Birmingham

With Ideas for Exploring Further by

Angela M. Horton
Lecturer in Primary Education, Exeter University

RMEP

RELIGIOUS AND MORAL EDUCATION PRESS

Religious and Moral Education Press
An imprint of Chansitor Publications Ltd,
a wholly owned subsidary of Hymns Ancient & Modern Ltd
St Mary's Works, St Mary's Plain
Norwich, Norfolk NR3 3BH

Stories first published 1981 under the title
Bible Stories for Today. The New Testament

This edition first published 1992

ISBN 0 900274-54-9

Designed and illustrated by Topics Visual Information, Exeter

Cover photograph by William Pridie

Typeset by ICON, Exeter

Printed in Great Britain by BPCC Wheatons Ltd, Exeter
for Chansitor Publications Ltd, Norwich

Preface
to
First Edition

In attempting to retell these Bible stories I have been conscious of trying to do four things.

First, I have tried to write for children. In so doing I hope I have avoided childish writing. The Bible is not childish. Its children grew up quickly in a world which was often harsh and uncompromising. Insipid characters were rare and reviled. Drama, excitement and danger were never far away.

Secondly, I have tried to be honest. The Bible narrative is based on history. That does not mean that all its stories are historical stories. There are stories of inner struggles as well as outer ones. Religiously speaking the former are more important than the latter. In my experience this seems to worry adults more than children, for whom the inner world is often very real.

Thirdly, I have tried not to moralize or sermonize. A good story tells itself, although sometimes its original context needs explanation. Experience has caused me to reject the belief that children should not be given these stories until they can understand them. Great stories, like great music, poetry and art, are never fully understood. Rather we go on unpacking layer after layer of meaning as the years go by. Interpretation goes on at a variety of levels. At the heart of all religion lies a mystery.

Finally, I have tried to keep a balance over the whole of the Bible literature. Harsh selection has been unavoidable, but I have given priority to those stories which contribute to the development of The Story. The Bible is a unified collection of religious experiences. That is the wonder of it. Against those experiences we can measure our own and grow accordingly. That, I believe, is why we have a duty to go on telling these stories. That is why our children have a right to hear them.

J.G.P.

For
Matthew Brault and his generation

Contents

Note: Where a new title has been given to an already familiar story the traditional title is given in brackets.

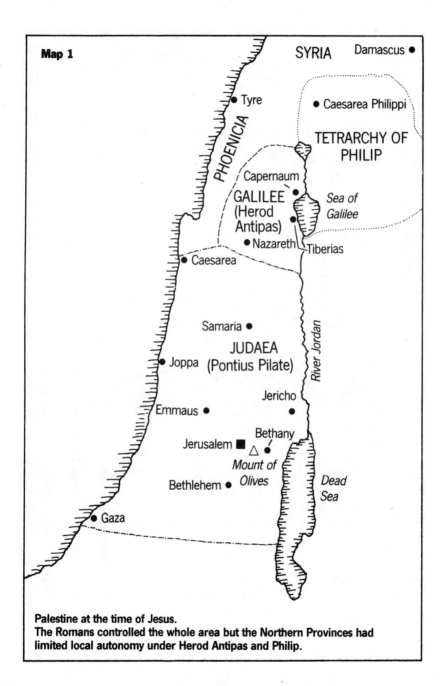

Map 1

SYRIA   Damascus ●

● Tyre   ● Caesarea Philippi

PHOENICIA

TETRARCHY OF
PHILIP

Capernaum

GALILEE ●
(Herod
Antipas)

Sea of
Galilee

● Nazareth
● Caesarea   Tiberias

Samaria ●

JUDAEA
● Joppa   (Pontius Pilate)

River Jordan

Jericho
Emmaus ●   ●

Bethany
Jerusalem ■ △ ●
Mount of
Bethlehem ●   Olives

Dead
Sea

● Gaza

Palestine at the time of Jesus.
The Romans controlled the whole area but the Northern Provinces had
limited local autonomy under Herod Antipas and Philip.

1

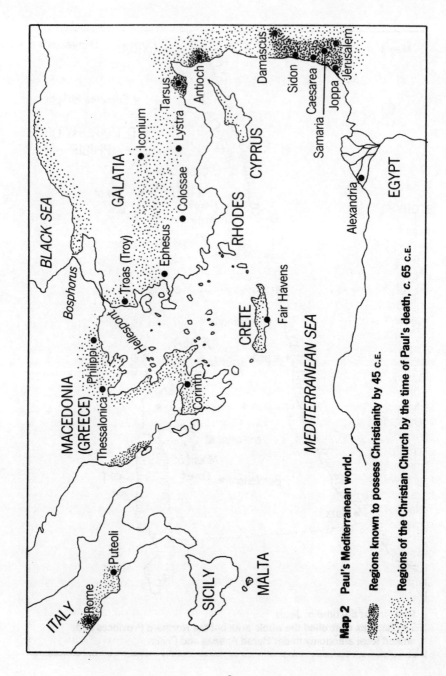

Map 2 Paul's Mediterranean world.

Regions known to possess Christianity by 45 C.E.

Regions of the Christian Church by the time of Paul's death, c. 65 C.E.

BLACK SEA

Bosphorus

Hellespont

MACEDONIA
(GREECE)

Thessalonica

Philippi

Corinth

GALATIA

Troas (Troy)

Ephesus

Iconium

Lystra

Colossae

Tarsus

Antioch

CRETE

RHODES

Fair Havens

CYPRUS

Damascus

Sidon

Samaria Caesarea

Joppa

Jerusalem

Alexandria

EGYPT

MEDITERRANEAN SEA

ITALY

Rome

Puteoli

SICILY

MALTA

Introduction
Story, Truth and Bible

STORY AND STORIES

'Read the Bible like any other book,' said the poet Samuel Taylor Coleridge, 'and you will quickly discover it is not like any other book you have ever read.'

This is exactly what we do not seem to be capable of doing any more, particularly in schools. Many teachers appear extremely uncomfortable with the Bible. They give all sorts of reasons which often appear more defensive than rational and frequently contradict one another. For example, many say that they cannot teach Bible stories because they do not believe them but they become confused very quickly when asked just what that means. To make matters even more complex the same teachers will very often be found using stories from other religious traditions, for example, from Hindu mythology, apparently with no qualms, even when they do not regard themselves as belonging to those faiths either.

Others will argue that it is not possible to gain the same enjoyment from Bible stories as from other literature because they are somehow 'special' or 'holy'. In other words interpretations are prescribed beforehand and consequently both children and teachers are inhibited from giving free rein to their own imaginations. Again these teachers are often at pains to point out that they do not regard themselves as believers. It is usually someone else's tradition they are safeguarding. In the main this group are what we might term alienated Christians. Jews (and we must remember that, apart from St Luke, who wrote one of the Gospels and The Acts of the Apostles, all the New Testament writers were probably Jews by culture before they were Christians by conversion) seem to have far less of a problem. By and large they can relax in their own Scriptures, which Christians refer to as the Old Testament, enjoy them, laugh with them in places, argue with them in others and generally treat them as a normal and indispensable part of any education which is concerned with passing on the culture. Christians, especially those of the Protestant tradition, seem to have the greatest difficulty in following Coleridge's advice.

There is a third group which simply says that this material is old fashioned, out of date and boring. They argue that neither teachers nor children see the point in using it any more. There are simply more important things to fill up curriculum time with. In its own way this attitude is as confessional as its opposite, based as it is on minds already

3

convinced that their evaluation is final and not subject to challenge or change. To this group there is only one answer and it is the Coleridgean one – give the Bible a chance, try it and see. These stories must survive on their own merit but honesty must surely serve to make us recognize that they have already survived longer than most and that perhaps there are reasons for that, contained within the stories themselves. It has to be said that the argument of this group is more persuasive when it is based on some knowledge of what is being rejected.

The first two arguments are more subtle because they involve factors other than straight reasoning. There is confusion, there is often a sense of guilt and there is, most of all, an awareness of deep ignorance. Coleridge was fortunate. He was involved right at the beginning of the whole opening up of the Bible to scientific criticism. In his time he probably understood what was starting to happen, especially in Germany, better than any other person in Britain but it did not worry him. He was a poet and he knew a great deal about the nature of poetry and how poets, as distinct from scientists, went about searching for and expressing truth. However, when he advised us to read the Bible like any other book it was not a scientific textbook or even necessarily a history book he had in mind. Read the Bible, he was saying, just like any other book of stories and then find out for yourself whether it is just like any other story-book. It seems a fair test.

In terms of school knowledge the question is one of entitlement. Rabbi Lionel Blue in one of his 'Thought for the Day' broadcasts on BBC Radio 4 illustrated this perfectly when he pin-pointed the familiar issue of telling stories which we may or may not believe in, but gave it an unexpected twist. He cited a Jewish woman who was held by some of her friends to be something of a hypocrite because she claimed not to have any religious beliefs but, nevertheless, in her own words, 'kept the observances' for her children. Her reply to her accusers was simple. 'What right have I to break the tradition? Maybe they will want to become believers even if I don't.' We cannot escape the charge of indoctrination simply on grounds of content. To deny access to this material is as prescriptive as to permit it. It is how we use it which makes the difference.

The school's job is primarily to inform. Quite apart from any questions of personal belief and faith, not to know these stories is to break with tradition, to cut a future generation off from much which has permeated the past and to leave it ignorant and alienated from much of its history, its literature, its music, its art and architecture and the general rhythm of its life, which is the legacy of its traditional religion and even of its attitude towards other faiths. The languages of Europe retain thousands of biblical images, even if many of them seem to be used nowadays mainly as profanities. Every city, town and village possesses its church. Less discernible but most persistent of all, many of our moral and cultural attitudes come out of the biblical experience whether we like it or not. The 'hidden curriculum' is a relatively modern invention of a society which perhaps would rather not know where its values come from.

At the same time those who do not know where they stand have problems in moving forward. The stories in this book are some of the most influential expressions of the values of Western civilization. That is why our children are entitled to know them and to explore them. Professionally speaking the individual teacher's personal beliefs

4

about the Bible are of no more significance than their personal opinions about Roundheads and Cavaliers, but then that too is a piece of English history impossible to teach adequately to pupils with no knowledge of the Bible.

Coleridge's first suggestion then was that we should simply try to tell Bible stories like any other story. His second point, however, is that when we do so we are likely to find that they are in some sense different. The important thing is to realize that the educational discovery has to be that way round. If what he says is true then children will discover it **for themselves**. If it is not true then that is the end of it for that particular child. What is not acceptable is for children to be told beforehand that these stories are different so that they are never fully attended to as story because other considerations get in the way. The child must always be free to gather insights which the teacher may lack. For what Coleridge is saying is distinctive about these stories is not that they are made special or in some way sanctified by any external body but that the material itself simply goes deeper than other literature.

There are, very broadly speaking, three categories of story. There is, first, the ephemeral 'soap opera' type which merely reflects, and thereby reinforces, social mores. Its primary function is to entertain and it rarely does more than that as it fills our television screens, magazines and many books.

Secondly, there is that to which we attribute the title 'literature'. Literature endures. It possesses a depth which goes beyond the circumstances of the story itself, and the term covers a whole range from Shakespeare to folk-tales. It holds a mirror up to life, points to something basic in the human condition and, in doing so, confronts us with ourselves. Literature has to do with ethics (ideals) as much as with mores (how we actually behave) and, for that reason, has an important part to play in moral education in its own right. We teach literature because children are entitled to be aware of the highest and the best that humankind has conceived, as well as of what humanity is really like.

There is then a third category, to which we give the name 'myth'. It does not help that our contemporary use of language has distorted that word to the point where it has become counterproductive to use it. Just as story-telling has become synonymous with lying so a myth is generally seen as something which is untrue, a classic example of what Wittgenstein called the 'bewitchment of language'.

Perhaps we need to start again and simply resort to using the original Greek word *mythos* if only because the term is vacuous and not soiled by prejudice from the start. *Mythos* represents the deepest story form of all. It comes nearer to poetry than anything else, which is perhaps why poets recognize its value more quickly than the rest of us. If we search for a modern analogy then the seemingly unlikely image of the warhead of a cruise missile is not inappropriate. We are told that it is very small, not much larger than a cricket ball, but when released it has the power to devastate whole cities and to radiate out even further. So it is, only in a constructive way, with myths or *mythoi*. In appearance they are simple and innocent little stories but they contain a highly compressed mass which, when released, influences whole civilizations, feeds whole literatures and endures not just down the centuries but down the millennia.

Thus Ted Hughes, the Poet Laureate and writer of children's fiction, can talk, in an essay entitled 'Myth and Education', of the religious myth as 'irreducible, a lump of the world', which 'can never be diminished by the seemingly infinite mass of theological agonising ... which has attempted to translate it into something more manageable'. Hughes, it should be said, has never laid claim to 'being religious'.

What matters in teaching these stories is simply that children should know and enjoy them. It is Ted Hughes again who talks of children 'entering and leaving such stories at will'. We do not have to tell children what they mean because there are layers upon layers of meaning and none of us is able, with absolute certainty, to say that we have the final, conclusive meaning. The stories must be left open and not closed off from future exploration. But we cannot enter into them and explore them at all unless we are told them in the first place.

So much, then, for story but we have still left the vexed question of truth untouched.

TRUTH AND TRUTHS

If truth remains the problem then it is a problem which is vested not so much in these stories as in ourselves. Pontius Pilate's question 'What is truth?' continues to reverberate down the centuries but it is unlikely that there was ever a time when the question was more urgent than it is now. It is education's task to open children's eyes to the various ways in which truth is communicated but we in the West in general, and in Britain in particular, are woefully unskilled these days in the use of any form of truth criteria other than those of mathematics and science.

Philosophers are acutely aware of our difficulties but my own awareness of the depth of the problem came to me in a personal encounter some years ago. It was the hyena story which brought it about.

I was teaching at the time in a primary teacher training college in a remote part of rural Zambia. Our students came from two contrasting areas. Those from the north had been educated in village schools out in the bush and were steeped in the culture of Africa. The others came from the towns of the Copperbelt, with its Europeanized culture and its Western-style schools.

The hyena story which, for reasons I can no longer recall, we were discussing that day came from the Nyanja people of Eastern Zambia and Malawi. It was a simple story of a hungry hyena vainly searching for food. It arrived, ravenous, at a fork in the path and hesitated about which way to go. It sniffed to the left and, in the far distance, at last smelt food. Beginning to move on, it hesitated, turned its head and sniffed to the right. Again, food. Which way should it go? The hunger pains became unbearable. It moved left and right, right and left undecided and indecisive, becoming more and more frantic in its movements like a demented disco dancer. In the end, with mounting frustration, it tried to go in both directions at once, tore itself in two and died!

Was the story true? The question, for some reason, was asked. Half of the group – the Copperbelt half it later transpired – immediately burst into laughter. Of course not! No one believed that old tribal rubbish any more. The others looked increasingly hurt. 'But it is true; it is true,' they began to mutter. The laughter only increased. 'Where do you think it happened?' they were asked. They were nonplussed and could not reply. 'When did it happen?' They were pressed and pressed on these points. Was there ever

6

a time and place where all this occurred? No, but they would not give in, repeating again and again, 'It is true, it is true.' Further words of explanation failed them.

In the end it came with a rush. 'It is true. Greed kills.'

In recounting this it is not my intention to suggest that the biblical narrative is of the same literary form as this African folk-tale. I simply make the point that there are certain types of truth which are better communicated by narrative than by proposition. The Bible contains many, many different types of account. The oversimplified question 'Is it true?' means something different in each case. Children have to be taught this differentiation.

The real problem is that many modern-day adults are themselves unsure of the various types of truth claims they are dealing with. This, I am convinced, is the main reason why so many primary teachers shy away from biblical material and make their excuses. It is perfectly acceptable to debate in what sense Orwell's *Animal Farm* or Swift's *Gulliver's Travels* (both written for adults and long used with children incidentally) may contain truth but when a Hebrew writer of the fourth century B.C.E. produces an exact literary parallel, which we have come to call the Book of Jonah, we are apt to go looking for whales in the Eastern Mediterranean and to be found arguing about how long a person could survive inside a fish as way of ascertaining 'truth'! It is noticeable, however, that in the Christian New Testament there is never a problem when such a story is introduced with words such as 'He spoke a parable to them …'. Even though there has long existed the Inn of the Good Samaritan half way between Jerusalem and Jericho, few would regard it as of any significance whether the incident within the narrative actually took place or not.

The Zambian experience revealed my problem as a Westerner. I instinctively asked the question 'Is it true?' and not the much more important questions 'Does it convey truth?' or 'What does it mean?' Because we do not encourage children to ask these latter questions they can grow up missing vast areas of insight from both the past and the present. We pride ourselves on the 'knowledge explosion', the 'new knowledge', while throwing away the key which makes old knowledge still available to us. (See Addendum, p. 10.)

The question 'Is it true?' is the basic question of a scientific culture. It assumes exactness, literalism and some form of empirical verification. By contrast the question 'Does it contain truth?' belongs to the world of the arts, to the theatre audience, the concert goer and the literary critic. No exactness is looked for; a degree of subjectivity is assumed because it is recognized that the artist, in whatever form, is attempting to express and draw our attention to an inner experience which it is beyond the possibility of literal words to express. For some strange inexplicable reason we seem unable to treat any material which bears the label 'religious' in the same way even though such material is the basic inspiration of the vast majority of our art, drama, music and literature.

The philosopher Ludwig Wittgenstein catches this point exactly and very simply when he says, 'People nowadays think that scientists exist to instruct them, poets, musicians etc. to give them pleasure. The idea that these have something to teach them – that does not occur to them.' *(Culture and Value, p. 36.)*

7

In another passage in the same book he turns to the New Testament as an example of something which is not 'just a story' but is not 'just history' either. Talking specifically of the Gospels he remarks on the fact that there are four different accounts and judges this to be a good thing simply because history is not the sole or perhaps even the most important truth test with this material.

It is important that this narrative should not be more than quite averagely historically plausible **just so that** this should not be taken as the essential, decisive thing, so that the **letter** should not be believed more strongly than is proper and the **spirit** may receive its due, i.e. what you are supposed to see cannot be communicated even by the best and most accurate historian; and, therefore, a mediocre account suffices, is even to be preferred. For that too can tell you what you are supposed to be told, roughly in the way a mediocre stage set can be better than a sophisticated one, painted trees better than real ones, – because these might distract attention from what matters.

(Culture and Value, p. 31)

Adults who very freely comment on whether they 'believe in it or not' might do well to ponder these words very carefully before passing on their own certainties to children. For the one outstanding characteristic of this material is that no one has total mastery of it. It is all too easy to tell others what the story means but that is to overlook the fact that there may be layers of meaning, some of which may be seen by the teacher but some of which may not. The one great fact about religious education, which distinguishes it from other subjects, is that a young child may well have insights denied even to a university professor! It is also important to note that a gospel is not just another biography. It is a proclamation. The word means 'good news'. The good news is that the story shows that Jesus of Nazareth was the long-awaited Messiah of the Jews. Those Jews who came to believe this were the first Christians and set about spreading the Gospel to non-Jews. One third of the Gospel Story takes place in a single week – what Christians now call Holy Week. Wittgenstein's point is that the four accounts are more like four dramas or plays than four history books.

It is here too that we might add a short note on moral education. During the 1970s and 1980s the work of Lawrence Kohlberg in the U.S.A. had a significant influence on thinking about moral education in Britain and elsewhere. Basically he argued that the growth of moral understanding was a case of natural maturation towards a high point, the peak of which was a sense of detached justice. All that teachers could do was to hurry the process along, although it was of great concern to him that only a very small minority of people progressed beyond a certain point.

Space does not permit any detailed analysis of Kohlberg's position. Suffice to say that writers on religious education were among his strongest critics. In particular, Craig Dykstra in his book aptly entitled *Vision and Character* (Paulist Press, New York, 1981) argues for a much more positive approach. By this he does not mean going back to old prescriptive ways of simply trying to tell children what to do in order to be good. Rather he means putting before them examples of people who have achieved the highest standards of morality, often by challenging conventional behaviour and taking action to improve society. It is no accident that Kohlberg himself had to go outside his own research findings to pinpoint such figures as Gandhi and Martin Luther King and that they happened to be religious figures. Such people live not so much by a creed of 'what is normally done' as by some sort of vision of what the world could be like. Character is formed by the confidence which comes from knowing one's own mind and living by certain convictions rather than just mindlessly following the crowd. Stories of religious people who acted according to a strong other-worldly sense of God can play a significant part in moral education seen in this way.

BIBLE AND BOOKS

It was as long ago as 1964 that Ronald Goldman, at the conclusion of a long piece of research, declared that 'the Bible is not a children's book'. This statement had a devastating effect on the use of this material. Had he declared at the time that there was far too much of it in most syllabuses then few, if any, would have questioned his judgement. As it is it now has to be said that in his declaration he was simply wrong. There is no other part of the world in which the basic, traditional religious stories of any culture are denied to children on the grounds that they cannot be fully understood. Nobody of whatever age or intelligence has ever fully understood them. They are not that sort of material. The Bible is not a historical textbook, although it contains a lot of history. It is, first and foremost, a library, a collection of different sorts of writings compiled over a long period of time, well over a thousand years.

What the Bible really is is a collection of religious experiences and spiritual insights. All the great, enduring questions of human existence are here, including major dreams and visions for a better world. These can only be told, as it were, from the inside.

All the great religions of the world have begun in the context of one person alone, whether it was Abraham under the stars, Moses at the burning bush, Gautama Buddha under the tree, Jesus in the wilderness (or on the Cross) or the Prophet Muhammad in the cave. Inward experience can be communicated only via the medium of imagery. Often this is non-verbal and takes the form of music, dance or visual art. When language is used it is the language of metaphor and simile. There is poetry and parable, there are personal letters and public pronouncements; occasionally there is only silence. Above all there is, for us, the need to know the difference. To reduce all this to mere learning of externals is to shatter vision, to destroy dreams and to reduce the inspiration of our forebears into the pathetically mundane.

A whole generation has now grown up since the Goldman research more or less imposed a ban on the use of the Bible in school. One result has been a generation of teachers who themselves find this material strange and bewildering. This collection was originally produced as one person's response to the Goldman fallacy. It has proved popular in many schools but it was quickly realized that many teachers needed something more by way of background. This revision has tried to meet that need in as simple a way as possible, bearing in mind that teachers nowadays have little time to read and none at all to study new areas in any depth.

9

HOW TO USE THIS BOOK

The stories are presented as before to be read to or by children either in the classroom or in assembly. In addition, however, we have now added two Notes sections to each story. At the end of each telling there is a section entitled 'About the Story'. These short passages attempt to explain why the story has been written in the way it has and to give other background information. The aim is simply to allow the teacher some degree of confidence in telling the story. **These sections are not intended for study by children.**

There follows a section entitled 'Ideas for Exploring Further'. They are just that. They are not intended as a substitute for any teacher's own original ideas and they are in no way intended to be regarded as exhaustive. What Angela Horton has attempted to do is to put forward ideas which add a genuinely religious dimension of thinking to integrated topic work as opposed to turning the religious-education component back into something indistinguishable from historical or geographical input. She has also, wherever appropriate, linked up the stories to named study units and/or attainment targets within the National Curriculum, showing how religious-education work can be accommodated with integrity in mainstream work thus helping to ensure some economy of that most precious classroom commodity – time. Books mentioned in the text are listed in Appendix 1.

Abbreviations References to areas of the National Curriculum are preceded by the symbol NC. The abbreviations AT, CSU and SSU stand for 'attainment target', 'core (History) study unit' and 'supplementary (History) study unit', respectively. Stories in the companion volume *Bible Stories for Classroom and Assembly. The Old Testament* are referred to as OT Story 1, etc.

AN ADDENDUM TO THE HYENA STORY

What I was privileged to observe happening in a very short space of time in an African setting has, of course, happened in Europe over a much longer period of time. One has only to look at the entry for 'story' in the full *Oxford English Dictionary* or in any good etymological dictionary to see this.

All of the earliest examples denote a form of communication which is directly related to truth. A story is a 'narrative true or supposed to be true'. It is 'the same as history, a branch of knowledge as opposed to fiction'. However, as we move into the eighteenth century and beyond, the definitions become more and more hedged about with qualifications. A story becomes 'a recital of events alleged to have happened'. It is 'a narrative of real, or more usually fictitious events', 'a particular person's representation of a matter', until finally we reach a point where the word 'story', once synonymous with truth, is now deemed to convey the exact opposite. The last dictionary entry, from our own century, is 'a colloquialism for a lie, as in the phrase "you story-teller"'.

It is as if the whole history of Western thought since the Middle Ages has been compressed and is contained within this one dictionary definition. What has changed is not the form of story so much as our concept of what constitutes truth. Our culture has undergone a change to the point that we are becoming cut off from the past, unable to penetrate its thought patterns. There are certain questions we no longer even ask or train our children to ask. This is at root our fundamental problem in teaching from all ancient texts. The Bible is no exception.

CONCLUSION

The Education Reform Act of 1988 gives little choice in the matter of whether or not the Bible is any longer taught. It forms a compulsory part of all Agreed Syllabuses of Religious Education. What is essential is that it should be treated within the traditions of the best imaginative educational practice and without anxiety on the part of teachers who, quite rightly, even if sometimes a little unreflectively, do not want to be seen in the role of propagating religious beliefs. All that is asked is that these stories be seen as important enough to warrant diligent attention in the curriculum and, in view of their place in our heritage, it would be hard to deny that request.

The crucial question is how they are presented. Maria Harris, an American teacher, sums up much of our argument very concisely when she says:

Religious education must be related to the search for truth. Such truth, however, is not so much the truth of fact, where the opposite of a true statement is a false statement, or even where some things are false and others true. It is rather the truth of art, where some things are adequate and others are more adequate.

As in the teaching of art, these stories will do their own work, or not, and that work is quite unpredictable. What is required of us professionally is that we do not deny the possibility to future generations. 'Whatever speaks to me is true,' said Coleridge, 'and there is more that speaks to me in the Bible than in any other book I have ever read.'

Jack Priestley
July 1992

11

1

A Dream of Things to Come

Luke 1: 8–56; Matthew 1: 18–21 (I Samuel 2: 1–10)

Mary was singing. It was an old song, but that didn't matter. Once, a thousand years ago, it had been sung by a woman called Hannah. That was when she had found out she was expecting a baby. Now the same thing was happening to Mary. Hannah's son had grown up to become the great prophet Samuel. What would Mary's child become?

Mary had changed the words of the song a bit. She had sung it so many times now that she no longer needed to think about it. But she couldn't stop going back again and again over the way things had happened.

It had all started with that vision – a really clear dream in broad daylight. One minute she had been sitting on her own. The next, everything had changed. The tiny dark room with its few pots and pans and hardly any furniture had suddenly been full of light, and there stood the messenger. She hadn't even had to ask who he was. She had known straight away. It was the Angel Gabriel. Not that knowing that had made her feel any better. She had been so frightened she had started shaking like a leaf.

Then she had heard as well as seen. She could still hear that voice inside her head.

'Greetings,' Gabriel had said, just like anybody who met you in the street. But then he had gone on: 'Greetings. God is with you. You are a very special woman.'

Mary had gone on shaking. She couldn't stop.

The messenger had paused. At last he had seemed to notice. 'Don't be frightened,' he had said.

Mary smiled as she remembered that. Frightened! She had been terrified.

'Don't be frightened. I have come to give you good news. You are going to have a child, a very special child. It will be a boy. You are to call him Jesus. He will be God's own son. God has chosen you to be the mother.'

At last Mary had found her voice. 'But who is going to be the father?' she had asked, in a tiny shaking voice.

'God himself,' Gabriel had replied. 'Oh, and one other thing. Your Aunt Elizabeth is expecting a baby as well.'

Then the messenger had gone. He had simply vanished as quickly as he had come. Mary had been left alone sitting in the dark room. Who would believe her? Nobody else had seen the messenger or heard him speak. Then there was Joseph. What would he think? She had been going to marry Joseph, a carpenter from Nazareth. Would he believe her story?

Aunt Elizabeth! Mary had jumped to her feet. Of course! At least she could visit her aunt who lived in Jerusalem. Nobody else had heard that news. Surely that would prove that she hadn't just made it up.

It had been a long journey but it was true. Aunt Elizabeth was going to have a child at last. The two women were together in Elizabeth's house.

'But how did you know?' asked Elizabeth. 'We haven't told anybody.'

Mary told her about her vision. Elizabeth was very quiet for a minute. Then she said, 'Something very strange is happening. I'm frightened and excited all at the same time.'

'You see,' she went on, 'I haven't told anyone because we had a dream too – or rather old Zechariah my husband did. You're very young. I'm old enough to be a grandmother but I've never been able to have children. Then suddenly one day in the Temple Zechariah saw an angel just like you did. "Your wife is going to have a son," he said. That's all. And the next thing I knew the baby was starting to grow inside me.'

The two women were silent again. They wondered. What was so special about them? One was getting old. The other was very poor.

Then Elizabeth spoke again. 'The angel said our son is to be called John,' she said.

'Mine is to be called Jesus,' replied Mary.

Mary stayed with Elizabeth for three months. Then she went home. There was still Joseph to worry about. He would not want to marry her now. But another surprise was waiting for her.

Joseph met her. 'We're going to get married after all,' he said. 'While you were away I had a dream. It was so clear. I can still feel it now. A messenger, an angel, stood right in front of me. "Marry Mary," he said. "The child she is going to have is a very special one. It belongs to God himself. She must call it Jesus. It's not your son, but Mary will need you to help look after him. You and Mary will have children of your own afterwards."'

Three dreams to three different people in three different places! And they all said the same thing! Elizabeth had been right. Something strange was happening. Mary too felt frightened. But she felt excited as well. She started to sing again. She didn't know it, but it was a song which would last for ever, a song which would change the world.

NOTES

ABOUT THE STORY

The New Testament can be described as the 'Christ Story'. 'Christ' or 'Christos' is a Greek word. Its Hebrew equivalent is 'Messiah'. Both terms mean 'the anointed one'. The Jewish people had long expected such a person to come but they had different ideas about what he would be like. Some expected a deliverer or saviour who would overthrow their political enemies. Others thought he (and it was always assumed that it would be a 'he') would be someone who was nothing less than God in human form. Christians believe that Jesus was that Christ (it is a title not a surname). These stories were written by Christians to show that to others.

Mary's Song

My soul magnifies the Lord, and my spirit has
   rejoiced in God my Saviour.
For he has regarded the lowliness of his
   handmaiden.
For behold, from henceforth, all generations
   shall call me blessed.
For he that is mighty has done to me great
   things, and holy is his name.
His mercy is on them that fear him, throughout
   all generations.
He has shown strength with his arm: he has
   scattered the proud in the imagination of their
   hearts.
He has put down the mighty from their seats,
   and has exalted the humble and meek.
He has filled the hungry with good things, and
   the rich he has sent empty away.
He remembering his mercy has helped his
   servant Israel:
As he promised to our forefathers, Abraham and
   his seed for ever.

(Adapted from the Book of Common Prayer)

Throughout these stories it is important to remember what scholars have for a long time called the 'Messianic Secret'. That simply means that the characters in the story do not know who Jesus is for quite a long time but the people reading the book do, right from the start. The Gospels were not written, like a modern novel or a biography, for general interest. They were written to tell the second generation of Christians and others the details of how Christianity had all begun. Both writers and readers, in the main, already 'knew' (that is, 'believed') that Jesus was God in human form. The story tells how those who had been involved in the events had come to that realization in the first place.

It is also important to recognize what is said about 'truth' in the Introduction to this book. Historical accuracy may be important but it is not always the most important criterion for judging whether an inner experience is real or not. That can be judged only by what happens as a result and the reality of the experience can never proved in the way we can prove that 2+2=4 or that Leeds is north of London. Nor, of course, is this unique to religion. For endless generations parents have questioned whether their children really are in love and ought to marry the person they want to. Only time shows who was right and not always then.

The Gospel Story begins with a dream, or rather, three dreams. Ever since Freud we have been made aware of how important dreams can be but the ancients knew that too. These are what we might call 'daydreams', although it would be more accurate to call them 'visions'. There is an old saying that nothing happens without first a dream. We have to have an image or a vision, however ill defined, of something which does not exist if we are ever to make it come into being. All art, all music, all drama and literature comes out of that fact. It is, however, something which affects us all. Without powerful imaginations we cannot start to make our own hopes come true; nor can we ever change the world.

Mary is poor and powerless but out of her can come something which will totally change the whole world. Whatever one's personal beliefs it is surely the case that this conception achieved that. It ties in too with the other dreams. Something awesome was happening which the characters in the plot did not begin to understand. It was to be earth shattering. Mary's song, known as the Magnificat (its first word in Latin), is one of the world's great statements about social revolution. The words themselves are powerful, which may be why establishments the world over have sought to soften their impact. Set to a Gregorian chant they can be made to sound bland and impotent but always they re-emerge. History is only as old as the latest new-born child. The world does not have to remain as it is: it can always be different. It is part of the task of education to prepare children for what we term the 'real world'. It is also part of the teacher's task to keep the children's imagination alive in the hope that they may create a better one.

IDEAS FOR EXPLORING FURTHER

Songs of Praise The Magnificat is Mary's song of praise to God in which she expresses the range and depth of her feelings. Ask which are children's favourite songs of praise, and why. Compile a class Top Ten, or get the whole school involved and focus on these songs during a time of worship. Invite children, as individuals or collectively, to write their own song of praise, perhaps using a word-processor to aid collaboration and ease of drafting text. (NC *English*: AT 2 – reading, AT 3 – writing; *Technology*: AT 5 – information technology; *Music*: AT 1 – performing and composing.)

Working for a Better World   Christians believe that one of the reasons why God became human in the person of Jesus was to show us how to help create a better world. Invite the children to think about what helps to make a poor/pleasant atmosphere in the classroom. What about the physical environment and the natural world? Make links with environmental education. (Cf. NC *Environmental Education; Geography*: AT 5 – environmental geography.) Can the children suggest ways of improving relationships between people, the classroom environment, an area in the school grounds, or devise a way to make life better or easier for someone they know? Consider a range of people from different countries and religious traditions, past and present, who have helped to make the world a better place during their lifetime (e.g. modern writers such as John Agard and Grace Nicholls, with their stories and poems which have helped many to appreciate another culture/tradition; Martin Luther King, who fought for the civil rights of black people in the U.S.A. in the 1960s; Mohandas Karamchand Gandhi (1869–1948), who struggled to help India to gain independence through a non-violent revolution; Edward Jenner, who developed the idea of vaccination in 1796; the Faith in Action series is useful here). NC *History* projects could include a study of people who have helped to get rid of evils and greatly influenced the way people thought in a particular age (e.g. CSU 3 – the Victorian William Wilberforce, instrumental in the abolition of slavery (1833), which encouraged people to see the Empire with new eyes; Anthony Ashley Cooper, Lord Shaftesbury (1801–1885), responsible for the legislation prohibiting the employment of women and children in mines (1842) and limiting the working day in factories to ten hours (1847); Joseph Lister (1827–1912), who introduced the principles of disinfection and antiseptics into surgery; Mary Seacole from Jamaica, who nursed in the Crimean War at the same time as Florence Nightingale; Elizabeth Garrett Anderson (1836–1917), the first British woman doctor; Alexander Fleming (1881–1955), who discovered penicillin, which led to the development of antibiotics). NC *History* also points to people who have made the world a poorer place by destroying something valuable (e.g. CSU 6 – Hernan Cortes' encounter with the Aztec civilization, CSU 4 – Nazi persecution of the Jews). Older children could make a list of things they feel would improve the world in more general terms and rank their choices. See also notes on Story 11.

2

Born in a Barn

Luke 2: 1–7

The donkey plodded along the dusty track. It was heavily loaded with bags. At its side walked a man. Upon its back sat his wife. Joseph and Mary were on their way to Bethlehem from the town of Nazareth where they lived.

Normally the man would ride on the donkey and the woman would walk, but this was not a normal journey. Mary was expecting a baby. It was due any day now. Joseph didn't want it to be born before they got to Bethlehem. He did not want to be travelling at all.

Nobody liked it but everybody had to do it. The Roman Governor had made an order and everybody had to obey it. It was this sort of thing which made the Jews hate the Romans.

'Every man will take his family and go back to his home village to be registered. Then he will be told how much tax he has to pay.' That was what the Governor had said.

Nowadays the Jews were all mixed up but every man knew which tribe his family came from. Joseph was proud of the fact that he came from the tribe of Judah. King David had come from the same tribe. That was enough to make them feel important. Usually he would have been quite glad to go back to Bethlehem, but this was the worst possible time.

The road seemed endless. They had to travel so slowly and rest often. Other people kept overtaking them. But at last the little town of Bethlehem came into sight. Not long now. It

18

would be nice to sleep in a bed again and to know that the baby could be born in a proper place.

The donkey picked its way down the hillside towards the town. Below, the streets looked very full. There were people everywhere. Just suppose. . . . No! Joseph did not even want to think about it. Suppose everywhere was full up.

Joseph led the donkey towards the first inn, just inside the town. He hammered at the door. The innkeeper opened it and glared at him. Before Joseph could say anything the man spoke.

'No room, no room,' he shouted, waving his arms. 'You're much too late. There are people knocking at the door all the time. We're full up.'

Joseph's face fell. 'I have to find a room,' he said. 'My wife is expecting a baby at any minute. That's why we had to travel slowly. Can't you squeeze us in somewhere?'

'Sorry,' said the innkeeper. 'It's not my fault. I can't get another one in here. There's two of you and it looks as if there might be three of you by morning.' He laughed. 'And it will be the same everywhere else,' he added as he shut the door.

Joseph went back to the donkey. What could he do? A voice behind him made him turn round.

'Excuse me.'

'What is it?' asked Joseph. He didn't want to be pestered by a woman selling things at a time like this.

'I overheard what you said to my husband at the inn,' said the woman. 'About your wife expecting a baby. I just came to say that the inn really is full, but if you are in trouble you can use the barn at the back. It's not much more than a cave in the hillside with a door across, but it's dry and the wind doesn't get in. We use it as a stable for donkeys and cattle.'

Joseph looked at Mary. She was very tired. She could not travel any farther. It would have to do. He turned to the woman, nodded and said, 'Thank you. You are very kind.'

Inside, the barn smelt of animals and old straw. But it was warm and cosy. It was getting dark. Joseph unloaded the donkey and made up a rough bed for Mary. He found an old

19

oil lamp and lit it. Its flickering flame threw shadows on to the walls of the barn. The animals in one corner looked at them but did nothing. Joseph and Mary settled down.

Late that night the baby was born. The woman from the inn came and helped. The new-born baby was wrapped in strips of clean rags. The woman placed him in the manger from which the cows normally ate their food. 'He will be safe there,' she said. 'It's off the ground so there's no draught and he won't get trodden on.'

She said 'good night' and went back to the inn.

Outside it was a dark and windy night. Joseph knew he would not get much sleep but he was glad to be indoors. There must be people still out on the hillside but they would not trouble him. Nobody knew they were here.

But he was wrong.

NOTES

ABOUT THE STORY

Only two of the Gospel writers tell us about the birth of Jesus – Matthew and Luke. Mark does not begin his story until Jesus is approaching thirty and starting his ministry. John goes back to the creation of the world and then, like Mark, switches to the baptism of Jesus (see Stories 6 and 7). Is this remarkable? Not really. When we celebrate the birth of a great person, such as Shakespeare, we usually have little interest in details of birth and childhood. On Guru Nanak's Birthday, for example, Sikhs celebrate the mature man who founded their religion. Mark and John do much the same thing. Matthew and Luke, however, recognize that for Christians this birth was supremely important. Christianity is not just about what Jesus did. It is fundamentally about who he was. John felt so too but did not bother himself with the details. Like the Magnificat in Story 1, he was concerned with the great cosmic significance of these events. However, when people build Christmas cribs they very rarely pay much attention to the doll they put in the manger.

For this story we have followed Luke's version of events. Each Gospel writer has his own emphases. Luke is always anxious to show that the Gospel (the Good News) is for everyone, everywhere and perhaps especially for those who are disadvantaged. More than any other writer he draws attention to the women in the story as well as the poor, the foreigner and the socially downtrodden. A concern for animals is not absent either. Luke sees this event as heralding the breaking down of barriers such as those between Jew and Gentile, men and women, and rich and poor. The Creator of the Universe becomes flesh (in Latin *in carne*, or incarnate) in conditions of homelessness. A new world, in which all social divisions are turned upside down, is being born in this stable.

The historical background is that of collecting the poll-tax. Under Roman practice all adult males had to return to their respective tribal homelands in order to be registered. Luke gives the year in the usual terms of the time. Caesar Augustus is Emperor and Quirinius the Governor of Syria. It was the first such tax-gathering during Quirinius' rule. Much later on, when Christianity became established, the calendar was restarted from this event but not accurately. Although it sounds silly to say so Jesus was born about 4 B.C. (before Christ) or 4 B.C.E. (before the Common Era, common, that is, to Jews and Christians). Nor did this event take place in December, which was midwinter in Palestine as much as anywhere else in the northern hemisphere. It was when Christians converted northern Europe that they found the great festivals of midwinter and converted them too. That is why we still have two festivals overlapping one another, both of which we now call Christmas. The great feasting celebrates the turning-point (relative to the earth) of the sun: the giving of presents celebrates what Christians see as the greatest possible gift to the world.

IDEAS FOR EXPLORING FURTHER

Children's Rights Collect pictures of young children from around the world, preferably showing them going about their daily lives (not just faces). Discuss the jobs they do and compare these with the work done by children in the U.K. Talk about the opportunities these children might have in life and about some of the problems they face. In addition, make a collection of items which show how many children around the world have much in common (e.g. family life, schooling, an interest in games, a lively imagination, an interest in stories).

Through collaborative writing (cf. **NC** *English:* AT 2 – reading, AT 3 – writing), invite the class to draw up a Children's Charter of Human Rights. (**NC** *Equal Opportunities.*) The book *Do It Justice* (ideas for introducing education in human rights, published by the Development Education Centre in Selly Oak, Birmingham) contains helpful ideas, as does the Save the Children project pack on the U.N. Convention on the Rights of the Child. If a word-processor is used, the items on the charter can be amended easily, and each child could print a copy and take it home. (Cf. **NC** *Technology:* AT 5 – information technology.) The pictures of young children could be placed around a world map and a string could link each picture with the place of origin. (Cf. **NC** *Geography:* AT 2 – knowledge and understanding of places.) A desire to find out more about the possibilities for one particular child might act as a springboard for a study of a European locality or one in the economically developing world.

Explain to children that 'responsibilities' go hand in hand with 'rights', and that this is true for all people whether children or adults. Ask pupils to make a list of what they consider to be their responsibilities both in the home and at school. (Cf. **NC**

Citizenship.) See also Stories 5, 46, especially the notes on community; the project booklet *Me and My Communities* (CEM).

Belonging   Jesus belonged within a family and a strong religious tradition. Discuss children's feelings of belonging: to their family, school, clubs, religious tradition, local/ national community. What does it mean to 'belong' to any group of people? Discuss what it feels like to be left out and why this occurs. Older pupils could consider political events of recent years (e.g. Germany, U.S.S.R., Yugoslavia, Czechoslovakia, pressures to alter the union between England, Scotland, Wales and Northern Ireland) and ask: 'What is a country?' Another important question might be: 'What does it mean to be a refugee?' Ask the children to imagine they have to leave home and go off in a hurry with other children to escape a dangerous situation. What would they take with them in one small bag? What would they miss most? (Cf. NC *Geography:* AT 2 – knowledge and understanding of places.) The Save the Children pack for primary schools *Refugees* could help to stimulate thinking. Compare childhood roles through the ages. (Cf. NC *History:* SSU on domestic life, families and childhood.)

3

The Night Visitors

Luke 2: 8–20

The night was dark. The clouds, pushed by the west wind, moved quickly in front of the stars. There was no moon.

Up on the hills a small group of shepherds kept watch. They listened for those small noises in the night which might tell them that a wolf or a jackal was after their sheep. There was nothing – only the sound of the wind.

Suddenly, without warning, something strange began to happen. The clouds to the east began to grow lighter. It could not be the dawn. It was still the middle of the night. The light got stronger and stronger. The shepherds became uneasy. They began to move closer together.

'What is it?' asked one. His voice shook.

'I've never seen anything like it,' said another.

The light in the cloud became brighter and brighter. By now the shepherds were huddled together, looking upwards. They felt safer together. They were brave men but they were all becoming frightened. The light grew brighter still. It seemed to move straight towards them out of the cloud.

'Get down,' whispered one of the shepherds. He was speaking to himself as much as to the others but they all fell to the ground. The light was now as bright as the full moon shining on them. Everywhere else seemed to be in darkness. One or two of the shepherds pulled their cloaks over their faces. Others buried their heads in their arms.

Some powerful force was near them. They could feel it but

they could see nothing – only the bright light all around them. It had stopped moving now but to the shepherds it was like a blinding torch in their eyes.

Suddenly out of the night a voice spoke to them. 'Don't be frightened,' it said. 'I have come to bring you good news. In the town of Bethlehem a baby has been born. He is the Christ child, the Saviour of the world. Go and worship him. You will find him lying in a manger.'

The brightness went out of the light. The shepherds looked up. They clambered to their feet and looked around. There was nothing there. But the vision was not over yet.

The sky glowed again. This time it was a softer light spreading right across the eastern sky. A distant sound of voices echoed across the hills. They sang, 'Glory to God in the highest; peace to all men on earth.'

Slowly the sound faded. The darkness returned. The shepherds rubbed their eyes and looked at one another. 'What's happening?' 'What was it?' 'Did we imagine it?' They all started to ask questions. Nobody gave any answers.

The babble of questions stopped. They were less frightened now.

'Come on,' said the head shepherd.

'Where to?'

'Down to Bethlehem, of course. It's the only way to find out if we've been imagining things.'

'What about the sheep?'

'They will be safe,' replied the leader, 'if God is really here.'

The shepherds hurried down the hillside. They came to the track which led into the small town. Everywhere was in darkness – except one small building.

'Somebody at the inn is still awake,' whispered one of the shepherds.

'It's not the inn, it's the stable next door.'

The shepherds stopped.

A stable! Of course. Where else would they find a manger? The voice had said that this baby was to be found in a manger of all places.

Starting to feel frightened again, the shepherds turned and crept towards the door where the light was. Slowly they pushed it open.

A smell of warm straw and animals met them. An oil lamp burned. There on the straw lay a young woman. Next to her sat a man. He stood up as the shepherds came in.

'What do you want?' asked Joseph. 'Please don't disturb us any more. My wife has just had a baby.' He pointed to a small bundle lying in a manger. 'She is very tired. She needs to sleep. We want to be left in peace.'

'Peace,' replied the head shepherd. 'Peace. That is what your child is going to bring. Peace to the world.'

Softly and quietly the shepherds told Mary and Joseph what had happened to them out on the hillside. Mary was silent. She said nothing but she remembered what had been said to her months before. She did not understand but she knew she would never forget this moment.

The shepherds left. They could not find all the right words to say, but it did not matter. They sang and danced around as they made their way back up the hillside. Something wonderful had happened. And the sheep were perfectly safe – just as they had left them.

NOTES

ABOUT THE STORY

The book which we now call *The Gospel according to St Luke* probably started to circulate about 80–85 c.e. There was, of course, no publication date and only one copy to start with. We just cannot know when Luke started writing it or whether he worked from notes made many years earlier. We do know that he himself came on the scene relatively late, just as St Paul was about to cross into Europe by moving out of Asia Minor (Turkey) into Greece (see Story 46). Many scholars think that Luke may well have started his research – as we would say today – while Paul was in prison awaiting trial (see Story 48). If that were the case he could have collected information from eyewitnesses, even from Mary herself. None of this is certain but his aim is. He was writing up a full account for Theophilus, a name which simply means 'God-lover', but which may well have belonged to a particular individual, in order to 'tell the truth concerning the things about which he [Theophilus] had heard'.

As with the previous story Luke's interest is in the ordinary people. The shepherds of the time spent their lives on the hills. A flock of sheep represented a family's fortune. Again and again sheep and shepherds are used as images in the Gospel Story. The shepherds lived with the sheep. At night they may have used rough pens as some protection against wild animals. Then they would themselves have slept across the opening, becoming the 'door' by which anything had to enter. Throughout Jewish history and Scriptures the sheep had always been an important image. For example the Messiah (or Christ) in the Suffering Servant passages of Isaiah was as 'A lamb led to the slaughter'.

So the shepherds come to Bethlehem. They are the first visitors, rough, hard-bitten and worldly, not accustomed to cooing over new-born babies. This story can be told as a very simple straightforward narrative, as it has been in countless nativity plays over the years, but it contains many undertones and symbols, which recur often as the full Gospel Story unfolds and are there in abundance at the end of it.

IDEAS FOR EXPLORING FURTHER

Birth Rites   Jesus was presented to all the peoples of the world, represented by the humble shepherds, through a message from God and an invitation to go and meet him. Why were the shepherds the first to hear the message of the angels? Did it indicate that this news was meant for everyone, no matter how 'ordinary'? Talk about the ways in which different communities welcome a baby into their midst and present the child to the people. Look at naming ceremonies for children far afield (e.g. in an African country). (Cf. NC *Geography:* AT 2 – knowledge and understanding of places.) Find out what members of different religious traditions do for the new-born both in Britain and elsewhere. What are the differences between birth rites and what are the common points? Perhaps record these using a Venn diagram. Studies in relation to NC *History* could include ways in which children were welcomed into the community through baptism, naming ceremonies, etc.

Occupations and Values   Ask the children to talk about and perhaps draw a picture of people whom they feel are doing very unimportant jobs. Discuss the skills required for these jobs and ask what would happen if these jobs were not done.

4

Strangers from the East

Matthew 2: 1–12

Everyone in Jerusalem was talking about it. The visitors had begun it with their questions.

They had ridden in from the desert, the three of them, on their camels. It was easy to see that they had come from the East. They were dark-skinned and proud. They were wise too. You could see that in their faces. And yet what strange questions they asked.

'Where is the new king?' they wanted to know. 'We have seen the signs across the western sky. Where can we find the royal child, born a little while ago?'

People shook their heads. There was no new king. There was only old Herod up at the palace. He wasn't new. He had been King of the Jews for a long time. Nobody trusted him, least of all the Romans who really ruled the country. It would be nice to get rid of him.

Who were these dark strangers? What did they know? What signs had they seen to make them so sure that something important had happened? What had made them travel hundreds of miles across the desert sand? Were they kings themselves? Or did they know secrets that were hidden from other men?

Herod heard about them, of course. And he was worried. He invited them to his palace. When they came in he was sitting on his throne, dressed in purple. He tried to look like a king but it wasn't easy. He was short and fat and very ugly.

His eyes moved quickly from side to side. 'Welcome, good sirs,' he said, trying to smile.

The three tall strangers bowed low. They were very polite. Herod liked that. He spoke again: 'What can we do for you? It has been said that you are looking for a royal child recently born. We do not know of such a child. Tell us more.'

The tallest of the three visitors stepped forward. He spoke quietly but clearly: 'We know a great event has taken place here in recent days. Somewhere a child has been born who will change the world. He must become a great king. We thought we must find him here in Jerusalem.'

Herod thought for a moment. Yes, they were clever. His own wise men were really rather stupid but they had told him what he wanted to know. These three did not know all the sayings about a Messiah, a great Saviour who would free the people. Could it have started to happen? Herod did not want any trouble. But if anybody could find out about such a child these three men could.

Herod spoke up. He chose his words carefully. 'The child you want will not be here,' he said. 'If such a king is born our sacred books tell us it will happen in Bethlehem. It is very near. You have my permission to go there straight away to see if you can find him.'

The three men thanked him and started to leave. Herod called them back. 'When you have found the child,' he said, 'come back here and tell me. Then I can go and visit him as well.'

The visitors bowed and left the palace. They mounted their camels and disappeared into the night. Once out of the city they turned to the south, towards Bethlehem. Above them the stars shone brightly. One star in particular was very bright. That had been their sign all along.

Bethlehem was only ten kilometres away. The journey was quickly over. Now they seemed to be right underneath the star. It took them no time at all to find Mary and Joseph and the young Jesus.

The three kingly men bowed low to get in the door of the

little house where the family now lived. It was a strange scene. They knelt on the floor and solemnly gave the gifts they had brought. They were not presents for a baby or a little boy. They were gifts for a king – gold and frankincense and myrrh. Then they bowed and left.

Back in Jerusalem Herod waited – and waited. Nobody came. He began to get impatient. A new king indeed! Let them find him and then he would soon show everybody who was the real king. Where had those men got to? He would have to look for them. He sent a messenger to Bethlehem.

A few hours later the messenger returned. He looked frightened.

'What is the matter?' demanded Herod.

'Your Majesty,' stammered the man, 'the three strange visitors went away the day after they left here. From Bethlehem they went straight back into the desert from where they came. No one knows where that is.'

Herod was furious. He knew he had been tricked.

But the messenger did not tell all that he had learned. It was said that the three men had been warned in a dream not to go back to Herod. They had done what they came to do, but no one knew which child they had visited.

NOTES

ABOUT THE STORY

We switch here from Luke's stories to one from Matthew. Matthew was a Jew through and through. Whereas Luke seems to have been eager to show that Jesus was for the whole world, Matthew's first concern was to demonstrate to his own people that this really was their Messiah.

In most school nativity plays the kings or the three wise men follow hard on the heels of the shepherds. (Note that Matthew's Gospel does not say how many people there were, only that there were three gifts.) The Church, however, has always separated the two visits by a much longer period. This story is the basis of the season of Epiphany (the 'showing forth' or 'presentation to the world'), which starts on 6 January, otherwise known as Twelfth Night and the date of Christmas itself for the Eastern Orthodox Church.

Whatever historical basis there might or might not be to this story – and there is simply no way of telling – some very deep symbolism is being expressed. We need to remember that children are often much more capable of dealing with a symbolic story than adults, whose education has often made them far more literalistically minded. These men are very different from the shepherds. They are dignified and cultured. The Jews were always a small race surrounded by richer and more powerful neighbours. These dignitaries come and pay homage to Messiah even in the form of a powerless baby.

We need to recall what was said in the notes on Story 1 about the Messianic Secret. This story is a celebration by those who know about the whole life of Jesus and its significance. The gifts are recognitions of achievement, not toys for a baby. Gold is a sign of kingship, frankincense is incense as used in the Temple, a sign of godliness, and myrrh was widely used in the preparation of a body for burial. In short we have a recognition of a God King whose death will have huge significance.

The earthly king of the time was Herod, a puppet of the Roman government and an unpopular, vindictive and insecure ruler. The intertwining of the pilgrimage of the three with his jealous stance provides stark contrasts and also a historical basis. Herod existed: of that there is no doubt. Did the Magi exist or have they in a mysterious way always and for ever existed, in much the same way that we might suggest that Adam and Eve have always existed like the Everyman tradition (see the Introduction to the companion volume, p. 5)? These stories are at one and the same time both very simple and deeply profound. Too many historical questions can mean too few spiritual ones.

IDEAS FOR EXPLORING FURTHER

Symbols   The gifts brought by the men from the East were symbols. Talk about how symbols can sometimes say more and speak with greater effect than words and literal things. Talk about symbols known to children: everything from school/football club badges and road signs to religious symbols and what they may represent. Invite the children to imagine themselves as among the first visitors to the infant Jesus. What would they have brought as a gift? What would that gift have represented? Would it have been something musical, a piece of art work, a geometric design? Consider, for example, *The Little Drummer Boy,* by E. Keats; *The Little Juggler,* by B. Cooney; *The Best Present,* by H. Keller; *The Clown of God,* by Tomie de Paola; *The Surprise,* by George Shannon. The characters in these stories could not afford an expensive gift but found that they could give of themselves. Is it important to give kindness, tolerance, patience, help and forgiveness to people? Can the children design and package a surprise gift for someone? (Cf. NC *Technology; Art.*) Or is there something the children can do for someone as a 'gift'? See also the CEM booklet *Gifts and Giftbringers.* (Cf. OT Stories 15, 20, 25, 27.) Talk about what we value as gifts: see Story 28.

Human Nature   Do we have to guard against the greed and jealousy exhibited so clearly in Herod? What other human qualities do we have to guard against? (Cf. OT Stories 47, 49.) Younger children could identify unpleasant characters from stories/ poems they know about, and also consider more noble ones (e.g. *St George and the*

Dragon, by M. Hodges; *Tyrone, the Dirty, Rotten Cheat*, by H. Wilhelm). Older children could consult newspapers and pick out articles/photographs which represent people's greed, jealousy, anger and hatred, as well as those which represent love, kindness, cooperation and thoughtfulness. Which kind of article predominates? Why? See also Stories 15, 30, 31, 41.

Journeys   (Cf. notes on OT Story 5.) For people of the different religious traditions, certain places have special significance, and they like to visit them (e.g. Iona, Canterbury, Walsingham, Lourdes, Stonehenge, Benares, Amritsar, Makkah, Jerusalem; see CEM booklet *Journeys*). Ask the children whether any places locally or further afield are especially important to them and why. What do they/would they like to do there?

5

When a Child Becomes an Adult

Luke 2: 39–52

'Where can he have got to? Have you seen Jesus anywhere? I can't find him.'

'No, I thought he was with you.'

'He hasn't been with me since we left Jerusalem yesterday. He's a man now, you know. He won't travel with the women and children any more. I thought he must be with all you men.' Mary's voice sounded anxious.

'But I haven't seen him since we left the Temple,' replied Joseph. 'That's a whole day and night ago.'

Everybody had stopped. There must have been a hundred or more people in the party. The Passover festival was over for another year. Now they were all going home together, back to Nazareth.

This trip to Jerusalem had been special. Jesus was thirteen. He had been presented in the Temple as a Bar Mitzvah. In the eyes of everybody he was now a man. When they got back he would sit downstairs in the synagogue with the other men. No longer would he be in the gallery with the women and young children. But where was he? Nobody had seen him at all.

'We shall have to go back,' Mary said.

Joseph groaned. She was right, of course, but what a nuisance! It would add another two days to the journey and they would have to travel alone. Why couldn't he behave like a grown-up if he wanted to be one?

Mary and Joseph separated their own donkey from the others, said goodbye to their friends and turned back.

Jerusalem was less crowded now. Many of the pilgrims and tourists had gone. But where could Jesus be? They searched the narrow streets near the place where they had stayed. No one had seen him.

Finally they climbed wearily up the steps to the Temple area. Surely he would not still be in there.

All around the huge courtyard sat groups of men. It was always like that. Joseph smiled. We Jews, he thought. Anyone would think we never had any work to do. Everybody was arguing. How they enjoyed it! As they walked between the groups Joseph and Mary could hear the chatter. 'Was it right to do that? Can't we do this? What did Moses mean when he said. . . .' Questions, questions, questions. They went on and on. The deep voices of the men arguing were all around.

Suddenly a much younger voice could be heard across the other side of the courtyard. Mary spun round and pushed her way between the groups. She knew that voice. But she could hardly believe what she saw.

A group of very old men sat in a circle on the courtyard stones. Their beards were long and their backs were bent. For many years they had met here to talk and to argue. They were some of the wisest men in all Jerusalem. But now they were not talking; they were listening. There at one side of the group sat Jesus. He looked so young but he sounded so grown-up. Some of the old men were nodding; others smiling.

Jesus looked up. He saw Mary looking down at him. The old men followed his eyes. Mary suddenly realized they had all stopped talking and were looking at her. She didn't know what to say. She was very angry and proud all at the same time.

'Son,' she said at last, 'what are you doing to us? Your father and I have been worried sick. We were half-way back to Nazareth before we missed you. Where have you been? What are you doing? We should be home by now.'

There was silence. Then Jesus said, 'But you must have

33

known where I was. Where else could I be except in the House of God, my real Father?'

Jesus stood up and smiled at the old men. 'It looks as if I shall have to be going now,' he said, 'but I shall be back.' He walked off with Mary and Joseph.

The old men looked at one another. 'When that young man becomes a bit older he is going to be quite famous,' said one.

The journey back to Nazareth was very quiet. Mary did not know whether to be worried or happy. What sort of person was this son of hers? He was so special that she was almost frightened. What would happen to him?

Jesus was thinking too. He knew he had to go back to Jerusalem and the Temple. He had done nothing wrong. He was a grown-up now. But for the time being he had to stay at home and work and learn much more.

--------------------- NOTES ---------------------

ABOUT THE STORY

This is the only story in the Gospels of Jesus as a child and it is an account of the rite of passage from childhood into adulthood. There is clear evidence from as far back as the second century – and no reason for not believing it to have been common practice long before that – that Bar Mitzvah coincided with a boy's becoming what today we would call a teenager, i.e. his thirteenth birthday. The Bat Mitzvah for girls has become a widely accepted practice only during the twentieth century.

The name Bar Mitzvah means 'Son of the Commandments', Bat Mitzvah 'Daughter of the Commandments'. It is every Jew's inheritance to take on responsibility for the Tradition. Today the essential part of the ceremony takes place in the synagogue and synagogues had existed for five hundred years before Jesus' time. However, the Jerusalem Temple was still standing and it would have been normal for any family to have made the special effort to go there for the great festival of Pesach (Passover) and celebrate this occasion at the same time in the central shrine of Judaism.

To become Bar Mitzvah was to come of age. Our modern Western idea of a long transitional period called 'adolescence' is very new indeed. In most of the world still the change is much more abrupt.

The on-going Jewish practice of Talmud is that of constant interpretation and reinterpretation of Torah, which is translated as 'Law' but is more accurately

'Tradition'. The young Jesus joins in with the enthusiasm of a modern seventeen-year-old who cannot wait to get on with the business of obtaining a driving licence. There may appear to be a certain precociousness about his action but it is obviously not seen as that by his elders. Nor need it be. When it comes to religious questions a young child can be as profound as any adult. This is why the Anna of *Mr God This Is Anna* sounds authentic. Anna died young, so young that she would never have got to Key Stage 1, but few theologians have had greater insights. It is sobering also to realize that almost all Jewish boys (and many girls too) have been made literate for the past three thousand years: for Western Gentiles universal literacy is barely a century old.

Luke is obviously anxious to show through this story that Jesus is separating from his earthly parents and embarking on his divine mission.

IDEAS FOR EXPLORING FURTHER

Childhood   Many children have heavy responsibilities throughout childhood. Consider childhood roles of the past. (NC *History*: SSU on domestic life, families and childhood.) See OT Story 22, about the young David.

Gender Stereotyping   Ask the children to draw (separate) pictures of a scientist, a banker, an engineer, a lawyer, a nurse, someone at home looking after a baby, a doctor, a Member of Parliament, a ballet dancer, a bus driver, a detective, an astronaut and a pilot. When the children have drawn their pictures, put them up on a wall. Talk about how many women and how many men are shown in the pictures. Discuss reasons for showing a man or a woman doing a particular job. Find out more about the pilot Amy Johnson, who was the first to fly from Britain to Australia. *Working Now: Photographs and Activities for Exploring Gender Roles in the Primary Classroom*, published by the Development Education Centre in Birmingham, is a useful pack for exploring these issues. Talk about whether girls can be good at science, maths, engineering, etc., and whether boys can also care for young children, do nursing, dancing, and so on. Letterbox Library (8 Bradbury Street, London N16 8JN) specializes in anti-racist and anti-sexist books. See, for example, *Katy's Kit Car*, by Robin Lawrie, about a young girl who rebuilds her dad's old banger when it breaks down; *Oliver Button is a Sissy*, by Tomie de Paola, about Oliver who hates the things boys are 'supposed to do' and, above all, loves dancing. At school Oliver is teased mercilessly until the talent show, where he wows everyone with his tap-dancing and becomes a star. Discuss the toys children play with and whether there are really any restrictions related to gender. (Cf. NC *Equal Opportunities*.) Another important issue is gender rules within the community. (See also OT Story 3.) Talk about this and issues related to toys, jobs and schooling for boys and girls in the past. (NC *History*: e.g. CSU 2 – Tudor and Stuart times, CSU 3 – Victorian Britain, SSU on domestic life, families and childhood.)

Coming of Age   (Cf. notes on Story 3 – birth rites.) Find out how people in different parts of the world mark a young person's coming of age (e.g. confirmation in the Roman Catholic and Anglican Church, the Jewish Bar Mitzvah, the thread ceremony of Hinduism, the turban ceremony of the Sikhs, graduation, getting a driving licence). Invite local representatives of different religious traditions (e.g. parents, ministers, young adults) to talk to the children about what is done in their community.

Responsibility   Talk to the children about citizenship. Ask what new responsibilities they might have when they are older. Will they have to face any new problems or dangers? How can these be confronted? Invite them to speculate as to the kind of contribution they will make to the community when they are adults (e.g. employment, voluntary work, sport). For what reasons do we choose jobs and different activities? See notes on Story 22 – occupations and values; Stories 2, 46. (Cf. NC *Careers Education and the World of Work; Citizenship*.)

Recognizing One's Gifts   See OT Story 8.

6

A Loud and Angry Voice

Matthew 3: 1–10; Luke 3: 7–11

It all began by the side of a river. The River Jordan flowed along the very edge of the desert. The nearest town was Jericho. Jerusalem was forty-three kilometres away up a long, hot, winding road.

The man who was causing all the excitement had the appearance of a man of the desert. His skin was brown and dry. He was tall and thin but very strong. His black beard was long and straggly. He wore only a loincloth. His shoulders, chest, legs and arms were bare. It was said that the only things he had to eat were locusts and honey from the nests of wild bees. But the most noticeable thing about him was his eyes. They shone like pools of liquid fire.

'He is a prophet,' the people were saying. 'There hasn't been anyone like this for hundreds of years.' Every day the crowds which came from the towns to see him grew bigger and bigger.

The man was John. He seemed like a prophet all right. He preached in a way which made people listen. His voice was loud and sometimes angry but it did not frighten people away. They called him John the Baptizer, or John the Baptist. From time to time he would walk into the river and baptize men and women. These were people who believed what he had to say. They were promising to live a better life. To show that they meant it John dipped them in the water. It

37

was a sign that they were washing away their old life. When they came out of the water it was as if they were starting a new life – like being born all over again.

Today the crowd was bigger than usual. People nudged one another. They pointed. 'Look who has come,' they said.

At one side stood a small group of priests. They had come all the way down from the Jerusalem Temple to see what was going on. They stood together, dressed in their fine robes. The people were a bit frightened of them. Would John be frightened too?

The crowd did not have long to wait to find out. John looked across at the little group of priests. He knew why they had come. It was to try and catch him out, not to listen to what he had to say. A look of scorn crossed his face. His fierce eyes seemed to burn right through them. His voice was strong and his words were hard. 'You nest of snakes,' he suddenly roared, 'who told you to come here?'

The crowd gasped. One or two grinned. Nobody ever spoke to Temple priests like that. The priests looked uncomfortable, but John gave them no time to answer. 'Are you running away from the Temple or from God?' he asked.

He turned to face everybody. 'God is angry,' he went on, 'and I'm not surprised. Do you know what God is like? I'll tell you. Just now he is like an angry fruit farmer with an axe in his hand at harvest time. He's just discovered that some of his trees have no fruit on them. He's going to chop some of you down.'

John paused. He looked all around. Very few people could look straight back into those powerful eyes. Then he spoke again.

'And be warned. It won't be any use saying "We're special, we've always been in this orchard". That will just make it worse.'

A man in the crowd spoke up. 'That's all very well,' he said, 'but tell us what we have to do. Should we make more sacrifices?'

'Yes,' said John, 'but not the sort of sacrifices they make in the Temple.' He pointed to the priests. 'You can start right here and now.'

Among the crowd were lots of poor people. Some of them were little more than beggars.

'Look,' said John to the man who had asked the question. 'Some people here have only a few rags, others have fine clothes and can afford jackets as well as coats. Some do not have enough to eat, others have too much. Share what you have with those who do not have enough. That's what God wants you to do.'

A few people began to move away, the little group of priests among them. They did not like what John was saying: they knew it was true but they did not want to do as he asked.

'This man is dangerous,' said one of the priests to another. 'We must find some way of getting rid of him.'

NOTES

ABOUT THE STORY

With this story (continued in Story 7) we move into the main narrative. The Gospels of Mark and John see the adult John the Baptist as announcing the coming of Christ (the Messiah). Traditional church services in the four-week period of Advent, leading up to Christmas, reflect this. Most school nativity plays or carol services dwell on the wise men and shepherds of Matthew and Luke.

John the Baptist caused great excitement because word had got around that he was a prophet. The Jews had not had any real prophets for at least four hundred years. What is a prophet? The word means quite simply a spokesperson. In religious terms a prophet was recognized as one who spoke for God, regardless of his own safety and security. Because what the prophets predicted turned out to be true they were often portrayed as if they were some sort of crystal-ball gazer or fortune teller. However, as an old cliché has it, they were *forth*tellers, not *fore*tellers.

The status of the prophets had grown out of the Jewish belief in theocracy, which simply means 'God rules O.K.?' They had come into prominence when the Israelites had demanded a king. They saw their task as reminding the people, including the kings, that everyone was subject to God's moral rule. (See especially OT Story 26.) They were ruggedly independent and often lived frugally so that they were beholden to nobody. They attacked power or, more accurately, the abuse of power. Particular targets were politicians, the military and priests.

39

Such people, of course, were hardly popular with the authorities and they were often imprisoned or killed. What made these dissidents different in Israel from elsewhere, however, was the public recognition that they did indeed represent the voice of God.

The message of John the Baptist (continued in Story 7) is a moral one. It is also very modern. Those who have power, even in quite small amounts, often use it for their own ends and not for the good of the community.

Is it also a religious message? Is there a connection between morality and religion? Few would deny that people can be moral without being religious. However, there are two meanings of the word 'moral'. It can simply mean 'how people behave'. Moral education is then seen to be all about helping children to fit into the world by behaving properly. There is, however, another meaning that has to do with ideals. For that we sometimes use the word 'ethics'. Moral education would then be concerned with looking beyond what is normally done to the highest and best ideas about how we ought to live. It would be about changing the world for the better instead of just fitting into it as it is. Where, though, would such ideas come from? The very word tells us: 'ethics' is made up of two Greek words which mean 'out of God or the gods'. Religion provides a vision of what might be.

This is what John the Baptist is concerned with. He sees a new beginning, a new world order in someone who is different and better than one normally finds in the world. That is religion at its best. At its worst, however, it is not even moral in the lower sense of the word. It might be possible to be moral without being religious but it is not acceptable to claim to be religious without being moral. Hypocrisy in religious leaders is a major failing, hence the vicious attack on these particular priests.

IDEAS FOR EXPLORING FURTHER

Listening to Points of View   Choose an issue about which class members may hold a variety of opinions and discuss these briefly. Ask the children how they think people living in John's time would have viewed both John and Jesus. Extend discussion to obtain a wide range of opinions. For what reasons might people have held their views? Talk about how reasoning and motives may be quite complex. Discuss how oral communication was very important in the past. Highlight its advantages/disadvantages and compare these with the pros and cons of using written communication and advanced technological communication systems. Discuss reasons for any overlaps. Pupils could compose different newspaper headlines or reports or make posters reflecting different viewpoints using a software package such as *Front Page Extra*, *Newspa* or any word-processing program. A word-processor might be helpful for devising questionnaires, composing, and poster making. Group older pupils with a view to 'interviewing' (and recording a conversation with) John the Baptist, a number of different ordinary people with a variety of opinions and others who might have been opposed to John and Jesus, such as Pharisees, Saducees, Herod, Roman soldiers, etc. Draw up interview questions in advance. Combine interviews to make a 'radio broadcast'. (Explain the anachronism of a radio broadcast and a newspaper.) Should everyone be respected and allowed to give their view? Should all views be respected?

Can views be given forcefully, and in a non-aggressive manner? (Cf. NC *English*: AT 1 – speaking and listening, AT 3 – writing; *Technology*: AT 5 – information technology.) See also Stories 39, 46, 47, 48.

Speaking Your Mind   Ask the children to think about occasions when it is important to speak your mind (e.g. safety issues, when someone is being abused, when there is clear injustice) and times when it is important not to say what you think or at least to phrase your opinions carefully (e.g. in order not to hurt people's feelings, not to make trouble between friends, because it would not actually serve any purpose and might make matters worse). Are there times when people should not offer an opinion at all (e.g. because they do not really know very much about the matter)? Does sounding angry always help a situation? In what ways can one be assertive without being aggressive? Discuss important issues in the local community and examine news-papers. Make a list of issues which are worth speaking out about and perhaps even write some carefully worded letters to the town/city council. Older children could act out different scenes to illustrate these ideas. Pupils could also be given pictures to criticize in small groups: first in a destructive fashion; then in a constructive fashion. The teacher may have to demonstrate this first. Of course, many pupils may have been taught to criticize each other's work constructively already through collaborative group work.

7

Someone Else Is Coming

Matthew 3: 11–17; Luke 3: 12–22

John the Baptist was down by the river again. The crowd was bigger than ever. John had finished preaching. People started to ask him questions.

One man stepped forward. He was a tax-collector and he had very few friends. 'I want you to baptize me,' he said. 'But first tell me how I can be different from what I am now.'

'Collect the taxes you have to,' replied John, 'but not a penny more.'

There was a murmur in the crowd. Everyone knew that tax-collectors usually took more than they were supposed to. The extra money went into their own pockets. That was why they were so rich and why people hated them.

A soldier stepped forward. 'And what about me?' he asked.

'You be happy with your wages as well,' answered John, 'and don't use your sword and your strength to bully people.'

The tax-collector and the soldier went into the water with John. The crowd went quiet as John baptized them.

In the silence a man turned to his friend and said, 'Do you think he's just a prophet? Perhaps he's the Messiah, the promised king we've been waiting for all these years.'

John overheard him. His voice came across like thunder. 'No,' he roared, 'someone is coming who is far greater than I am. Why, I wouldn't even dare to get on my knees to undo his shoes.'

Just at that moment another figure stepped forward. Like John he was tall and strong. Unlike John he was gentle and quiet. One or two people knew him as a carpenter from the town of Nazareth in the north. His name was Jesus.

He stood in front of John. 'Baptize me,' he said quietly.

The two men faced each other. Their eyes met. John was the first to look down. 'I can't,' he gasped.

The people were very surprised. In front of Jesus he suddenly didn't look very strong any more.

'I can't,' he repeated. 'It is you who should baptize me.'

'Do as I ask,' said Jesus. 'This is where I must start.'

John stood still for a moment. Then he turned quickly and they both went into the water. John placed his arm round Jesus' shoulder. He held him as he lay back in the water and then helped him to his feet again. The crowd had gone very quiet.

For a moment Jesus stood as if lost in a trance.

'What's the matter?' whispered John. 'Are you all right?'

'Now I know for sure,' answered Jesus. 'As I came up from the water I had a clear vision of God. A voice said to me quite clearly, "You are my beloved Son and I am well pleased."'

He turned to John.

'I must go away for a while,' he said.

The river was not deep. Instead of coming back to the crowd Jesus turned and waded across to the other bank. Beyond lay the desert. The crowd started to drift away.

Just then some soldiers galloped up. They made straight for John and drew their swords.

'You are under arrest,' said the officer.

'What for?' asked John.

'For treason,' came the reply. 'You have said evil things against Herod the king and against other leaders of the people.'

John stood where he was. A few of the crowd were still near. Will he run or will he fight? they wondered.

John just laughed. He looked straight back at the officer and held out his hands.

'Do what you like with me,' the people heard him say. 'My work is finished.'

He walked away with the soldiers to go to prison.

NOTES

ABOUT THE STORY

Whilst hypocrisy is a particular failing in priests and others whose jobs have a particular moral quality, it can be present at all levels. This story starts with John the Baptist responding to questions from tax-collectors and soldiers. These are public servants. In this instance they had the whole power of the Roman government behind them. Sometimes the temptation was too much. Like civil servants the world over, ideally they existed to serve the people but it was all too easy to serve themselves first, to line their own pockets or to show off their power.

The dilemma when Jesus presents himself for baptism is bound up with this charge of hypocrisy. We need to remember that the two had grown up together. John knew that Jesus possessed total integrity; he had nothing to repent for.

However, Jesus too bears the hallmarks of a prophet. They were not all loud and outspoken. The most effective ones were often those who did rather than said. It is a question of actions speaking louder than words. The good person repents for the evils of the community as if they were his/her own.

In some versions of this story Jesus comes up out of the water, sees a dove and hears a voice saying, 'This is my beloved son in whom I am well pleased.' The difficulties which this may present are dealt with in the next story. Jesus goes straight on into the wilderness. John's work is done. He is arrested. The sequel can be found in Story 15.

IDEAS FOR EXPLORING FURTHER

Celebrating Difference   Jesus was different; people either loved or hated him. How do we react to things which are new, strange or different? Think about how we receive 'strange news' today (e.g. reports concerning the landing of a space craft on the moon or crop circles, or information about newly explored lands). Collect pictures of little-known animals from wildlife magazines. Do we condemn some animals just because they seem ugly to us? Or can we find ways of celebrating their different features? How do we receive strangers in our community? Are we welcoming, or do we shut them out of our lives? Is it true that all people can enrich our community? Think about Albert Einstein (1879–1955), who was a Jewish refugee from Germany but made a tremendous contribution to the world of science and mathematics; or Claudia Jones (1915–1964) from Trinidad, who in 1958 became the founder and editor of the *West Indian Gazette*, the first newspaper of its kind in Britain. A large number of sports personalities whose families originated in other countries have joined the British sports teams and distinguished themselves. (Cf. notes on Story 3 – birth rites, Story 45.)

44

8

The Easy Way and the Hard Way

Matthew 4: 1–11; Luke 4: 1–13

Jesus walked into the desert. During the day the sun was very hot, but at night when the moon and the stars came out it suddenly went very cold. There was nothing to eat. It did not matter. He wanted to be alone – alone with the sun, the moon, and the stars, to feel close to the earth and close to God. He knew he was God's chosen messenger. How should he behave? He knew he had the power to do anything. How should he use his power? He wanted to pray and to think. Nobody else could help him now.

As the days went by, strange pictures came to him. One night the Devil stood in front of him. Jesus was feeling very, very hungry.

'Here you are,' said the Devil. 'Here are lots of stones. If you are really the Son of God change them into loaves of bread. You needn't go hungry again and you can give to others. You can always live well and people will respect you.'

Jesus thought. It was tempting. If he used his power in that way he would never have to worry about food and he could make himself very popular. No! It would make his life easier than other people's. The Devil was wrong.

'Man does not live by bread alone,' said Jesus. 'To live well means much more than just having plenty to eat. There are more important things in life.'

Another day Jesus saw himself standing on the highest point of the Temple in Jerusalem. The Devil was there with him. As they looked down they could see all the people looking upwards.

'Go on,' said the Devil. 'Jump off. If you are God's son, God will look after you. He will probably send a squadron of angels along to catch you and lower you gently to the ground. Think how the people will cheer. They will know for certain who you are.'

'No,' said Jesus. 'It is written in our Scriptures that we should not tempt God. I would be the sort of messenger who asks for special favours. I will not behave like that.'

Finally Jesus saw himself on top of a high mountain. He could see for miles and miles. It seemed as if all the world were underneath him.

The Devil came to him again and said, 'Look, just be like me and you can control the whole world. Force people to obey you. Tell them to love your God. If they refuse, destroy them. Be like me and conquer the world.'

'No!' shouted Jesus. 'Never.' He knew this was the biggest temptation of all. The message he had to give was that people should love one another. As John the Baptist had told them, they must help each other. Jesus knew what he had to do. He had to preach God's message of love, but he had to live it as well. Men and women would only believe him if he believed in it himself.

Jesus turned and went back towards Jordan and home. He had come through the desert. It was time to put into practice what he had learned. He must love all the time. He must do what was best for other people and not think of himself. He had to show people what God was like, not just tell them. It would be hard but he knew now what had to be done.

ABOUT THE STORY

Religion begins in the individual soul but it cannot just stay there. We have to recognize that Jesus endured this intense experience all alone. Then he himself had to communicate it afterwards. Telling others about deep inner experiences often requires vivid picture language. The dove-and-voice incident omitted from the previous story is another possible case in point.

Is the story true then? Refer again to the Introduction. For most of us the 'truest' moments of life are when we 'know for certain' what we have to do. Do we educate children, however, in learning to trust or mistrust their own inner convictions? Or is our curriculum only about externals?

How could the story have been 'proved'? Had there been television crews following Jesus around what sorts of picture might they have come back with? We can never know but we can make intelligent guesses. There is no spot in the Jordanian desert from which we can see all the countries of the world or even very many neighbouring countries: the pinnacle of the Temple too was miles away. The truth lies in the consequences. The world was to be changed as a result of this experience.

The issue within the story is very straightforward. It affects all of us especially as teachers. It is simply this: the method must be in keeping with the message. In this case the message is that God is love and so the method too must be one of love. There can be no short cuts. Talking about love is no substitute for loving. Talking costs very little and a few stunts, like photo-opportunities, can get a quick, if shortlasting popular response. Actually loving means getting hurt but that is the way it has to be. Would we still be discussing it two thousand years later if, out of this mental anguish, a different answer had been arrived at?

IDEAS FOR EXPLORING FURTHER

Caring   How do parents, relatives, friends show that they care about pupils? Supposing these people just said, 'I love you,' or 'I care about you,' but *did* nothing to show it. Do people sometimes have to put themselves out or make sacrifices for others to show that they care? Ask children to make a list of things they could do at home or at school to show that they care about the people there. Can pupils plan a surprise for someone to show that they care about them (e.g. an elderly person, someone on the school staff, someone at home)? What do pupils feel like when they are preparing the surprise? Is it all plain sailing and easy? What do they feel like when the surprise is being delivered and afterwards? Was it worth making the effort? (Cf. NC *Health Education:* family education, psychological aspects of health education.)

Dreams and Reality   Discuss the proposition that 'Nothing happens without first a dream or vision'. Talk about messages in stories and visions (refer back to the Introduction and to the different truth questions about the hyena story: 'Is it true?' or 'Does it contain truth?'). See notes on Story 20, OT Stories 5, 35, 45.

Quick Fixes   Speculate about what might have happened if Jesus had allowed himself to be a military leader as some Jews wished. Tape/write a story about this. (**NC** *English:* AT 3 – writing.)

Give small groups of children a card on which there is a brief description of a problem situation (e.g. two friends are arguing over who should have exclusive use of a toy; the headteacher is angry because there is so much litter in the playground and has asked some children to clear it up; a special visitor is coming to the school and the governors have asked the children to brighten up/improve the school grounds). Ask children to find two solutions to their problem: one easy, with a quick, immediate effect; one which requires more effort and will have a greater impact in the longer term. Help children to justify their strategies and to talk about short- and long-term outcomes.

9

Let's Go Fishing for People

Matthew 4: 18–22; Mark 1: 16–20; Luke 5: 1–11

Jesus made his way back home. He would start his work there
with people who knew him. His home was near Lake Galilee.
Many of his friends were fishermen on the lake. They had
known one another since they were children. As a carpenter
Jesus had sometimes helped them to mend their boats.

There were always people down by the lake. Jesus went
down to the edge of the water. He started to talk to people. A
crowd began to gather. Soon there were so many that Jesus
could not make himself heard. He was being pushed into the
water.

Nearby was a boat. It belonged to a fisherman called Simon.
Jesus knew Simon well. He was a strong man who worked in
all weathers. Everybody liked him because he worked his
heart out at everything he did. Not that he always did the
sensible thing. Sometimes he was so enthusiastic that he didn't
stop to think. He was like a man trying to beat a door down
when the key was in the lock all the time. Today he looked
very fed up.

'Can I borrow your boat, Simon?' asked Jesus.

'Of course,' came the reply. 'But I hope you're not going
fishing.'

'Why not?' asked Jesus.

'Because the fish have all gone on holiday,' replied Simon.
'I've been out there all night in the freezing cold and I haven't

caught one. I might as well have gone to bed like everyone else.'

Jesus laughed. 'I'm not catching fish at the moment,' he said, 'but may I borrow your boat just the same?'

'Help yourself,' said Simon.

Jesus got in the boat and pushed it a few metres from the shore. Now he could see all the people. His voice carried clearly across the water.

'God is a loving father,' said Jesus. 'We are his children. He wants us to love one another.'

Jesus talked on and on. He told stories and everyone listened, even the fishermen. Simon was busy mending his nets but he stopped and listened too. So did his brother Andrew.

Jesus finished talking. He rowed in to the shore. 'Come on,' he said to Simon, 'jump in.'

They rowed out from the shore.

'Throw your nets in there,' said Jesus.

Simon looked at him, shrugged his shoulders and threw his net overboard. Then he leaned over to pull it in. The boat nearly went under. The net was so full of fish Simon could not hold it. 'Help!' he shouted.

Andrew, Simon's brother, and two other fishermen on the shore jumped into another boat and rowed out. Together they towed the heavy net back to shore.

Simon did not know what to say but, being Simon, he said it just the same. 'You show me up, Jesus,' he said. 'There's something so different about you that I feel bad when you're around. You don't want to stay here with the likes of me.'

'I'm not staying around here,' said Jesus. 'I want to go fishing.'

'What!' exclaimed the four fishermen. 'Not again! We've got enough here to last a week.'

Jesus laughed again. 'No, I've got much bigger things to catch,' he said. 'I'm going fishing for people. I'm going to catch them for God. Come with me.'

The four men looked at one another. How would they live? What about their families? But, as Simon had said, there was something special about Jesus. It was a challenge. Before the other three could speak Simon had said, 'Yes, we'll come.'

They finished unloading the fish, drew their boats on to the shore and got ready.

'Where are we going?' asked Simon.

'We'll start over there,' said Jesus, pointing across the lake, 'in the town of Capernaum.'

They began to walk.

'Oh, one other thing,' said Jesus.

'Yes?' said Simon.

'I'm going to give you another name,' said Jesus.

'Oh, what?' asked Simon.

'Petros,' said Jesus. 'Rock.'

'Why?' asked Simon.

'Well, your friends might say you had a head like a lump of rock sometimes,' replied Jesus. 'But the real reason is that you're as solid and reliable as a mountain. That's why I want you.'

The others laughed and nodded. 'Petros, yes, Peter. That's a good name.'

NOTES

ABOUT THE STORY

This is a simple and straightforward story and, in itself, needs little explanation.

Galilee was in the north, generally regarded by the Establishment in Jerusalem as of little interest. It had a more mixed population and, because of the trade routes, an often broader outlook on the world than could be found in the much more self-confident but occasionally aloof capital and centre of Jewish affairs. The occupying Romans saw Galilee as a potentially rebellious area but their attitude towards the whole of Palestine was one of nervous apprehension.

The story as told here seeks to bring out two things in particular. First, there is the call of the first disciples. 'Disciple' is not a word we employ much nowadays but its associated word 'discipline' is still in very common use. A disciple is simply a follower. Just how one gets and keeps followers is the important thing. Saddam Hussein and Mother Teresa perhaps represent the range of contrast. These disciples of Jesus have grown up knowing him and still choose to give up everything and go with him on a barely understood mission when invited to do so.

51

Secondly, there is the character of Simon Peter, who is to become one of the key players in the drama. Probably of only average intelligence and impetuous with it he is, nevertheless, loyal and persistent and still there at the end. This 'bear of very little brain' character, a humble and ordinary fisherman, is destined to become a leading figure in a world-changing movement, a fact which if advertised would doubtless have caused endless mirth in polite Jerusalem circles. However, a long thread of Jewish tradition was on his side (see OT Story 50). Religion, unlike theology, is not assessed on intelligence criteria.

IDEAS FOR EXPLORING FURTHER

Team Work   The twelve disciples were effectively a special team which worked with Jesus. Ask children to work in pairs and to say or write down one positive reason why Jesus might have wanted their partner to be a member of his team. Make two paper team cups or shields. Indicate on one the positive, and on the other the negative requirements for working as a team. Try out some of the cooperative activities published through the Cooperative Education Network (address on p. 229). See also *Let's Play Together*, by Mildred Masheder, an exciting collection of over three hundred cooperative games. Alternatively, read stories which show people working well together (e.g. *The Enormous Turnip*, retold by Vera Southgate; *Jamaica Tag-Along*, by J. Havill). Ask the class to undertake a very big task (e.g. an enormous collage, a large model). Invite pupils to break the overall task into component tasks and assign individuals to carry them out. Once the task has been completed, discuss what was required for team work. Were any difficulties experienced? How could they have been resolved? See also notes on cooperation for OT Stories 17, 38, 50.

Look at how the school is run by a team of people which, when you include parents, governors and other members of the community, is fairly substantial. Perhaps make a diagram or flowchart to illustrate this. In addition, consider how teams of people operated in the past: for undertaking all kinds of production jobs, such as printing, making clothes, running monasteries, food production/farming; domestic life; organizing a royal progress for Elizabeth I; going into battle; Victorian factory life. (Cf. **NC** *History*.) Talk about how teams of people have to work together today in the business world, industrial firms and other forms of employment. (Cf. **NC** *Economic and Industrial Understanding; Careers and the World of Work*.)

Religious Commitment   Find out how people from different religious groups show commitment to their beliefs both in daily life and through specific activities (e.g. the work of the Salvation Army; Hindu respect for animals, such as regarding the cow as sacred; Muslims praying five times a day; the Jewish tradition of keeping Shabbat (the Sabbath); the way all the major religious traditions give money or goods to help the poor and support ecological issues). (Cf. **NC** *Geography*. AT 5 – environmental geography; *Environmental Education*.) See the books for teachers listed in Appendix 1 (e.g. *Islam and Ecology*, by Fazlum Khalid with Joanne O'Brien).

Recognizing One's Gifts Ask children to say or write down one sentence of the form 'I/X have/has the gift of …' about themselves or another person to encourage discussion about differing talents. Read *The River That Gave Gifts*, by Margo Humphrey. See also OT Story 8.

Gender Stereotyping See Story 5.

10

Teaching in Capernaum Synagogue

Mark 1: 21–39; Matthew 5: 38

It was a Saturday, the holy day of the Jews. The law said that no one was allowed to do any work on the sabbath day. Everyone in Capernaum was going to worship in the synagogue. Jesus went to the synagogue too.

The congregation sang some psalms. The sacred scroll was brought from its place by the wall. It was carried into the pulpit. There it was read aloud. Then the leader of the synagogue looked down and said, 'I have asked Jesus, the carpenter from Nazareth, to speak to us this morning.' Jesus was well known in Capernaum. It was not far from Nazareth where he had lived for nearly thirty years.

Jesus stood up, walked to the front and climbed into the pulpit. Sermons were often boring. This one was different. As Jesus spoke, the people in the synagogue became very still and quiet.

'In the Scriptures,' said Jesus, 'it says, "An eye for an eye, a tooth for a tooth". But I say to you, don't hurt anyone who does anything bad to you. If an enemy hits you, let him hit you again. When someone does bad things to you, you do good things.'

'What's he saying?' whispered a man in the congregation. 'Our religious leaders don't normally say things like that.'

'They usually send me to sleep,' answered his friend. He looked round. Up in the gallery even the children with their mothers were listening. Some were too young to understand,

54

but they could feel that something different was happening.

Suddenly the silence was broken. A man down in the congregation had jumped to his feet. 'What are you trying to do to us?' he shouted up at Jesus. 'Are you trying to get us wiped out?'

Jesus stopped and looked down at the man.

'I know who you are,' the man shouted, 'you're God's holy man.'

By now Jesus had come down from the pulpit. He stood facing the wild-eyed man. Jesus spoke quietly but firmly. 'Keep quiet,' he ordered. 'Let him go.'

It was as if the man had a devil in him. He shook all over, and slowly, still shaking, he sank on to the seat. For a few minutes he sat there shaking and whimpering like a baby. Suddenly he was calm again and his friends held him and gave him water to drink.

The service was over. Jesus left with his fishermen friends. Other people stayed behind chattering. 'What was that all about?' they asked one another. 'He seemed very sure about what he was saying.'

'Did you see what happened at the end?' said one man. 'It was as if a devil recognized him and then had to do what Jesus told him. There's something very strong about that man from Nazareth. He's quite different from other religious teachers.'

The people went home still talking about what had happened. Soon the news was all over the town. Everyone wanted to see Jesus but he could not be found anywhere. First he went back to Simon Peter's house. Early next morning he went out of town on his own to be quiet with God. When his friends found him they said, 'Come on back into town. Everyone's looking for you.'

'No,' said Jesus. 'Let's go somewhere else and not stay in one place.'

ABOUT THE STORY

The synagogue ritual here is instantly recognizable today. It has been going on every Shabbat (Sabbath) for more than 2500 years. Shabbat lasts from nightfall on Friday until nightfall on Saturday. Originally the Jews had the Temple as the one central place of worship. Worship there involved sacrifices and centred around festivals. The Ark of the Covenant, containing the Ten Commandments, was kept in the Holy of Holies but all that had been destroyed six hundred years before Jesus' time when the Jews had been conquered and taken into exile. Both (rebuilt) Temple and synagogues were to exist side by side until 120 C.E. although the Ark had gone for ever. In Christian churches we can see how both forms of worship continue to co-exist. In some traditions, especially in the Roman Catholic and 'high' Church of England, the Communion service centres on re-enacting the sacrifice of Jesus on the Cross as the body (bread) is broken and the blood (wine) is poured out. The non-sacrificial, reading, singing and preaching service dominates elsewhere, especially in Reformed Churches such as the Baptist and Methodist Churches, where the Communion service emphasizes sharing a meal and remembering. (See Stories 18 and 30.)

The president of the synagogue had invited Jesus to read and preach. We do not know what this sermon was like. What has been included here is a part of what are normally called the Beatitudes (beautiful or blessed attitudes) from the Sermon on the Mount (Matthew 5–7). It was based on very traditional material but its emphasis was new. Jesus did not break with the past. Rather he went to the very heart of what the tradition was all about instead of depending on later interpretations by other people, which had taken the sting out of it and made it bland.

Jesus obviously already had a reputation; he would not have been asked to preach otherwise. However, here he shows the strength to overcome powerful forces which are raised against him. His interrupter is well known too and deemed to be devil-possessed. Whatever form of mental disorder we might name today, Jesus leaves him calm and changed as no one else has been able to do. This causes great excitement but the temptation to be known for this sort of action has already been faced and challenged. Jesus decides to move on and away from his home area.

We should note also, however, the authority of his speaking. Just as 'disciple' is related to 'discipline' and retaining followers so 'authority' is related both to 'author' and to 'authoritarian'. Jesus' authority comes from being an author. He speaks off his own bat rather than quoting other people. His teaching is fresh and creative. He walks away from any authoritarian reputation which might arise as a result of his having commanded evil spirits to come out of the demoniac.

IDEAS FOR EXPLORING FURTHER

Judaism   Find out more about the Jewish traditions in which Jesus was steeped. See, for example, the packs on Judaism produced by Westhill College, Birmingham, or CEM, as well as the video *Judaism Through the Eyes of Jewish Children*, available from Chansitor Publications Ltd (for addresses see p. 229). If possible, visit a synagogue or ask a Jewish leader to talk to the children about it. Consider what the Jewish sacred writings (the Torah) and Christian Bible have in common.

The Spread of Religious Ideas   Ask older children to think about Judaism and Christianity as world religions. (See the CEM pack *When Christians Meet.*) Mark on a world map where Jews and Christians are to be found. What caused these religious ideas to spread? (Cf. **NC** *History:* CSU 4 – Second World War.) See Stories 38–50, OT Stories 10, 34, 35, 40.

Places of Worship   Consider what people do in places of worship and why. Draw out the points which seem strange or difficult to comprehend, with a view to increasing children's understanding of what happens there. Look at the CEM packs on Christian buildings, Hinduism, Islam, Judaism. What are the common points about the various places of worship and what are the differences? Look at a local religious building and identify how it has changed over time. Visit a few local churches belonging to various denominations to provide children with some breadth of experience. How have different generations expressed their ideas about God through architecture, decoration, painting, and so on? What first-hand evidence of past ages is to be found inside the church and in the graveyard? (Cf. **NC** *History:* SSU on houses and places of worship, local history, AT 3 – historical sources.) Investigate the reasons for the siting of the church, where building materials came from, the way the local settlement has developed, its precise location in the local area, how its construction altered the environment, the kinds of habitat that exist in the church grounds, how site conditions can influence surface temperatures and local wind speed and direction, evidence of weathering. (Cf. **NC** *Geography:* AT 1 – geographical skills, AT 3 – physical geography, AT 4 – human geography, AT 5 – environmental geography.) Consider the materials used in a local place of worship and make links with **NC** *Science:* AT 3 – materials and their properties. See also OT Stories 17, 25, 37, 38.

11

Healing the Man with Leprosy

Mark 1: 40–45; Leviticus 13: 14

One day Jesus met a man suffering from leprosy. Such people were very sick and sad people. Because of their illness they were sent out of the towns to live on their own in caves. No one went near them for fear of catching the dreaded illness. Sometimes a friend would go out and leave food by the road. When the road was clear the sick person would come out and collect it.

This man came out on to the track right in front of Jesus. Jesus' followers stepped back but Jesus stood still. The man looked a dreadful sight. Parts of his ears and his nose were already being eaten away by the disease. He had bound old rags around his fingers and feet. His clothes were dirty. He knelt down in front of Jesus. 'Help me,' he said. 'I've heard about you. You have all sorts of power inside you. If you want to, you can make me better.'

Jesus looked at him. Once this man had been happy. Now he was dying very slowly. And he was all alone. Every time anybody came near him he was supposed to shout 'Unclean, unclean!' Jesus felt very sorry for him. He could do something about it. Then he remembered those days in the desert. Should he use his powers? Yes, it was all right if he really used them to help others. The temptation had been to use them to show off and get attention.

Jesus put out his hand. Behind him Peter and the other fishermen gasped. Nobody ever touched a person with this disease. But that was exactly what Jesus did. He placed his hand on the man's head and said, 'Of course I want to – be clean!'

The man stood up. Something had happened deep inside him. Strength was seeping back into tired limbs and muscles. He knew he was going to be well again. He began to smile. He laughed. He became excited and started to shout and leap about.

'Stop,' cried Jesus. 'Stop and listen to me.' His voice was stern.

The man stood still; the smile left his face. Jesus looked very serious. Would he take back the power he had given?

'What I have done for you is something that only you and I know about,' Jesus said. 'You are to say nothing to anybody. I healed you because I was sorry for you, that's all. I don't want anybody else to know about it.'

'But I'm so happy,' said the man. 'I want to go back into town and tell everybody.'

'You can tell them you are cured,' replied Jesus, 'but don't tell them how it happened. You know our laws. Sometimes people are thought to have leprosy and they are mistaken. What happens then?'

'It is written in the law of Moses,' the man answered, 'that I should go to the priest. He will look closely to see that my skin is clean. Then he will shut me up for seven days. If I am still all right there will be a ceremony of cleansing. Then all the people will welcome me back.'

'That's right,' said Jesus. 'Go and keep the laws, but remember: show people you are well again but don't tell them how it happened.'

'I won't, I won't,' shouted the man as he ran off down the road to the town.

But he did. He couldn't keep it to himself. He told everyone and they all began to look for Jesus to do things for them.

NOTES

ABOUT THE STORY

With this and the following story we come to the vexed question of miracles. To some extent we often create the problem for ourselves by feeling that we have to offer explanations in detail about what might have happened. The truth of the matter is that we do not know and cannot know. We need only to tell the story with an air of mystery about it. What we do seem to know here and elsewhere are the consequences. Jesus acquired a strong reputation as a healer and miracle-worker. He was taunted about it even while in his death throes but he seems persistently to have attempted to stop people following him on the basis of this reputation. In other words he did not attach the importance to the miracles that many of his followers have done.

Once again the basic experience is essentially private and personal. Whilst it is easy to dismiss it, the old Cambridgeshire Agreed Syllabus definition of a miracle as 'any event which brings about an overwhelming sense of the presence of God' has much to commend it. Often a surprising number of children will talk about 'miracles' within the family once they are absolutely certain that no one is going to laugh at them.

Social acceptance is central to this first story. The touching is a key element. Leprosy sufferers the world over were, until well into this century, treated in much the same way as this one. They were expelled from all human contact and were as likely to die from starvation, neglect and lack of shelter as much as from the disease itself. Leprosy is marginally infectious at certain stages but for centuries was thought to be highly contagious. The disease was last recorded in Britain in 1798 but at one time there were hundreds of lazar (after Lazarus, the most famous of the biblical lepers) houses in this country. The Lizard (Lazarus) Peninsula in Cornwall took its name from the colony at its tip where ships deposited suspected cases at the first landfall to avoid being put into quarantine at other ports. The leper trail, bypassing towns and villages such as Helston, is still traceable in places.

Modern drugs now make the disease curable although much prejudice against ex-sufferers still persists. The nineteenth-century Father Damien is one of the best-known figures linked with the disease in Christian history. A Belgian missionary, he went to the Hawaiian Islands in 1863. He was struck by the policy of herding leprosy sufferers on to Molokai Island and in 1873 showed his commitment by joining them. As well as catering for the spiritual needs of the leprosy sufferers he campaigned for better housing, water and food supplies even after contracting the disease himself from constant and prolonged contact. He died of leprosy on 15 April 1889 but his life attracted great attention and hastened research work on the disease. (See *Island of No Return*, by Geoffrey Hanks, in the Faith in Action series, which also contains several titles describing more-recent work with leprosy sufferers.)

IDEAS FOR EXPLORING FURTHER

Feelings and Emotions   Discuss with pupils how they feel when they are ill and list their feelings. Talk about those people who are able to bring help when children are ill

60

and explore the range of emotions which children might experience when assistance is brought. (Cf. NC *English*: AT 1 – speaking and listening.) Incorporate the appropriate words into a large collage picture. If possible, make arrangements for groups of pupils to visit a children's ward at a local hospital – a useful experience in itself to prepare children for possible hospitalization, but also so that pupils might consider what they might do/take along to cheer sick children. (Cf. NC *Health Education*: family life education, psychological aspects of health education.) Look at a variety of advertisements or pictures of goods (e.g. wheelchairs, eating equipment, lifting gear, special telephones and door bells) which have been carefully designed to help disabled people. Children might like to interview some people who are physically disadvantaged in order to discover that they are nothing less than whole people inside a body which does not work as it should. (Would 'differently abled' be a useful term in this context?) Hopefully too, pupils will become more aware of such people's needs and try to design something which might give pleasure or be of assistance. (Cf. NC *Technology*.)

Joy   Help children to gain insight into the leprosy sufferer's joy by asking them to recall an occasion when they were so happy about something that they simply **had** to tell someone about it. Ask the children to write a sentence, a story or a poem about the experience and attach these to brightly coloured balloon shapes to suspend from the ceiling or to make into a frieze around the room. Older children could devise their own symbol for joy and relate their written work to it. (Cf. NC *English*: AT 3 – writing.)

Medical Knowledge: A Gift from God?   Reconsider the phrase 'Nobody ever touched a person with this disease' and the contemporary popular belief: 'Healing someone with leprosy! It can't be done!' Help the children to find out about medical cures which were discovered by people for whom the phrase 'It can't be done' had no meaning (e.g. the Canadians Frederick Banting and Charles Best, who made insulin available to humans for the treatment of diabetes in 1922; the Germans Paul Ehrlich and Emil von Behring, who developed immunization against diphtheria at the beginning of the twentieth century; the American Jonas Salk, who developed the Salk vaccine against polio in 1955). Find out about the Persian doctor Abu-Bakr Muhammad Ibn Zakariyya Ar-Razi (also known as Rhazes), who lived in the tenth century, gave one of the first descriptions of measles and wrote an encyclopaedia on medicine; the Persian Ibn Sina (also known as Avicenna), whose work *Canon of Medicine* was translated into other languages and became an important text in European medical schools; the Indian surgeon Susruta, who in the fifth century had numerous surgical instruments for his operations and more than seven hundred medicinal plants for drug treatments. Discuss the contributions of Egyptian and Greek physicians. (Cf. NC *History*: CSU 5 – Ancient Greece, SSU on Ancient Egypt. See *The History of Medicine*, by S. Parker.) Discuss the courage and perseverance of medical scientists shown in the way they often had to work in very poor conditions and had to overcome enormous obstacles. (Cf. notes on Story 1; NC *History*: CSU 3 – Victorian Britain, inventions and scientific discoveries.) Talk about the ways in which people might feel 'called' to undertake this type of work. Find out more about cancer research. Older children could debate the views of those who, for religious reasons, like Jehovah's Witnesses, refuse to have blood transfusions themselves or to allow their children to do so. The beliefs of Christian Scientists could also be reviewed.

Prayer   Within an appropriate context and with care and sensitivity, invite children to name/talk about anyone they know of who may be in need of healing or help at that time and/or recall (using pictures/newspaper articles) people locally, nationally and around the world who have health concerns. In order to keep these people in mind for a while longer, construct a 'prayer tree' with the name of each person or group being entered on a leaf or flower shape or on a segment of trunk. Alternatively, write a prayer for a particular land on paper cut to the shape of that country and use the shapes to form a map which indicates areas of the world where people have serious health concerns. (Cf. **NC** *English*: AT 3 – writing; *Geography*: AT 1 – geographical skills, AT 2 – knowledge and understanding of places.) See also OT Story 20.

Combatting Stereotypes   See Stories 3, 7, 14, 45, OT Stories 11, 18, 36, 40, 41.

Learning from Difficult Times   See notes on Story 12 – perseverance, Story 24.

Miracles   See OT Story 30.

12

The Day the Roof Fell In

Mark 2: 1–14

Jesus was back in Capernaum. Immediately the news spread
that he was in town. Jesus wanted to talk to people – to tell
them what he knew of God. He didn't even have a chance to
get out of the house. Faces appeared at the windows.
Children were held up to see him. When the door was
opened everybody crowded in.

Jesus started to talk to them there and then. Some listened
but many just pushed and shoved to see this man in the news.

Outside, the crowd spread across the road and went all
round the house. Suddenly while Jesus was talking, the roof
above his head began to give way. A foot appeared through it
and all the people in the house screamed. They tried to push
back to the door but the crowd outside was still pushing to get
in.

The foot disappeared. Then another pile of dust and clay
came down a little farther along. The foot came through the
ceiling again. It happened a third and fourth time. Now there
was a big hole in the roof. For a minute everybody in the room
could see the blue sky through the hole. Next a man's face
appeared at the hole, looking down at Jesus.

Some people in the room laughed. The roof wasn't falling
in after all. It was just some of the crowd who couldn't get in.
They had climbed up on to the flat roof where the owner slept
on very hot nights, and made a hole. One man wasn't pleased.

63

He was the owner of the house. But there was nothing he could do except shout – and nobody took any notice.

The face disappeared and another foot came through a metre away. It happened again and again. Were they taking the whole roof off? The hole was getting very big indeed.

'If you're sleeping up there tonight be careful your bed doesn't fall through,' called a voice.

More people laughed – but then suddenly a bed did fall through. What was more, it had a man on it. The laughter stopped dead.

The bed didn't fall on the people. It hung in the air, swaying backwards and forwards. The people in the room could see that it was held by ropes at each end. Nor was it a proper bed. It was a thin mattress, not much thicker than a blanket.

Slowly the man was lowered to the ground right at Jesus' feet. Jesus looked up and saw four faces peering through the hole. He had to smile. Everyone in the room had stopped talking.

'Sorry,' said one of the faces. 'He's our friend. He's paralysed. We just had to get him to you but the crowd kept us out. You will do something for him, won't you?'

Jesus looked at the man. He was very young. He lay on the floor. He could not move. Jesus spoke. He said something strange. 'My son,' he said, 'your sins are forgiven.'

At the back of the room there was a whisper. Two scribes stood there. They were very religious men. Their job was to write out the law. Because they did that all the time they got to know all the laws better than anybody else. People were frightened of them.

'Did you hear that?' said one to the other. 'He said "Your sins are forgiven". Whatever next?'

'Yes, I heard,' replied the other scribe. 'Who does he think he is – God? Only God can forgive sins.'

Jesus overheard them. 'What are you mumbling about?' he asked. Everybody turned to look at the scribes. 'What does it matter whether I say "Your sins are forgiven" or "Get up and go"? It's all the same thing. I have the power to do it.'

64

All this time the young man had been slowly getting to his feet. He shook and wobbled, but one or two people helped him.

Jesus turned back to him. 'Off you go,' he said. 'Just roll up that mattress and be on your way.'

The crowd parted and the man staggered to the door.

Up on the roof there was a shout. 'He's done it!' Footsteps clattered across the roof and down the outside stairs.

Jesus began to talk again, but some people began to drift away. Their excitement was over. They had had their fun. A few stayed behind. They wanted to get to know Jesus better.

Along with Peter, Andrew, James and John another eight men were asked by Jesus to stay with him all the time. So there were now twelve of them. As one of them said, 'Jacob had twelve sons who started the twelve tribes of Israel. Now Jesus has twelve followers. Perhaps God is starting to build his nation all over again.'

———————————— **NOTES** ————————————

ABOUT THE STORY

This is a second healing miracle but the story contains other elements which are important in terms of the whole Gospel Story.

Despite his protests Jesus' reputation has become based largely on his healing powers. Attempts to withdraw to home territory fail. There is no place to hide. To picture what happens in this story children need some understanding of the construction of Palestinian houses with flat roofs and outside staircases. The roof would be thick for insulation purposes but quite easily breakable, probably made of branches and interwoven sticks and fronds as a base for a clay covering.

Since Freud we are perhaps much less surprised today by any suggested connection between physical paralysis and deep guilt. However, as with the previous story, it is idle to speculate too much about the details. We should not pretend to knowledge we do not have.

It is in this story that the scribes make their appearance. They were much the same as biblical lawyers. Those who constantly had the job of writing out the Law (a sacred task in Judaism) soon became experts in it. Jesus' assurance that 'your sins are forgiven' is interpreted as an absolution. Only God can forgive sins. However, Mark, as the author of this story, is working at two levels. We are back to the Messianic Secret.

65

(See notes on Story 1.) Mark assumes that the reader already understands that Jesus is God. The characters in the story still do not but they are getting near to finding out. Then the trouble will really begin.

As told here the story has another hint. Jesus has been gathering other disciples. Now he has twelve. That is enough. Twelve is important. Israel, the people of God, had twelve tribes. Messiah should have the same in order to start the new 'people of God', which is what the word 'Israel' literally means.

IDEAS FOR EXPLORING FURTHER

Sin and Evil   Begin by exploring the meaning of the word 'sin' by talking/drawing/writing about characters in fiction, myths and legends whom children believe behaved wrongly and might be said, therefore, to have sinned. Consider people from different periods of history who have been deemed by some to be evil (e.g. Viking invaders, Henry VIII, Guy Fawkes, Adolf Hitler). Is it easy to say whether people are good or evil? (Cf. NC *History*: AT 2 – interpretations of history.) Older children could look at newspapers and take cuttings of stories which seem to them to illustrate the idea of sin. Throughout this type of work, encourage debate. Help children to understand the complexity of defining what is a 'sin' in human terms and help them to understand that people have different moral values. (Cf. *That's Not Fair: A Resource for Exploring Moral Issues in Primary and Middle Schools,* by Barry and Trish Miller.) Make a rogues' gallery of monsters, mythical characters or others deemed to be evil-doers by members of the class.

Story and Drama   Invite the children to work as a class with the teacher as scribe, or in small groups, to think through a modern-day parallel story. The aim is to experience a similar kind of dramatic tension and to understand better the thoughts and feelings of the people involved. For example, what would pupils do if they had a young brother or sister who urgently needed an expensive, life-saving operation abroad, but their family could not afford this? What would pupils do to get publicity? How would they go about fundraising? What difficulties and frustrations would they have to face? At what points would they need more courage than usual? What would their small triumphs be and what would it feel like when the patient was finally *en route* to the relevant hospital? (Cases like this are reported in the newspapers now and again.) The children could record the story orally on a cassette tape, act it out informally or write a script for it first. (Cf. NC *English*: AT 1 – speaking and listening, AT 3 – writing.) Throughout the work, discuss what joys, sacrifices/efforts the characters had to make on behalf of their friend, as well as their fears and worries. Later, relate the thoughts, feelings and experiences encountered through this work to Story 12 itself.

Caring   Draw out children's ideas about how, in the real world, they might look after a friend in need at home or at school. See also notes on Story 11, OT Stories 30, 45, and Paul Gallico's story *The Small Miracle,* about a young Italian boy who has to work at attracting the attention of the Pope himself in order to get help for his sick donkey.

13

Breaking the Rules

Mark 2: 23 – 3: 6

Jesus was not always happy and smiling. Sometimes he got
very angry. One of those days was another Saturday, the
Jewish sabbath day.

A long, long time before Jesus was born a lot of rules had
been made about making the sabbath different from other
days.

The rules were supposed to make sure that nobody had to
work on that day. Everybody should be able to rest and
everybody should be free to go to the synagogue. The first law
simply said, 'Remember the sabbath day and keep it holy'.
Sometimes people would not know whether something they
wanted to do was right and holy or not. Then they would go
to a lawyer and say, 'Can I do this on the sabbath day?' The
lawyer would look in his books and think, and say 'Yes' or
'No'. Usually he said 'No'. By the time Jesus was born there
were over one thousand five hundred things which couldn't be
done on Saturdays. Someone with a bad leg wasn't even
allowed to use a stick. That was carrying things, said the
lawyers, and carrying things was working – which was wrong.

The rules which once made people feel free now made them
feel like slaves. There were so many rules that whatever they
did they were bound to be breaking one of them.

On this particular Saturday two things happened. First,
Jesus and his twelve special friends were walking to the

synagogue. On the way the path went through a cornfield. As they walked along one or two of Jesus' disciples reached out and picked some ears of corn. They rubbed them in their hands, blew away the husks and ate the kernel which was left. They were chatting happily.

Suddenly Andrew looked up. 'Oh, dear, look out, we're being watched,' he said.

The others followed his gaze. There at the end of the field were two Pharisees looking all prim and proper.

As Jesus and his friends reached them one of the Pharisees spoke. 'We saw you,' he said, 'working on the sabbath, breaking the law.'

'What have we done now?' groaned one of Jesus' followers.

'You were rubbing ears of corn,' said the Pharisee. 'That is the same as grinding, and grinding corn on the sabbath is forbidden.'

Jesus interrupted. 'The sabbath,' he said, 'was made for people. It is to allow them to be free and to rest. A moment ago we were happily enjoying ourselves. We weren't harming anyone. You make it sound as if people should be made to fit in with the rules.'

The Pharisees did not answer. They looked down their noses at him, turned away and went into the synagogue.

Jesus and his disciples followed them in. The service had not started. A small group of people stood in the middle of the large room. 'Here he is,' somebody said. The group looked round at Jesus. In the middle of the group was a man whose left arm was all deformed. He could not use his hand. It was obvious that he and his friends wanted Jesus to heal him.

'Come here,' said Jesus to the man. 'Let me have a look.'

The man stepped forward. Jesus turned round. There at the back of the synagogue by the door stood the two Pharisees. There was no expression on their faces. They stood with their arms folded, looking straight at Jesus.

'Tell me,' said Jesus angrily, 'is it wrong to do good on the sabbath day?' He stared back at the Pharisees, waiting. They did not answer.

Jesus turned back to the man. 'Stretch out your hand,' he ordered.

Slowly the man did so. He had not been able to bend his left arm for many years. Now he strained and strained. Slowly, very slowly, the arm came out straight. He smiled, then laughed and threw his arms round Jesus. His friends all started talking excitedly. It was time for the service to start. The people went back to their seats. As they did so they noticed for the first time that the two Pharisees had disappeared.

They had slipped out of the door as soon as the disabled man had stretched out his hand. As the first psalm was being sung in the synagogue they were already hurrying off deep in conversation.

'This man is very dangerous,' said one. 'We must get rid of him as quickly as possible.'

'But how?' said his companion. 'He gets more popular with the people every day.'

'I don't know,' came the reply, 'but let's go and see some of Herod's friends. They have ways of getting rid of people. Perhaps they can suggest something.'

NOTES

ABOUT THE STORY

This story provides two examples of good religious practice turning sour. It is what can happen when something which begins as a spiritual response becomes translated into rules and attempts are made to define it. The two examples here are Shabbat (Sabbath) and Pharisees.

Both probably began as ways of helping Jews to cope with great pressure – the pressure of foreign domination – and to retain their identity. One day a week, from sunset on Friday to sunset on Saturday, was set aside from work. It was, and still is, a time when Jews belonged primarily to their families and to the synagogue community. Among Jews today it is often a relaxed occasion, a total break from normal work routine and literally a period of re-creation. It means doing no work. It is when officialdom tries to define what that means that the relaxation disappears and anxiety creeps in lest some rule or other is being broken. What is meant by work? Can you lift or carry anything or even take a walk? The list of prohibitions mounts up and guilt takes over. Here Jesus goes back to basics, repudiates the negative aspects and restores the positive. Is it ever wrong to do good? The legal minds cannot answer.

Pharisees were not priests. The movement had been founded some two to three hundred years previously. A rough parallel would be English Puritans. The Pharisees originally tried to live a simple, distinctive life-style which set them apart from what they saw as a brash, alien culture largely imported from the Greeks. In this way they helped keep Judaism alive. Then they started to define themselves. Many, although by no means all, started to become narrow-minded bigots, full of self-righteousness and of condemnation of others, more concerned with laying down the law than with simply living and being. Rules and regulations replaced any inner peace and joy which was there. Jesus goes back to those essential ingredients of true religion.

IDEAS FOR EXPLORING FURTHER

Rules   Invite the children to think about one (or more) of the following types of rules:

- rules made in the home;
- rules made at school;
- rules which govern traffic and behaviour in the locality (e.g. road traffic signs, 'No parking' signs, 'One-way street', 'Put your litter in the bin', 'Dogs must not foul the footpath', 'No cycling on pavements');
- club rules (e.g. Cubs/Scouts, Brownies/Guides, sports clubs);
- national laws;
- the Ten Commandments;
- rules belonging to the major faith traditions.

Talk about the purpose of rules (e.g. helping people to remember important things; helping to keep people free from certain ill effects). (Cf. **NC** *Health Education.*) Within the category of rules being considered by the children, are there any rules which are not in line with this? If so, why is this? What might be done about it? Give small groups of children a selection of rules written on paper or card. Ask pupils to rank them according to which they feel are the most/least important. In discussion afterwards, talk about:

- the reasons for the children's choices;
- the fact that people have different opinions about rules;
- the importance of having rules which are in the interests of the majority and are to the detriment of as few people as possible;
- any occasions when it might be necessary to break a rule and the difficult decisions which are sometimes related to this.

Older children may like to think about controversial rules/laws of the past (e.g. Hitler's laws concerning race, particularly the laws governing the Jews in the 1930s and early 1940s; the laws of Tudor monarchs governing religious affairs). (Cf. **NC** *History:* CSU

4 – Britain since 1930, the Second World War, CSU 2 – Tudor and Stuart times.) Pupils could also reflect on present-day controversial issues such as whether it is necessary to have a law to limit the influx of refugees into a country or to limit immigration in general.

In any of these discussions, encourage children to understand that people have to make choices about the type of rules/laws they want for their community and that these rules/laws are based upon a set of values which need to be examined. See also *Tyrone, the Dirty, Rotten Cheat,* by H. Wilhelm; OT Stories 14, 29, 39.

14

A Roman Officer Asks a Favour

Matthew 8: 5–13

The land in which Jesus lived was not a free land. The soldiers of the Roman army were everywhere. The Jews hated the Romans but they were too weak to get rid of them. They hoped that one day a leader would come and lead an uprising against them.

In every town there was a Roman officer in charge. He was usually a centurion, an officer who commanded a hundred men.

One day, to everyone's surprise, the Capernaum centurion appeared as Jesus came into the town.

'Now what's going to happen?' asked people in the crowd. 'Is he going to arrest Jesus?'

There were gasps as the centurion suddenly stopped in front of Jesus and said, 'Will you help me?'

A Roman officer, of all people, asking a Jew for help! No one had ever heard anything like it.

'How can I help you?' said Jesus.

'Well, it's not really me,' said the officer. 'It's my servant. He's very ill. Already he can't move his arms and legs. I don't like the look of him at all.'

Jesus replied, 'I will come straight away.'

At the back of the crowd, people began to mutter among themselves. 'Fancy helping Romans.' 'The only good Roman is a dead one.' 'Let them all get the sickness, then we shall be rid of them.' They were suddenly silent as the officer spoke again.

'No!' he said to Jesus. 'You don't have to come all the way to my house. I am not worth that. All you have to do is to say the word and my servant will be healed from here. I've watched you over the past few weeks. I know power when I see it. After all, I have a bit of power myself. I've a lot of men under me. All I have to do is say "Come here" or "Go there" and they do as they are told.'

There was a pause. Jesus turned to the crowd behind him.

'Listen to that,' he said. 'I haven't heard anything like it from my own people. This Roman is a better man than many of us. Belonging to a particular race or group isn't going to save us. God sees us as individuals. There are good Romans and bad ones just as there are good and bad Jews. That is true of all people everywhere.'

He turned back to the centurion. 'Go home,' he said kindly. 'You will find that when you get there your faith has made your servant well again.'

The centurion turned and pushed his way through the crowd. When he got home it was just as Jesus had said.

The people who followed Jesus were now arguing among themselves. 'It is a new teaching,' said some. 'He says that God loves everybody who has faith, even Romans.'

'Never mind what he says,' argued others. 'Look what happened. There was a Roman officer telling everyone that Jesus was more powerful than he was himself. This is the man we want. Forget his words. This man could help us smash the Romans. He's got real power and they know it. Let's make sure he uses it.'

ABOUT THE STORY

At the time of Jesus the Jews had been a conquered people for over six hundred years. Their independence had ended when the Babylonians had conquered them in 598 B.C.E. The Babylonians had themselves been conquered by the Persians (see OT Story 36), then the Greeks, under Alexander the Great, had conquered the Persians (see OT Story 42) and finally Greece had been conquered by Rome. Throughout all this time tiny Judah was simply a small piece of property which kept changing hands. Amazingly its people retained their identity and their faith. (Ten of the twelve tribes of Israel had disappeared in 737 B.C.E. – see notes on OT Story 32. The two small tribes of Judah and Benjamin made up the remaining country of Judaea, from which the word 'Jew' has come.)

Rome was strong and highly organized. It also tended to be nervous and could be very brutal. Jews and Romans kept their distance from one another. Within a local garrison the centurion, in charge of a detachment one hundred strong, would be a figure to be respected and feared. Most Romans ignored the local culture but, like a minority of British army officers in colonial India, this one obviously took a deep interest in 'the natives'. He shows humility and respect in public. He also recognizes power when he sees it.

Here Jesus shows the irrelevance of race and of social status. There is a common humanity which goes much deeper. However, he is both misunderstood and misinterpreted by those who cannot overcome their own stereotypes. A Roman officer has displayed weakness to a Jew and revealed his humanity. The situation can be exploited, especially if Jesus can be forced into a position of appearing to lead a rebellion. Although it is not referred to directly here it is at least possible that this is what was going on in the mind of at least one of Jesus' own disciples, Judas Iscariot.

IDEAS FOR EXPLORING FURTHER

Combatting Stereotypes Talk about how Jews and Romans felt about each other and possible reasons for this (e.g. the cruelty, greed, aggression, unfairness of the Romans as perceived by the Jews; the lawbreaking, tendency to revolt, envy of the Jews as perceived by the Romans). Explore these ideas further as follows:

(i) Talk with younger children about how appearances may be deceiving. Read stories which have characters who may look and sound good, but who, in fact, are not, and vice versa (e.g. Snow White's stepmother, the wolf in 'Little Red Riding Hood', the old woman in 'Hansel and Gretel'; *Beauty and the Beast*, by W. Crane; *The Frog Prince*, by J. Ormerod; *Sir Gawain and the Loathly Lady*, by S. Hastings).

(ii) Discuss with the children what they know about a group of people with which they are fairly unfamiliar (e.g. differently abled people, travellers, ethnic-minority groups in Britain, people living in other countries). As the discussion evolves, write down the children's comments. Talk about where the children get their ideas from (e.g. the old expression 'They say that ...' (rumour), TV, radio, visual material, films). Do these sources provide the whole, or only part, of the information required for a full understanding? Using pictures of the chosen group as a focus for discussion, ask: what definite information the pictures provide; what reasonable guesses may be made about the people and place in the picture; what questions must be asked in order to gain information which would help us really understand the people and the place.

(iii) Think about the prejudices we may have about other countries as a result of past wars or disagreements (e.g. Anglo-Irish difficulties, the war with Iraq, the Falklands War, divisions caused by the Second World War, attitudes created during the Cold War). Collect newspaper headlines and reports. What kind of language is used? Is it particularly emotive? Do some words have unpleasant connotations?

Draw out how easy it is to make judgements about people and places based on superficial and incomplete evidence. Relate the discussion from these activities back to the point made by Jesus in this story about a Roman officer – that God sees everyone as an individual and does not judge by external appearances. See also Stories 24, 45, OT Stories 11, 18, 36, 40, 41. (Cf. NC *English*: AT 1 – speaking and listening; *Multicultural Education; Citizenship*.)

15

A Birthday Party That Went Wrong

Mark 6: 14–30

King Herod was a frightened man. He was frightened of the Romans. He was frightened of his fierce wife, Herodias. He was frightened of the people because he knew they thought he was weak. Most of all he was frightened of God because of all the wrong things he had done.

He should never have married Herodias in the first place. She was the wife of his brother, Philip. But she was very attractive and he had just made off with her. He was still a king after all, so his brother couldn't do much about it.

Everything had gone wrong after that. John the Baptist had started it. Why had he had to tell everybody that even a king couldn't go round stealing other people's wives? Herodias had been furious. 'Arrest him and kill him,' she had said. 'I can't do that,' Herod had replied. 'Why not? You're king, aren't you?' 'This is Israel,' he had answered. 'Even the king has to obey the laws. They come from God. That's why the people cheer John. He's like the old prophets who stood up to the kings in the name of God.' She had scowled and gone into a sulky mood.

'All right, all right,' he said finally. 'I will have him arrested. At least that will shut him up. But I will not kill him. There are limits. Kings of Israel can't go round killing God's prophets.'

John was arrested. He was shut up in prison. Herod didn't know what to do with him. Then there was that dreadful night. He would like to forget it but he couldn't. It was his birthday. 'Let's have a party,' said Herod. 'Let's invite all the

Roman officers, the palace officials, the magistrates, in fact all the important people for miles around.'

It was a splendid party. There was lots of food. There was lots of wine as well. Herod enjoyed being the centre of attention. As the night went on he drank more and more wine. He got very drunk.

All of a sudden he banged his fist on the table. The plates and cups rattled. Everybody stopped talking. 'Let's have some music,' roared Herod. 'And bring on the dancing girls. Have some more wine, everybody.' He reached out for another jug himself.

The dancing girls came in. Herod watched. He was enjoying himself. One of the dancing girls was particularly beautiful. She danced better than all the others. When the music stopped Herod shouted, 'Bring that girl over here.' By now he was very drunk indeed. He did not even recognize the girl. She was Salome, the daughter of his own wife Herodias, born before he had married her mother.

'You are a beautiful dancer,' said Herod. 'Listen, everybody, I'm going to show you how generous I can be.' He turned back to the girl. 'You can have anything you want,' he said, smiling all round. 'Just name it and it's yours, anything at all – up to half my kingdom,' he added.

The girl paused. 'May I have a minute to think about it, Your Majesty?' she replied.

'Of course, of course,' said Herod. 'And then come back and sit up here with me.' He laughed.

The girl left the room. She went to find her mother. A minute later she was back.

'Well,' said Herod. 'What will you have?' The room went silent. In a loud, clear voice the girl said, 'I want the head of John the Baptist on a meat-plate, right here and now.'

'What!' exclaimed Herod. He glared round the room. All eyes were on him. He went red in the face. Everybody had heard his promise to the girl. What could he do? Herod spoke to the guards at the door. 'Bring what she asks,' he ordered.

The guards turned and went out.

Ten minutes later they returned. John had been beheaded in the prison yard. Herod's guests screamed as they saw the head on the dish. The girl seized it and rushed out to her mother, who smiled cruelly.

Some followers of John the Baptist came next day and took his body away to bury it. Then they went to tell Jesus.

A few weeks later news came to Herod that a new preacher was drawing crowds of people to him. He was called Jesus of Nazareth.

'What's he saying?' asked Herod.

'Very much what John the Baptist said,' was the reply. 'He's calling you an old fox.'

'It's his ghost,' groaned Herod. 'It's John the Baptist come back from the dead to haunt me. Will I ever get rid of him?'

NOTES

ABOUT THE STORY

This is the climax of the story of John the Baptist. (See Stories 6 and 7.) It is a clash between legal authority in the form of King Herod and moral authority as seen in the unconventional wild man from the desert.

For a comparison it is worth looking back at the Old Testament story of Naboth's Vineyard (1 Kings 21; see OT Story 29). Deep in Israel's subconscious was the idea of direct rule by God (theocracy). Prophets were seen as God's spokespersons although there was often a dispute as to whether or not any one particular prophet was genuine. There had always been, however, an even deeper suspicion of kings. (See OT Story 21.) There are some similarities with our modern idea of the Rule of Law.

In the past this story has often been regarded as unsuitable for children because of Herod's display of drunkenness and lechery. For better or for worse such characteristics are nowadays more widely experienced and understood if only through television. Here they come through as signs of weakness. As a king Herod was a disaster. He tried to please everyone and subsequently ended up being despised by all and sundry. John is summarily executed but it is his strength of character which has long outlived Herod's reputation. Within the story he is just another political prisoner disposed of behind prison walls but this does not solve Herod's problem; it only makes it worse. He cannot hush it up and news that Jesus is continuing John's message haunts him as Banquo's ghost came to haunt Macbeth.

78

The story might also raise questions as to who was the more guilty, the drunken Herod or the sober Herodias? Was Salome, a teenager, just an innocent victim of circumstances? Are only adults responsible? How easy is it to get carried along with the crowd? This is an old story: it is also a surprisingly modern one.

IDEAS FOR EXPLORING FURTHER

Choices Talk about the choices which faced Herod at different points in the story: (i) before he had married Herodias; (ii) upon hearing about John the Baptist's teaching; (iii) with regard to the amount he drank; (iv) when he felt like showing off by being over generous; (v) when faced with Salome's request. Think through the alternatives and their possible consequences. Discuss what God might have wanted Herod to choose and what might have been the result.

Relate the issue of choices to the children's own lives: situations at home and school where children have decisions to make and consequences to accept. Talk about pupils' desire to belong to a group and to be liked/admired by group members. Discuss the problems of peer-group pressure and raise issues related to taking drugs, glue sniffing, drinking, etc., all of which can cloud one's thinking and affect one's judgement. Draw attention to the fact that, as this story demonstrates, an apparently quick 'solution', a quick 'fix' does not really help in any way, but only creates more difficulties. (Cf. NC *Health Education*: substance use and misuse. See also Story 16.)

Working as a class, in pairs or as individuals, help the children to make a 'decision tree'. Write on the trunk the question at issue (e.g. 'Shall I sniff glue with my friends because they want me to, even though I don't fancy it?'). Draw a number of branches and write on each of them *one* of the alternative decisions that could be made (e.g. 'Yes, I will do just as the group wants'; 'Well, I will only do it once'; 'Well, perhaps I'll do it just occasionally'; 'No, I won't do it and I'll explain my reasons'; 'I really hate this idea, so I will tell a relative or my teacher'). At the end of each branch, draw the leaves or flowers or fruits of the plant with each one bearing key words relating to the possible consequences of each particular decision. Help the children to understand that one of the key features of being a human being is to have the capacity to make choices and decisions. This entails responsibility.

See also Stories 4, 16, 31, OT Stories 3, 28.

Alternatives See Story 47.

Leadership See Stories 17, 20, OT Stories 10, 21.

Actions Have Consequences See OT Story 4.

Temptation See Stories 4, 30, 31, OT Story 49.

16

The Story of the Loving Father

Luke 15: 11–32

Jesus was talking to the crowd. 'God loves every single one of you,' he said. 'He knows you all by name. God is like a good shepherd who knows all his sheep. God loves even more than that. He is the most loving father there ever was. Listen,' said Jesus. 'I'll tell you a story.

'There was once a man who had two sons. Both of them were now grown up. They knew that when he died they would share out what their father owned. The elder son would have two shares. The younger son would have one share, according to the custom. One day the younger son went to his father and said, "I want to enjoy life while I am young. Would you give me my share of the money now?" His father was very upset, but in the end he agreed. He counted up all his money and gave a third of it to his young son.

'A few days later the young man started to pack his things.

'"Where are you going?" asked the father.

'"Anywhere to get away from here," said the son. "I don't want to live on a dull old farm. I want to enjoy life."

'The father was very upset, but the son was grown up. What could he do?

'The younger son set off. He went into the big city. He had plenty of money. He could buy almost anything. He bought drinks for people, and presents for lots of girl-friends. He soon

80

became very popular. Lots of young people came and stayed at his house. He gave lots of parties and he didn't do any work. It was all great fun until one day he suddenly realized that nearly all his money was gone. Never mind, he thought, I've got lots of friends now. They will help me.

'"Could you lend me some money?" he said to a group of friends that evening.

'"Sorry," they said, "We don't have any with us at the moment. Tomorrow, perhaps."

'Next day they didn't turn up. He never saw them again. They had never really been friends at all.

'Now he was all alone in the big city. He had no money and nowhere to stay. Life was very miserable. He started to beg. Nobody wanted to know him. In the end only one person would help. He was a pig-farmer. He had no friends either. Good Jews never touch pig-meat.

'The young man spent his days in the fields with the pigs. He mixed their food. It was made from old left-overs mashed up. Nobody gave him any food so he had to eat pig-swill.

'One day he suddenly thought, Why am I doing this? My father's farm-workers eat better than me. I will go home. Then he thought, No, everybody will laugh at me. I can't go home. My father wouldn't want me after the way I behaved.

'He watched the pigs eating. He got more and more hungry. Pig-swill! Ugh! The thought made him feel sick. Anything would be better than that. He left the pigs and started off home.

'For several days he walked, feeling very weak and weary. Finally, he came over a hill and there in the valley was the old farmhouse. He started down the hill.

'In the distance he saw someone moving from the house towards him. He walked on. The other person came on as well. They got nearer and nearer to one another. Perhaps it was a traveller leaving his father's house. As he got close he realized it was an old man. Could it be? Yes, it was his father coming out to meet him. He began to run. Father and son met on the track. The old man threw his arms round his son.

81

'"I've looked out for you every day," said the father. "I always knew you'd come home one day."

'The son suddenly felt ashamed. The old man kept saying, "My son, my son". The son shook his head. "No, father, I can hardly be called your son any more. See how poor and thin I am. I have disgraced you."

'"Nonsense," said the father. "Come on. Let us go indoors."

'In the house the son was given clean clothes. His father even gave him a gold ring. A servant was called. "Kill the fatted calf," said the father. "Tonight we shall have a great feast."

'Out in the fields the older brother was working as usual. Towards evening he came home. As he got near the farmhouse he could hear music and singing. "What's going on?" he said to a servant.

'"Haven't you heard?" came the reply. "Your young brother has come home. Your father is so pleased that he has killed the fatted calf and is having a big party."

'"What!" screamed the older brother. "My silly little brother comes home after spending all his money and we have a party. Has my father gone mad? I've worked my fingers to the bone keeping this farm going and nobody has ever given a party for me. Well, I'm not going. Go and tell my father I'll have nothing to do with it."

'The servant went into the house. A few minutes later the father appeared. He came over to the elder brother who was sulking. "Come on in, my son," he said.

'"Not me," said the elder brother. "I'm fed up. I've worked hard ever since he went away and you've never had a party for me. Now he comes home and gets treated like a king."

'"Listen, my son," said his father. "Don't be miserable. Everything I have belongs to you. The farm is all yours. The party is not for your brother, it's for me. I'm the one who is happy. I had two sons. One got lost. I thought he was dead. Now he's been found alive. I am a happy man. Come and be happy with me."

'After a while they went indoors together.'
Jesus finished speaking. He never told the people what his stories meant. He left them to work out the meaning for themselves.

NOTES

ABOUT THE STORY

In the past this story has suffered from over use. Surprise was a major reason for using parables in teaching and that works only the first time a particular parable is employed. The Greek words *para* and *ballo* mean simply 'I throw alongside'. In fact the word *ballo*, from which we get our English word 'ballistic', carries quite a lot of force. We might even say, 'I hurl alongside'. Today in modern Greece the word is used, for example, when a farmer pitches a fork of hay alongside a tethered donkey.

Parabolic teaching is a creative method. Good teachers invent their own parables. Most of us copy those of others but then they quickly cease to be parables and become conventional stories. Jesus was a superb creator of parables. Often they are short, little more than metaphors, but some, like this, are full story length. One of the purposes of parable is to lull the listener into a passive, accepting frame of mind and then to give an unexpected twist which gets through a new thought and cries out for a response.

Care needs to be taken here as elsewhere with working from a father–child relationship. The whole point of this story is to show what a loving father *should* be like. However, for most of the time this reads like a standard family soap-opera situation with 'bored with home', 'I know best', 'want to be free' ingredients. It is important to remember that it is one of a series of stories about losing things and the key figure is the father, not the son.

The twist, however, comes right at the end with the entry of the older brother. Does he deserve more love or not? Would Jesus have been a better son if he had stayed at home and remained a carpenter? In most farming societies, until very recently, it was normal for younger children to have to seek their living away from the family estate. Certain elements of this story are given female parallels in Story 25.

IDEAS FOR EXPLORING FURTHER

Taking Things for Granted   Talk to the class about how the younger son in this story seems not to have fully appreciated his home and his relatives or the good things which made up everyday life. He took many things for granted. He imagined there were better things 'out there'. He wasn't satisfied. He wanted more. But, upon his return, having been disappointed by what was 'out there', he became aware of his

83

father's great love for him and saw his home and his work life with new eyes. Talk to the class about their life at school and about the local area. What do they particularly enjoy? Does everyone in the world have the same facilities or opportunities as they do? What do the children take for granted? Draw a picture map or sketch plan of areas in the school or parts of the locality (using printed plans or maps to help if necessary). Place on it or around it children's pictures/pieces of writing which indicate things which they particularly value. (Cf. **NC** *Geography*: AT 1 – geographical skills.)

Create a modern equivalent to this parable, perhaps about young people who leave home, encounter some challenging experiences and end up destitute in London in a cardboard city. The book *Fergus Travels South*, by Avril Rowlands, is one example of this. (Cf. **NC** *English*.)

Disappointment   Explore with the children the meaning of the modern adage 'The grass seems greener on the other side of the fence'. Can the children recall times when they thought something was going to be 'great' and then it turned out not to be so 'great' after all (e.g. toys they had wanted, visits, parties, food)? Is there anything to be learned from disappointments? Challenge the children to use their ideas and experiences to illustrate the adage in two-dimensional or three-dimensional form. (Cf. **NC** *Technology*.)

Metaphor/Picture Language/Meaning of Stories   See the Introduction, Stories 21, 24, 49, OT Stories 8, 9, 35, 41, 49.

Choices   See Stories 4, 15, 31, OT Stories 3, 28.

Alternatives   See Story 47.

17

The Storm on the Lake

Mark 4: 35–41

'Let's go and have a short holiday,' said Jesus one day to his disciples. 'We could row across the lake. There are no towns on the other side. We could be on our own there.'

They got out the boat. Everybody climbed in. The strong fishermen took the oars.

Jesus was very tired. It was already getting dark. He was in the back of the boat. It was going to be a long row. Jesus got down and lay in the bottom of the boat. He had been teaching all day. There had been crowds and crowds of people all around him. Now he could sleep. One of his disciples handed him a cushion. He put it under his head. Soon he was fast asleep.

The disciples rowed on into the dark night. Nobody could see any land. People in the town had gone to bed. There were no lights to be seen anywhere.

Up above there were a few stars. Soon they too disappeared.

'It's getting cloudy,' said one of the fishermen, looking up. Just then there was a ripple across the water. A breeze blew. The boat rocked very gently. They rowed on.

A minute later there was another movement on the water. This time the breeze that touched their backs was a little stronger. The boat rocked on the little waves.

One of the disciples who was not rowing shivered. 'It's gone cold,' he said.

The fishermen looked at one another. They knew the lake well. They knew what could happen when the wind swung round to the north. It would come off the snow-covered mountain, Mount Hermon, straight down on to the lake. There could be a bad storm.

The wind came again – stronger this time. The boat pitched. 'Where are we?' said a voice.

'Just about in the middle, I should think,' came an answer.

It was no good turning back. 'Then let's get there as quickly as we can.'

The fishermen leaned into their oars. The boat began to move more quickly through the water. They knew how to row. They had done it all their lives.

The wind was dead against them. The water splashed up the side of the boat. The spray went over them. This time the wind did not stop. It went on blowing, stronger and stronger. Now everybody could see the waves. The sea which had been black a minute ago was now a moving mass of white. The wind began to blow the spray off the tops of the waves. Everyone was getting wet and cold. Jesus alone in the bottom of the boat was dry. He was still asleep.

Stronger and stronger blew the wind. The boat started to go up and down. Not all the disciples were fishermen. Some were not used to boats. The wind was now a gale. The water rushed past the side of the boat. Suddenly a wave came over the side. 'Help!' yelled the man sitting there, 'it's coming in.'

'Sit down,' said one of the fishermen.

Too late. Others started to panic. 'We shall all drown,' they shouted. 'Help! Help!'

As they stood up the boat leaned over.

'Sit down,' roared Peter.

'Save us! Help! We're drowning!' yelled the others.

Jesus slept on in the bottom of the boat.

Suddenly he was wide awake. He looked up into a frightened face. One of his disciples was shaking him and shouting, 'Master, master, wake up! Do something. Don't you care whether we drown or not?'

Jesus sat up. All round him was panic. The wind howled. The boat moved from side to side. Men were jumping up and down.

Jesus looked up. In a loud, firm voice he shouted above all the noise, 'Keep still. Calm down.'

The movement stopped. The men in the boat sat down.

'What is the matter with you? Haven't you got any faith? What makes you so frightened?'

Suddenly everybody realized that the wind had dropped too. The boat still moved from side to side but the sea was black again. It was calmer too.

The fishermen rowed on. They were all silent. Jesus settled down again in the back of the boat.

'Who is this Jesus?' whispered a voice in the dark.

'You may well ask,' came a soft reply. 'Even the wind and the waves do as he says.'

The boat went on safely to the shore.

NOTES

ABOUT THE STORY

The importance of miracles, we need constantly to remind ourselves, is in their effect, not in any explanation we have to offer. Those who were present were convinced by them and often became followers as a result. Jesus did not perform them for that reason but because there was a need to be met.

In the healing miracles that need is apparent. With the nature miracles, of which this story is a classic example, it is harder to see what it was all about. All we can be sure of is that it was still being talked about fifty or sixty years after the event as an important episode in the life of Jesus. There are difficulties. It seems to go right against what was decided at the time of the Temptations (see Story 8). Again we do not know what level of symbolism might be contained within the story. What we can show, however, is a clear ambiguity. When Jesus uttered the famous words 'Peace. Be still', or, as we have worded it here, 'Keep still. Calm down', was he really talking to the water, as the text clearly says, or was he actually talking to the disciples? The Greek words that are used – although Jesus himself almost certainly spoke Aramaic – are quite strong and could almost take the translation 'Shut up and calm down'. What we cannot know is what every teacher could tell from experience would make all the difference, namely the tone of voice used.

Sudden storms on Galilee are not uncommon. Its length is only about eight kilometres but it lies under the shadow of the mountain to the north and sudden downdraughts can cause immediate turbulence. Many of these disciples were fishermen who knew the lake in all its moods and the authority of Jesus is enhanced by this incident. In its context this story helps build up the picture that this man is not only different but someone of very special authority over all things.

IDEAS FOR EXPLORING FURTHER

Leadership Ask children to design and make a 'Good Leader Award' for a favourite leader (to be worn, placed on or in a car, or used as a decoration). Some key words or phrases which indicate why that person has been chosen could be placed on it. (Cf. **NC** *Technology*.) See Story 20, OT Stories 10, 21.

Invite older children to think about this story again in short sections and to draw out the responsibilities of being a leader. For example:

- looking after the team's health by ensuring everyone gets a break and a rest;
- arranging times for the group to meet together alone, so that they can talk together;
- discussing goals and how to reach them;
- arranging transport;
- knowing when to take a rest yourself so that you can work effectively;
- encouraging the team to develop their skills so that they can perform well even in difficult circumstances;
- encouraging the team to look after each other's safety;
- encouraging cooperation amongst team members;
- dealing with each individual's personal worries;
- helping to settle disputes fairly;
- communicating clearly with everyone.

Discuss whether it is always easy to be a leader. What are the advantages and disadvantages? (Cf. football-club managers, leaders of political parties, company directors, owners of shops and restaurants, leaders of pop groups, captains of sports teams.) Consider also the qualities of great leaders of the past. (Cf. **NC** *History*.) In pairs, children could select one of these examples (or choose another, or use the story as an illustration), and indicate in words and pictures the weight of their chosen leader's responsibilities. Writing a letter to a local leader and holding an interview (perhaps with someone with responsibility for the environment and planning – cf. **NC** *Geography*: AT 5 – environmental geography) could provoke useful discussions. Composing an acrostic poem based on the word 'leadership' or 'responsibility' might be a suitable challenge for some pupils. Other children might like to work in small groups to devise a dramatic scene where a leader is faced with a particular problem and has to sort it out. Reasons for decisions can then be discussed. (Cf. **NC** *English*.)

18

Feeding Five Thousand People

John 6: 1–15

Everywhere Jesus went the crowds followed him, even out into the countryside.

It was Passover time. Every year the Jews celebrated the day when the Angel of Death passed over their forefathers in Egypt. They remembered the time when they had left Egypt and followed Moses into the desert.

The festival of Passover came in the spring.

On this particular Passover Jesus had gone with his disciples into a quiet place in the hills. He wanted to be alone with his special friends. There was a lot he had to say to them.

However, he soon realized they were not alone. People began to appear over the tops of the hills. He had been found. The news of where he was had spread everywhere. People had come to find him.

All day long they came, until in the afternoon there were hundreds of people in the tiny valley. Soon the sun would go down and it would begin to get cold.

Philip turned to Jesus and said, 'You'd better send these people away. It's a long way back to the town. Most of them have had nothing to eat all day.'

'Well, give them something to eat, then,' said Jesus in reply.

'Give them something to eat?' repeated Philip. 'But there's no food here at all. We should have to go into town and buy it. Besides, there are so many people that we wouldn't have nearly enough money. It would cost far more than we have.'

At that moment Andrew came up. 'They are not all without food,' he interrupted. 'I've just found a young boy who had the sense to bring some with him.'

'How much?' asked Philip.

'He's got five small barley loaves and two fish,' replied Andrew.

They laughed.

'That won't go far, I know,' added Andrew.

Jesus spoke. 'Tell the people to sit down on the grass,' he said.

The disciples went off into the crowd. After a few minutes they got everybody organized. People were sitting in groups, about fifty in each group. It was then that they realized there were not just a few hundred people but about five thousand.

Suddenly everything went quiet. Jesus had stood up. In his hands he held the bread and fish. He raised them up and lifted his head towards the sky. No one could hear what he was saying but he was obviously praying to God.

He stopped and began to give out food to the people nearest to him.

'Hard luck,' said a man at the back to his friend. 'We shan't get anything.'

'No, but I'm surprised how far it's going,' replied his friend.

The first man looked up. Jesus had gone right along the front row. He was starting on the second. They waited. Jesus got to the end of the row and started on the third.

'I'd never have believed it,' said the man again.

By now Jesus was walking down the fifth row. A strange silence had come over the crowd. On and on walked Jesus, up one row and down the next, giving everyone food.

And then it was over. Everyone had something to eat. Jesus went back to his disciples. 'Go and collect up what's left over,' he said. 'Nothing must be wasted.'

The twelve disciples each had a bag. They filled them up with scraps.

By now the silence had been broken. At first it was a whisper. Now everyone was chattering. The excitement

90

grew and grew. The crowd showed no sign of going home. Just the opposite.

A few men began to move among the crowd. 'This is the man we have been waiting for,' they were saying. 'This is our promised king. Here is the man of power. With Jesus leading us we can destroy the Romans. Come on, let's crown him as our king here and now.'

Men began to jump to their feet. They surged through the crowd towards Jesus. Suddenly they stopped. Where was Jesus? One minute he had been there, the next he had gone.

It was almost dark now. Jesus had seen what was happening. In all the excitement he had slipped away into the dark. He walked over the hill and into the next valley. On and on he walked.

NOTES

ABOUT THE STORY

Jesus does not escape. The crowd follow around the shore. This miracle of the feeding of the five thousand is seen as crucially important to the Gospel Story. It is the only miracle which appears in all four Gospels. John is most explicit about why this should be and it is his account which is followed here. At the end of it he comments that the crowd tried to take hold of Jesus and make him king but that he managed to sidestep their efforts and get away into the surrounding wilderness.

In telling this story we come back again to asking just what sort of truth claims are being made here. Being Westerners and living in a science-based culture our attention tends to centre on the question 'How?' Theories abound. Did the boy's production of the five loaves and two fish prompt others to admit that they had sandwiches under their shalwas? Had the disciples nipped back into town to do some quick shopping? These sorts of questions have been asked repeatedly. They are almost certainly very wide of the mark.

There can be little doubt that there is a deep symbolic element in all the accounts of this miracle. It is almost certainly that sort of truth we should be looking for. There is something of a Eucharistic or Holy Communion atmosphere about the telling of this story. Are those who take part physically or spiritually 'full up' at the end? The real power at work is the effect of Jesus' presence on the crowd. It is as if Israel has discovered a new leader and a new identity. Twelve disciples collect twelve baskets of left-overs from orderly groups of people. Are they in some mystical way the twelve tribes of Israel?

91

The five loaves and the two fish have been well-known icons in Christian art from the very earliest days. That this story is historically based on an incident which took place at this point in the whole narrative is highly likely. It is a critical moment. The crowd tries to proclaim Jesus as king. He rejects this and slips away. Why? The next story gives an answer. But later generations knew the eventual outcome and probably saw in this event some sort of rehearsal for the Last Supper.

IDEAS FOR EXPLORING FURTHER

Meals   Ask children to recall any special meals they have had. With whom did they eat? What did they talk about? How did they feel? Ask them whether they feel closer to someone if they go to their house and share a meal with them. Think about daily family meals, parties, barbecues, picnics, harvest suppers, Christmas dinners, midnight feasts. What do children value about these? Ask whether any of the children have been abroad and eaten a meal in a family home. What did they see/learn from the experience? Do opportunities for eating together provide anything else other than receiving food (e.g. companionship, information, new ideas, jokes, seeing things from a different point of view, a chance to share secrets or worries, a chance to show concern and sympathy, a sense of belonging and/or community)? Would this be the same the world over? (Cf. Jesus visiting the home of Zacchaeus for a meal and the effect this had on the tax-collector: Story 22.) Children could record their thoughts and feelings about special meals in picture/poetry/prose on fish- or bread-shaped paper and assemble these in or around a large drawn, painted or collage basket. Talk about how the basket might represent the idea of 'togetherness' or 'unity'.

Symbolic Food   Think carefully about how some people celebrate/remember important events through meals (e.g. the Jewish Shabbat (Sabbath) meal, the Jewish Pesach (Passover) meal, the Holy Communion). Ask an appropriate visitor to speak to the children about such a meal. Make a visual representation of it and indicate the children's understandings of the symbols being used. Find out how food is used for symbolic purposes in many different cultures. (Cf. **NC** *Geography*: AT 2 – knowledge and understanding of places.) Consider also the symbolic use of food in the past, especially herbs. (Cf. **NC** *History*: SSU on food and farming.) For additional ideas about symbols, see also Stories 4, 30, OT Stories 20, 27.

Miracles   See Stories 11, 12, 14, 17, 34, OT Story 30.

19

Who Am I?

Mark 8: 27–38

At last Jesus and his disciples were alone. They walked and walked, mile after mile, day after day. Most of the disciples had never been this far before. They were right outside King Herod's territory and near the capital city of his brother, Philip.

'Where are we going?' asked Peter as they trudged along.

'Just anywhere to be away from the crowds,' replied Jesus.

'Why?' asked Peter.

There was a silence. Jesus had stopped. He stood still and the twelve men with him stopped as well. Nobody else was in sight. Away in the far distance was a tiny village on top of a hill. The little white houses shone in the bright sunshine. It was too far away to see any people. Nothing moved. The sun was hot. Even the birds were still.

At last Jesus spoke. 'I want to ask you a question,' he said. 'It's this. Who do the people think I am?'

The men smiled.

'That's easy,' said James. 'Mostly they say that you're John the Baptist.'

'Especially since Herod had him executed,' added Matthew. 'In fact, I was told that Herod has been saying so himself. He wants to see what you look like, that's for sure.'

'I've heard other names mentioned,' interrupted Andrew.

'Oh, which ones?' asked Jesus.

'Elijah,' said Andrew.

93

'It's almost the same thing,' said James. 'When John the Baptist first came to the River Jordan people said he was Elijah come back.'

'He was one of our greatest prophets, that's why, and in the story he never actually died. Our people have always believed that when real trouble came Elijah would return and rescue us.'

'So that's how they see me, is it?' asked Jesus.

'Of course,' said the disciples together. 'The people might argue about names but they all think you are a prophet, like our great leaders of the past.'

'Let me ask you another question,' said Jesus. 'Who do *you* think I am?'

Peter for once had kept quiet up to now. But he could not hold himself any longer. 'You are the Messiah,' he said. 'The Christ, greater than all the prophets.'

There was a silence. Then Jesus spoke again. 'Sit down,' he said. They all sat down in a circle on the grass.

'Listen,' Jesus went on. 'Listen very carefully, because what I have to say is very important.'

The disciples went very quiet.

'I won't use the word "Messiah",' said Jesus, 'because people have a picture of Messiah as a soldier on a white horse charging at the Romans in battle. I shall call myself "Son of Man" instead. Now the Son of Man is going to suffer a lot. He's going to be hated by the leaders of our own people. He's going to be killed. But that won't be the end. He will come back from the dead.'

Peter exploded. 'What are you talking about, Jesus?' he said. 'I told you, you are Messiah. You've got all the power in the world. Nobody's going to kill you. You can wipe them all out with a wave of your hand. That's why the crowds follow you.'

'Peter,' said Jesus angrily, 'you haven't listened to a word I've been saying. You've got the Devil in you. I know that's why people follow me. That's what makes me so sad. I tell them God wants love and they cheer. Then the next minute

94

they expect me to go round leading them into battle and killing people. If God wants love, then I've got to love – even my enemies. And the people won't like that. They can't understand it. That's why we've come away from the crowds.'

Peter was silent. He could see Jesus was angry with him. He would do anything for Jesus. He would fight and kill and die in battle. But could he just let himself be killed without a fight? He found that very difficult to understand.

'We must go on loving people whatever they do to us.' That's what Jesus was saying now. 'Whoever wants to follow me is going to lose his life.' It was too much for Peter. He'd always been a fighter but he wasn't sure he was brave enough for this.

Jesus stood up. 'Come on,' he said. 'Let's go into that village and get some food.' He put an arm round Peter's shoulders. 'One day you'll understand,' he said.

And they walked on.

NOTES

ABOUT THE STORY

Jesus leads his small group of disciples out into the deeper regions of the sparsely inhabited desert area to the north-east of Galilee.

This is a turning-point in the Gospel Story. From now onwards Jesus' whole method changes. He ceases to preach to large crowds. Instead he becomes the teacher of the twelve and talks to others as individuals. At this point too the Messianic Secret comes out. What the reader has known since the beginning those within the story come to be aware of for the first time.

At first Jesus asks an innocent question about gossip. What have they heard other people saying about who he really is? Another John the Baptist is an expected response. Elijah is a far more profound reply. In Jewish mythology Elijah had never died. He had ascended in a chariot and would return at a moment of great crisis to restore Israel. Even today it is customary at the Pesach (Passover) feast for a place to be set for Elijah at the family table.

Then comes the crunch question: 'But who do you think that I am?' Peter, impetuous as ever, rushes the response. Jesus is nothing less than Messiah (*Christos* in Greek). Immediately we see why Jesus has abandoned the crowds. The popular view of Messiah was that he would be a military leader who would raise up an army and drive away the Romans. There were, however, other, deeper views. Religiously, as opposed to politically, Messiah was to be a Suffering Servant. Jesus starts to explain. Peter does not listen. He blurts out again the popular view and receives a good telling-off for his trouble.

The task for Jesus now is a teaching task. Words are of use only if they are understood. To be understood they have to be demonstrated as well as spoken. It is necessary for Jesus to be and to do what he also says. There are no short cuts.

This may seem a difficult story for children but it is not. It is more difficult for adults who are sure they know what words mean. Children are more accustomed to being unsure and to 'playing with words'.

IDEAS FOR EXPLORING FURTHER

Getting to Know People   Talk to the children about how easy/difficult it is to get to know people. Can one judge people just by looking at them from the outside? (Cf. combatting stereotypes: Story 14, OT Story 18.) How important is it to have shared experiences (e.g. shared a story, played a game together, drawn a picture together, built something together)? Ask children either to pair up with someone in the class they do not know very well, or to pair up with a friend. Ask the pairs to choose something to do together. While they work alongside each other, ask each child to try and find out or to notice something that the other child particularly likes or does well. Individual children could also be asked to draw/write/make a tape about themselves or one of their peers, explaining something about their family, their pets, their favourite food, sports, TV programmes, their dislikes, etc. Let the children share their experiences. Try to foster children's self-esteem and mutual understanding and respect. Invite older children to consider how complex human beings are and to appreciate that there are many different facets of a personality.

Interpretations of Jesus   Collect different pictures of Jesus. What do these pictures seem to be saying about Jesus: his character, his work, his relationship to God and human beings? Talk about different opinions and interpretations. Include in the collection some pictures from a variety of cultures. (See the CEM pack *When Christians Meet*.) What are the similarities and differences in the way Jesus is portrayed?

Jesus and Other Faith Traditions   Help the children to find out how Jesus is viewed by the majority of people belonging to the major faith traditions:

Christians   believe that God made himself human in the person of Jesus as a unique event.

Muslims   believe that Muhammad (pbuh) was the last and most perfect of a series of messengers of God, which included Abraham, Moses and Jesus. The Christian claim that Jesus was also divine is strongly rejected.

Hindus believe that when evil becomes too great in the world, God takes the form of a human being in order to save humankind. Therefore, for many Hindus, God made himself human in the person of Jesus, as he had done before: for example, in the form of Rama and Krishna.

Sikhs believe there is only one true God and live according to certain rules laid down by ten special gurus (teachers). Jesus does not play a part in their religious tradition.

Jews The vast majority of Jews do not recognize Jesus as the Messiah (the leader and deliverer of the Jews). They are still waiting for the coming of the Messiah.

Buddhists Jesus does not have a place in the Buddhist religion.

20

The Vision on the Mountain Top

Mark 9: 2–9

Jesus and his disciples were in the mountains.

From the high places they could look right across into the desert as far as the eye could see. Sometimes the tops of the mountains were covered in clouds.

It was on a day like that that Jesus said to Peter, 'I want you to come with me. And bring James and John with you.'

'What about the others?' asked Peter.

'They can stay here, in the valley,' replied Jesus. 'They will be glad of a rest.'

'Where are we going?' asked Peter.

'Up the mountain,' came the reply.

Peter looked up. The mountain Jesus was pointing to was the biggest in the area. It went up into the clouds. It was very steep.

The four men set off. Jesus led the way. It was a hard climb. At first it was hot. Up and up they went. From time to time they looked back. Each time their friends in the valley below seemed to get smaller.

Suddenly it got cold. They had walked up into the cloud. It was like thick mist, grey and damp. Still Jesus walked on. Still the path went up and up. Every time the three disciples thought they had reached the top they found another bit to climb.

Suddenly they were in the sun. They had climbed through the cloud. Now they were above it. The sun was really bright.

All below them was a sea of white as the sun shone on the top of the cloud.

Jesus still walked ahead. He stopped. At last he really was on top of the mountain. The sun was behind him. The white clouds were below him, stretching out as far as the eye could see. Other mountain tops looked like little islands sticking up out of a brilliant white sea. It was as if Jesus were standing on top of the world.

The three men had fallen behind. They looked up to where Jesus had stopped. What they saw made them jump. They caught hold of one another.

'Look,' gasped Peter. 'What's happening?'

There was no answer. James and John just stared ahead.

The figure of Jesus stood out against the sun and the clouds. He seemed to shine like a brilliant light. And he was not alone. In the bright light which seemed to come out from him, two human figures were to be seen, one on each side.

'Who are they?' whispered Peter.

'The one on the left must be Moses,' said James. 'And the one on the right is Elijah,' gasped John. 'The law and the prophets.'

'And Jesus is above them both,' went on Peter. 'What shall we do?'

Before James and John could reply, Peter at last found his voice. It still shook. They were all very frightened.

'Master,' Peter called out, 'it is wonderful for us to be here. We will put up three shelters – one for you, one for Moses and one for Elijah.'

He stepped forward. As he did so the vision disappeared. The three men blinked. When they looked again there were just themselves and Jesus up ahead of them. The cloud had come up. The sun had gone for a moment. Everything was normal again.

They followed Jesus down the mountain. The three men walked deep in thought. Had they imagined it? No. All three had seen it. It had been a vision that none of them would ever forget. They had seen the great Moses and Elijah bowing down to Jesus. This man they were following, this Jesus, was no ordinary man.

He was waiting for them now. They caught up with him.

Jesus spoke. 'What you have seen today you must keep to yourselves,' he said.

Even Peter did not argue this time. Jesus went on: 'When the Son of Man has come back from the dead, then you can talk about it. Then people may understand.'

In some strange way Jesus was greater than anyone who had ever been. Peter, James and John could not explain it. They couldn't find the right words.

When they reached the foot of the mountain again Peter, James and John did not tell the others what had happened.

NOTES

ABOUT THE STORY

Usually known as the Transfiguration, this story is about moving between two worlds, the world of fact and the world of values, the world of history and the world of faith, between the primary world of the here and now and the secondary world of eternity and vision. It takes place at two different levels, literally because it involves climbing a mountain and figuratively, as the word 'transfiguration' suggests, because it deals with appearances and what is beyond. It is confirmation of what has occurred in the previous two stories.

Did they actually climb a mountain? More than likely. Mountains are often symbolic of nearness to God for obvious reasons. Moses went to Sinai for the Commandments; Elijah returned there at a time of great crisis (see OT Stories 14 and 31). The sacred cloud (*shekinah*) was also a common Jewish symbol of God's presence.

As they pass above the cloud which cuts them off from the physical world Jesus becomes transformed in their perception of him. He is not just Jesus the Nazarene. The three disciples see him for what he really is, the Christ. He stands above the two great bastions of Jewish faith, the Law (Torah), symbolized by Moses, and the Prophets, symbolized by Elijah.

After the vision the three disciples literally come back down to earth. Few will believe them so there is no point in talking about their experience – yet. In time others will get the message. They themselves would die for the vision they had now seen.

The question 'Did it really happen?' is likely to arise. It is a faith question, not an empirical one. Would television cameras have recorded it all? No more than the vision of Martin Luther King that the time would come when blacks and whites would live happily together in the U.S.A., we might assume. From this moment on the three disciples were changed people, motivated by total conviction. 'Where there is no vision,' say the Jewish Scriptures, 'the people perish.' To try to reduce a story such as this to simple literalism is to debase it beyond recognition.

IDEAS FOR EXPLORING FURTHER

Authority of Jesus   Why were the disciples so amazed that Jesus seemed to be greater and to have more authority than either Moses or Elijah? Invite the children to find out as much as they can about these people, particularly in terms of God giving the Law and drawing up a Covenant (agreement) with his people through Moses, and in relation to the status of Elijah as a prophet. (Cf. 1 Kings 17–21, 2 Kings 1–2; see also OT Stories 11–15, 29–31.)

Sudden Realizations   Use stories where one of the characters is involved in a number of surprising/confusing incidents and suddenly comes to an important realization which makes a great deal of difference to the way they see things. Compare this with how Peter, James and John must have felt when they suddenly realized the power and authority of Jesus. Some children may be able to recall an occasion when they suddenly realized something and be able to describe it for the rest of the class. Similarly, they may remember times when they have seen 'another side' of a person whom they thought they knew well. See also Story 43.

Mystery   Although Peter, James and John understood something very important for the first time, nonetheless the vision on the mountain was a mystery. Discuss with the children how even adults do not understand everything there is to know about the world and life in it. Help the children to draw up a list of questions to which we have no definite answers or no answer at all. (E.g. Why are we born? What happens when we die? Why is there so much suffering? How was the world/universe created? Why can we not cure many diseases?) Explain how many of the jobs done by adults (scientists, medical researchers, astronomers, etc.) are trying to push back the frontiers of knowledge and are part of a huge search to try and solve key mysteries which affect all people. Show the children how the major religious traditions indicate that people have asked these questions before and sought answers to them. Compare, for example, stories about the creation of the world, and stories which show how people can help each other with problems of different kinds.

Children could also look at stories which come from outside the major faith traditions and gain a deeper understanding of the beliefs and values of people in a number of distant places. (Cf. **NC** *Geography*: AT 2 – knowledge and understanding of places.) For further ideas about the nature of truth, visions and dreams, see the Introduction and OT Stories 5, 8, 9, 35, 41, 45.

101

21

The Man Who Owed a Million Pounds

Matthew 18: 21–35

'Tell me,' said Peter as they walked along, 'How often should I go on forgiving someone? Do you think seven times is enough before I start getting my own back?'

'More like seventy times seven I should think,' replied Jesus.

'Seventy times seven!' exclaimed Peter. 'I couldn't remember that many times.'

'Exactly,' said Jesus with a smile. 'Listen,' Jesus went on. 'Let me tell you a story.'

The disciples stopped and gathered around.

'In God's eyes,' Jesus began, 'it's a bit like this. Once upon a time there was a king who decided the time had come to get all his money sorted out. Quite a lot of his nobles and officers had borrowed money from him. He asked them to give it all back.

'One particular officer owed the king an enormous amount of money, something like a million pounds. And he had spent all of it. The stupid man had nothing left at all.

'"Take him away," said the king when he heard, "and sell him in the slave-market. Then sell his wife and all his children as well. That will get some of the money back."

'The officer fell on his knees. "Please," he said, "give me time. Please don't do it. I will repay the money, every penny of it. Please don't sell my wife and children. I have been a fool, but please have mercy, have mercy."

'The man begged and begged. In the end the king felt sorry for him.

'"All right," said the king, "I can see that you are really sorry. You have learned your lesson. I will be generous. I will cross out the debt you owe me."

'The officer could hardly believe his ears. He could not thank the king enough. He stood up, bowed low and left the palace. He thought he was the luckiest man alive.

'On the way out of the palace he bumped into one of his fellow officers. "Hey," he said, "you owe me some money, don't you? You haven't let me have back that five pounds I lent you last month."

'"No, I'm sorry," said the man. "But don't worry, I haven't forgotten. Things are very difficult for me at the moment. I hope to let you have it back in a few days." He began to walk away.

'"Not so fast," shouted the first officer, grabbing him by the collar. "I want my money back and I want it now."

'"But I haven't got it."

'"Then you'd better think of a way of finding it. I'm going to have you put into prison until you do. If I let you go I might never see my five pounds again."

'"But how can I ever find the money if I'm in prison?"

'"That's your problem," was all the reply he got.

'The poor man was taken and put into prison until the debt was paid.

'Other officers who had been in the palace heard the argument. They were very angry. They told the king what had happened. He sent for the officer. "You terrible rogue," the king shouted at him. "How could you be such a hypocrite? I let you off a million pounds and you go straight out and put a man in prison just because he can't pay you your five pounds. I know how to deal with people like you. Take him away," he told his servants. "Throw him in the prison and see that he stays there until he has paid back every penny he owes me. That will be for the rest of his life. Let the other prisoner go free."'

Jesus finished. They walked on. Peter remembered a piece of a prayer that Jesus had taught them one day: 'Forgive us our sins as we forgive other people's.' He had a lot to think about.

NOTES

ABOUT THE STORY

This is a parable which needs very little commentary. Those who might want to argue about whether or not the Transfiguration 'really happened' will surely acknowledge in this case that it really does not matter in the slightest if this story happened just like this or not. In a very real sense it has happened and continues to happen at all times and in all places. This is a good point at which to ask again, 'What is the difference between a story that is true and one which is true to life?' What are the criteria for judging whether a thing is true or not? 'Don't tell stories' and 'You story-teller' have come to mean 'I think you're telling lies'. In previous generations, however, we passed on morals through stories like this.

The central theme here is hypocrisy. We get the word 'hypocrisy' from the world of ancient Greek drama. It related to the putting on and taking off of different masks. In other words it has to do with acting different parts instead of being real.

IDEAS FOR EXPLORING FURTHER

Forgiveness   Ask children to bring in comics, cartoon books, or stories and to pick out some incidents for which one character needs to forgive another. (**NC** *English*: AT 2 – reading.) In each case, discuss how easy it would be for the wronged character to forgive the wrongdoer. Ask children to rank some of the incidents according to how difficult they might be to forgive. Also, for each incident, discuss/list any possible mitigating circumstances which might have caused the wrongdoer to act in the way they did. Emphasize the complexity of 'judging' the behaviour of others and relate this to the work of magistrates and high-court judges. Discuss the saying 'He that is without sin among you, let him first cast a stone ...' (John 8: 7). Which of us has never done wrong and needed to be forgiven?

Prisons   Invite older pupils to debate whether or not prison is the best place for all offenders against the law. Talk about how many prisoners have been ill-treated while young or are victims of circumstances which caused them to turn to crime. Discuss how we all have a choice to do right or wrong and may have to make that choice in difficult circumstances. Think about crime and punishment in the past (cf. **NC** *History*), and the work of nineteenth-century prison reformers such as Elizabeth Fry (Newgate prison for women, 1813 onwards). Why do prisoners riot today? What are their real needs? See also Story 50.

Choices   See Stories 4, 15, 16, 31, OT Stories 3, 28.

22

Zacchaeus

Luke 19: 1–10

Zacchaeus was a nasty little man. Nobody liked him. He was the chief tax-collector in Jericho. No one likes paying taxes, but usually the tax-collector isn't blamed. Zacchaeus was different. He was a Jew and he collected the taxes for the Romans. He was a traitor to his own people, but they could not touch him because the Romans protected him. So they had to be content just with hating him instead. Zacchaeus got his own back by charging more than he had to. If the Romans wanted ten pounds from a man, Zacchaeus would charge him eleven pounds and keep one for himself. He became very rich. He was also very unhappy.

One day Jesus came to Jericho. The news spread and people flocked into the streets to see him. Nobody told Zacchaeus. By the time he found out, the crowd was already thick at the side of the road. Zacchaeus was a very little man. From the back of the crowd he could see nothing. 'Let me through,' he demanded, pushing between the people.

They started to give way and then one said to another, 'It's that nasty little Zacchaeus', and they moved together again, squeezing him out.

Zacchaeus jumped up and down. He tried standing on tiptoe but it was no good. Farther down the road the cheering started. Jesus was coming. The crowd pressed forward closer than ever. Zacchaeus was going to miss seeing Jesus. No one would let him through. He looked to left and right. The crowd stretched as far as he could see, but along the road was a sycamore tree. Zacchaeus ran to it. He jumped up to a low branch and began to pull himself up. Now he could see over the heads of the people in front. Just in time. Jesus and his disciples were coming down the road. Zacchaeus began to wave. Jesus came nearer. Right in front of Zacchaeus Jesus stopped. He saw Zacchaeus and smiled. The people turned round to see whom Jesus was looking at.

'Oh, not him,' said one.

'Look out,' said another to Jesus. 'He's a traitor who will have the cloak off your back to give to his Roman masters if you go near him. Don't have anything to do with him.'

Others started to boo and shout, 'Go home, Zacchaeus.' Jesus was no longer smiling. He could feel the hatred around him, the crowd hating Zacchaeus, Zacchaeus hating every-body back.

Jesus spoke. 'Zacchaeus,' he said, 'come down out of that tree.'

Zacchaeus began to wish he had not come. The crowd had gone quiet. Was Jesus going to give him a lecture on being honest? Serve him right.

'What for?' asked Zacchaeus.

'What for?' repeated Jesus. 'Because I'm hungry and thirsty and I thought you might take me back to your house for something to eat and drink.'

There were gasps of amazement from the crowd. Making friends with a nasty little thief like Zacchaeus – did Jesus know what he was doing? 'I thought he was supposed to be a religious man,' said one.

'So did I,' replied his friend, 'but no decent person would go near that little traitor, let alone eat and drink with him.'

The crowd began to break up. Their mood had changed. A few minutes before they had been cheering Jesus. Now they watched him with doubt and suspicion.

Jesus knew what he was doing. Zacchaeus needed a friend. Hating him only made him worse. He hated people because they hated him. Someone had to make friends with him, then perhaps he wouldn't be so frightened of people. Back at Zacchaeus' house, with supper over, Zacchaeus said to Jesus, 'Look, I feel very bad. I've treated people very unfairly. I'm going to count up all my money and then I'm going to give half of it away. I shall look at my books too. If I've taken too much from anybody I shall give him back four times as much as I've taken.'

Jesus knew he had made a lot of enemies by making a friend of Zacchaeus but he said, 'Thank God, somebody has been saved today and is going to be happier now. That's what I came for, to help those who have lost their way and made life miserable for themselves.'

NOTES

ABOUT THE STORY

The early ministry had taken place around Galilee. Galilee had, for a long time, been regarded with suspicion by the southerners who lived around Jerusalem in Judaea. It was a typical north–south divide. To Judaeans the people of the north were something of a mixed breed who were never quite acceptable. Galilee had for a long time been a hotbed of potential revolutionaries. The Romans, too, eyed it with mistrust. However, for just that reason there were many in Judaea who were interested in trouble coming from Galilee. Jesus now begins to move south, away from his own area and comes to the river-crossing at Jericho. His earlier reputation has gone ahead of him. Crowds turn out to see him and he encounters Zacchaeus.

Tax-collectors are rarely popular. Zacchaeus belonged to a particularly despised breed. He was a Roman *publicanus* or minor government official, often misleadingly translated as 'publican' in English. What it meant was that he was seen as a collaborator working for the occupying power. A Jew himself he nevertheless collected taxes for the Romans. As a result (or was it really the cause?) he was a loner. The Romans employed and protected him but never befriended him. His own race simply saw him as a traitor and many would simply have been waiting for the opportunity to get him. In response to this air of hatred he got his own back by overcharging on his commission.

Of all people the reputed rebel from the north is bound to snub him. Jesus calls him down and initiates an invitation to become his house guest. The result is a total shattering of expectations and complete bewilderment. What Jesus has been trying to explain to the disciples in private, namely that he is to be a loving servant rather than a

107

high-status figure, is now beginning to be made public. The Suffering Servant concept of Messiah has to be shown. Destroying hatred is what matters, not destroying the hated. Zacchaeus needs acceptance. In giving it Jesus brings down rejection upon himself from those whose attitudes are fixed.

IDEAS FOR EXPLORING FURTHER

Occupations and Values Make a list of the jobs that children would like to do when they are older, together with the reasons why each is particularly valued. Should we choose a job just because it will allow us to earn a lot of money? Help children to think about the choices which might be open to them. Which jobs does no one wish to do? Why are these not valued? Do they need doing? Should we be grateful to the people who do them? Zacchaeus abused his position. Ask older children about ways in which jobs today may also be abused (e.g. 'borrowing' equipment, use of telephones and photocopiers, taking extended tea and lunch breaks, pretending to be ill and yet accepting payment for work not done). What would pupils do if they were expected by their employer to cheat, upset or harm people? What issues are involved in being a responsible consumer of goods and services? (Cf. **NC** *Economic and Industrial Understanding*.) See also Story 27 for Jesus' response to people who cheat the public.

Consider jobs of the past. Which were most valued and why? Talk about gender issues. (Cf. **NC** *History*: all study units.) Make comparisons with the present day. What has caused the changes? Discuss how changes have affected the way in which people live and their values for living in general. Is it true that some people today are more materialistic, money-oriented, spend less time with the family, etc.? (Cf. **NC** *Geography*: AT 2 – knowledge and understanding of places, the way in which employment in an area is related to environment, land use, climate and location; *Careers Education and the World of Work*: identifying ways in which different types of work are like and unlike each other, contrasting work in different cultures and at different times, identifying sources of work satisfaction and dissatisfaction. Links can also be made with **NC** *Health Education*: environmental and psychological aspects of health; *Citizenship*.)

Meals See notes on Story 18.

23

Can You Thread a Needle with a Camel?

Matthew 19: 13–27

On and on Jesus walked. The disciples followed. Jericho was behind them.

'Where are we going?' asked Peter.

'Jerusalem,' Jesus answered.

'Jerusalem!' gasped the others. 'We can't go there. It's too dangerous.'

Jesus walked on. The men looked at one another. They shook their heads. What could they do?

'Come on,' said Judas. 'Let's catch him up. Who knows, perhaps it will be more dangerous for his enemies than for us.'

The others did not like Judas very much. But it did not matter. Peter, James and John were already hurrying after Jesus. There was nothing for it but to follow.

There were more people about now. And news had gone ahead. In every village there were people in the street or standing on rooftops. The disciples felt better. For months they had been away in the desert and mountains of the north. They thought Jesus would be forgotten in the south. They were wrong. Jesus was something of a hero. Everybody wanted to see him. Lots of people wanted to join his band of special disciples.

One young man ran out in front of Jesus and stopped him. 'Tell me,' he said, 'what really good thing must I do in order to live life to the full and live for ever?'

'What a strange question,' said Jesus. 'I wonder why you

ask it. You know the answer. If you want to live life to the full, keep to the rules of Moses.'

'Which ones in particular?' asked the young man.

'Don't kill,' said Jesus. 'Don't steal. Don't tell lies. Be loyal to your own wife. In other words, treat other people as you would like to be treated.'

'All right,' said the young man. 'I've done all that. But I'm still missing something. My life isn't as full as it could be. Are you sure there isn't something else I should do to feel really free?'

Jesus looked at him. He was a well-dressed young man, wearing an expensive coat. He had a gold ring on his finger. His hands were soft. Jesus could see that he was really quite rich. He was a very lucky man, but still he was not happy.

'I think I know what you ought to do if you want to feel really free and alive,' said Jesus.

'What? Tell me,' said the young man eagerly.

'Go and sell everything you've got. Then give all your money to the poor. You are a prisoner to all your possessions,' replied Jesus.

The young man looked as if he were going to cry. 'What, everything?' he asked.

Jesus nodded.

The young man turned away. He knew Jesus was right. He knew too that he couldn't do it. He worried about all the things he owned. But he couldn't get rid of them. He pushed his way through the crowd.

Jesus shook his head sadly. He turned to his disciples. 'Rich people are often to be pitied,' he said. 'They seem to have everything for a full life, but they don't. It's often harder for rich people to live to the full than for poor people. Sometimes I think it would be easier to thread a needle with a camel than to make a rich man happy.'

Some of the crowd laughed at the idea of pushing a camel through the eye of a needle.

'Are you saying that nobody who is rich can ever know God properly?' asked Peter.

'No, not really,' said Jesus. 'I'm just saying it's very very difficult for them. That young man couldn't have been nicer, could he? He said he'd do anything to be happy. He was kind to people, but he couldn't put people before all his possessions. Poor people and children don't have that problem – that's all. Poor people live nearer to God than rich people. And children often live nearer to God than grown-ups. All I'm saying is that if we want to live life to the full we've got to be just like poor people or children. With them nothing gets in the way.'

'Come on,' added Jesus, 'let's get on to Jerusalem.'

NOTES

ABOUT THE STORY

The scene is set to go into Jerusalem. It is highly dangerous but there can be no going back. Some of the disciples are growing anxious, if not fearful. This story and the ten which follow need to be told with a certain air of suspense. The crowds are still out but their attitude is fickle; they are not the 'home crowd' as in Galilee and they cannot be depended upon.

The rich young man is an example of this. He is keen to follow but what is required now is a higher level of commitment than he can accept. Jesus knows that his own life is on the line. Later generations were to use this story in support of the monastic life with its demands for giving up everything in order to live the Christian life without distraction. At extreme moments, as in times of persecution, it has been argued, only those with nothing to lose and with no other obligations can be wholly depended upon.

From this moment on confrontation is inevitable. Jesus is walking deliberately into the very centre of power of those who will resist all challenge to their authority. He is not belligerent but he will not go away. The Temple, the Holy City, the God of the Jews are his as much as they are anybody's.

The well-known simile of a camel going through the eye of a needle is probably just that – a vivid word picture, a piece of teaching hyperbole. Attempts to establish that there was a narrow gate called 'The Eye of a Needle' are of no importance. As a figure of speech it is probably of the same order as phrases like 'as useful as a chocolate teapot'.

111

Into this account has been woven the possibility that Judas was beginning to see in his own mind the chance of forcing Jesus' arm. Overlooking, or simply not understanding, all that he had been taught about Jesus' whole concept of Messiah, he could well have thought that Jesus could be compelled to lead a popular rebellion against Rome.

Note For a Hindu parallel, see the reference to 'threading an elephant through the eye of a needle' in the story on pp. 2–3 of *Hinduism and Ecology*, by Ranchor Prime.

IDEAS FOR EXPLORING FURTHER

Sacrifice Ask each child to name and draw a picture of a favourite pop star, film star, sports or TV personality, etc. – someone with whom they would like to spend a week. In addition, ask pupils to draw their most valued possession(s) and to say or write down what they value most about them. Would the children be willing to give away those valued items in exchange for spending a week with their favourite person? Would they be willing to give up everything if Jesus asked them to? Are these easy or hard decisions to make? Talk about adults who have given up everything to go and help people in need (e.g. Mother Teresa). Try to identify the things which such people would say are the rewards for making themselves poor for Jesus' sake and for the sake of others. Are they poor in one way, yet rich in another?

The Monastic Tradition Find out about monasteries. Discuss how many people in holy orders have taken a vow of poverty, chastity and obedience in order to be able to devote themselves better to serving God. Talk about what this might mean in real terms. Invite a monk or nun to explain why they chose as they did, what it is like to 'give up everything' and to describe their daily life. Consider how the Church became rich in the Middle Ages and talk about reasons for the dissolution of the monasteries in the reign of Henry VIII. (Cf. NC *History:* SSU on houses and places of worship, CSU 2 – Tudor and Stuart times. In this connection, read the version of this story in the King James Bible.)

Helping People Jesus said that when someone helps other people, it is as if they are helping him. When asked to help people (e.g. with jobs in the house and garden), we often say, 'Sorry, I'm too busy.' What things get in the way of our helping people/ serving God today? What excuses do we make? Are they really valid? Or are we just being selfish? Is it true that one way towards finding happiness is to make others happy?

112

24

The Story of
a Good Samaritan

Luke 10: 25–37

One day Jesus was talking to a crowd of people. He was telling them that they should love their neighbours. A man in the crowd stopped him. 'That's all very well,' he said to Jesus, 'but just who is my neighbour?'

Instead of giving him a quick answer Jesus began to tell a story. . . . It all took place on a road. Jesus and the people knew the road well. It was steep and twisty and ran through wild country where nobody lived.

One day a man was travelling all on his own along this road, going down from Jerusalem to the town of Jericho. It was hot and he was very tired and dusty. Suddenly a gang of robbers jumped out from behind some rocks. They pulled the man away from his donkey, beat him up, took all his money and ran away. Only just alive, the man lay at the side of the road in the hot sun.

Slowly he came back to life. He could not sit up. His head ached. His bruises and cuts were sore and he felt terribly thirsty. The sun got hotter and hotter but he was too weak to move into the shade. The blood had dried on his head and arms. His clothes were filthy with dust. He looked more dead than alive.

Just as he was giving up hope he heard footsteps. He opened his eyes and saw a priest coming up the hill. The priest was looking down and mumbling prayers to himself. He was on his way to the Temple in Jerusalem. When he noticed the man

113

lying by the roadside he stopped. The man looked dead – or, if he were alive, he was probably dying. The Jewish law said that anyone who touched a dead body was unclean. The priest would not be able to join in the service at the Temple if he touched the man. What could he do? Perhaps the man would die whether he helped him or not.

'Help me,' groaned the man.

The priest lowered his eyes. He pretended not to hear as he crossed to the other side of the road, still muttering prayers to himself. He hurried past on the way to Jerusalem.

The sun became hotter and hotter. The man grew weaker and weaker. Then he heard a noise. What was that? More footsteps. Gathering his strength the man called out again, 'Help me, help me.'

The traveller this time was a well-dressed man; he looked rich. He did not even hesitate. He took one look at the blood-stained figure and made his donkey break into a trot to get past as quickly as possible.

Surely the wounded man would die now. The sun was beginning to go down. There would be no more travellers that day apart from more thieves who moved at night. The man closed his eyes and slept.

He woke up suddenly and cried out 'Help me. Give me water!' almost before he realized what he was doing. A donkey with a rider was almost treading on him in the half-light. The donkey stopped. The wounded man sighed with relief. Then, as he looked up, his heart froze. The man on the donkey was not a Jew like himself. He was a Samaritan. Jews hated Samaritans and Samaritans were sworn enemies of the Jews. Would this Samaritan just kick him again or would he cut his throat? No one would see. He lay still and waited as the Samaritan got down.

Suddenly there was a tearing sound. What was happening? He opened his eyes again. The Samaritan was tearing strips of cloth from his cloak. A minute later the wounded Jew felt the cool, refreshing touch of water on his forehead. The Samaritan was using the strips of material as bandages soaked in

114

water. Then there was more water being forced past his cracked lips. Very gently the Samaritan picked up the poor Jew and placed him on the donkey. Slowly they went on up the hill.

A few miles farther on they came to a lonely inn. The Samaritan knocked on the door. The innkeeper opened it.

'I have found this wounded man,' said the Samaritan, 'can I leave him here?'

'He looks a right mess,' said the innkeeper. 'He'll need some looking after. And who's going to pay, may I ask?'

The Samaritan pulled his hand from his saddle-bag. 'Here,' he said, 'take this. It's all the money I have on me. But I shall be coming back down this road in a few days. If your bill is more than that I will give you more money then.'

With that he went on his way.

NOTES

ABOUT THE STORY

We do not really know just where this well-known parable fits into the sequence of the whole Gospel Story. It has been put here because, like the Zacchaeus incident (Story 22), it would have made at least as many enemies as friends. Like the parable of the Prodigal Son (Story 16) it has suffered from over use which, in turn, has made it highly acceptable. We have to assume that originally it caused deep resentment to many who heard it.

In our own language the very phrase 'good Samaritan' conjures up feelings of kindness and concern for others. When this story was first told it was to a crowd who would largely have regarded the only good Samaritan as a dead one. Relationships between Jews and Samaritans had been bad for a good five hundred years and would at least have rivalled the hostility between Jews and Arabs in our own day. (See OT Story 38.)

Priests were unpopular, so were Levites. (Luke says the second passer-by was a Levite although we have avoided introducing the term in this retelling.) Again we see the technique of parabolic teaching. Jesus takes the crowd with him up to the point at which the Levite passes by – hisses and boos might have been the order of the day. But then – a Samaritan! It could easily have been a humble, ordinary, poor Jew but the audience was already hooked and emotionally exposed.

Was the story based on a 'true' incident? Who knows? Does it matter?

IDEAS FOR EXPLORING FURTHER

Combatting Stereotypes   See Stories 3, 7, 11, 14, 45, OT Stories 11, 18, 36, 40, 41.

Learning from Difficult Times   Brainstorm with the children what the Jew might have learned from this very testing time. For example:

- to think ahead, to anticipate trouble and to travel with friends in future;
- not to judge whether people are 'good' or 'bad' by their job or social status;
- not to 'follow the crowd' and to believe everything he hears about Samaritans – there are good and bad people everywhere;
- that because he has been shown kindness, he in turn should show kindness to others – even people he doesn't like very much;
- that he has more strength to survive hardship than he imagined;
- that some people, like the Samaritan, are willing not only to help people once, but to go on beyond that to help again (in this case, by giving money);
- that sometimes God feels very far away, but he is not really – he was there in the presence of the Samaritan;
- the depth of meaning of the words 'thank you'.

Ask the children to think about what can be learned from times when they are ill. Do they discover how much people care about them because they receive cards, letters or presents? Do they learn that they have to be patient and wait to get better? Do they discover a new interest in something because they suddenly have more time to try out a different kind of activity? Do they find that it helps them through the difficulty if people show good humour? How important is perseverance during difficult times? Read stories which comment on this (e.g. *Brave Irene*, by William Steig).

Ask relatives and friends to recall experiences from the Second World War. Did they learn anything valuable from those difficult times? (E.g. that other people were more willing to help than they had thought; that sharing was important; that good humour saw them through dark days; that resources could be saved and re-used; that it was possible to invent quite interesting meals even with only a few ingredients; to give full value to small luxuries and treats.) (Cf. **NC** *History:* CSU 4 – Second World War.) See Story 50.

Feelings and Emotions   Discuss how the Jew would have felt during this eventful day. Make an imaginary picture map or sketch plan of his route from Jerusalem to Jericho. (If possible, find out something about the landscape/terrain in that part of the world.) Mark on the map where the Jew met thieves, where he lay to await help, the route to the innkeeper and the Jew's route from there to Jericho. Draw the Jew on the map at each key point and give him a 'thought bubble' containing key words about how he felt at that moment. Include the priest, the rich traveller (the Levite) and the Samaritan with their feelings too. (Cf. **NC** *Geography:* AT 1 – geographical skills.) See also Story 11.

Metaphor/Picture Language/Meaning of Stories   See Introduction, Stories 16, 21, 49, OT Stories 8, 9, 35, 41, 45.

25

Mary and Martha – Different Ways of Showing Love

John 12: 1–8

It was nearly Passover time again. Lots of people were making their way to Jerusalem for the celebration. They came from all over the country. A lot of people from the north were there. Some even came from other countries. The streets were full of tourists. All the inns and hotels were full. The city of Jerusalem was full of people and so were some of the villages just outside.

Bethany was five kilometres away from Jerusalem by road. The road went round the bottom of a hill which was covered in olive trees. It was called the Mount of Olives. A footpath went through the trees and over the hill. It was a steep path but a good short cut. Anyone who was fit could do the journey in less than half an hour.

Jesus and his disciples were very fit and strong. A tiny hill like the Mount of Olives was no problem for them. Bethany was a perfect place to stay. Every morning they could walk into Jerusalem with hundreds of other pilgrims. Every evening they could go back to Bethany when large crowds of people left the city.

A lot of people in Jerusalem did not like Jesus. They were powerful people too, lawyers and Pharisees as well as Herod's officers. The Roman soldiers were everywhere, on the look-out for any trouble. It would be good to be out of the city at night-time. Jesus was not afraid of his enemies but he was not going to make it easy for them to catch him.

117

There was another reason for Jesus and his disciples to stay in Bethany. Jesus had lots of friends there. Quite a few of the people he had healed lived in the village.

The road up from Jericho to Bethany was steep and hot. Jesus and his disciples were tired and dusty after the long walk. They arrived in the village and went to the houses where they would stay for the week. Jesus went to the house of Simon who had suffered from leprosy.

In Bethany there lived two sisters who knew Jesus well. One was called Mary, the other Martha. Mary sat and talked to Jesus. Martha busied herself in the kitchen, making supper. When supper was ready Jesus sat round the table with all his friends. Mary went out of the room. She came back with a bottle. She sat on the floor beside Jesus.

All of a sudden the room was full of the smell of beautiful perfume. Everybody stopped talking. They looked to see what Mary was doing. It was the job of the lowest servant to wash the feet of visitors with water. Mary had taken the top off the bottle and was washing Jesus' feet with the most expensive scent. She used up the whole bottle as if it were water. It had cost her a small fortune.

'What a waste!' snorted a voice. It came from Judas who looked after the disciples' money. 'If you didn't want to keep that you could have sold it and given the money to the poor,' he said to Mary.

Mary did not answer. She had undone her long black hair and she was using it to dry Jesus' feet.

'It's worth pounds and pounds,' continued Judas.

Now Jesus spoke for the first time. 'Leave her alone,' he said sharply. 'Mary is showing how much she loves me in the best way she can. Martha has shown her love by working in the kitchen. Others may show the same thing by giving to the poor. You will always have poor people around. You won't always have me.'

Mary looked up and smiled. Jesus at least understood.

Judas turned and walked out of the house. He was angry.

ABOUT THE STORY

The long introduction to this retelling has been included to set the scene for the stories of Holy Week which follow. We must assume that Mary and Martha are long-time trusted friends. Jesus is going into Jerusalem very purposefully and in full awareness of the dangers but there is nothing casual about his approach. Plans have been made and, apparently, kept secret. During the day he would be surrounded by pilgrims to the city. At night he would be among friends. Anyone who wanted to capture him would have to know when and where he might be alone or nearly alone.

The Mary and Martha story is usually used to show the contrast in two personalities. They were the sisters of Lazarus, whose story is told in John 11, but in the other Gospels (called the Synoptics because they see things together or in the same way), this is the main detail that we have about them. They would appear to be single, an unusual state of affairs at the time. Are we to imagine early deaths of parents, and a brother and two sisters living together with Martha, maybe as the eldest, taking on the traditional mothering role? Perhaps, as with many others dedicated to a life of service, Martha's weariness and frustration come to the surface – a reaction showing the basic humanity behind a saint. Mary is obviously not helping much, but is that because she sees hospitality as paying attention to the visitor rather than having everything just so?

The incident with the jar of perfume raises all sorts of questions. It would be customary to wash the feet of a visitor but normally only with water. How far is it good to offer the best and the costliest in response to God – as in great art, architecture, music, etc. – and how far is it, at the same time, of greater importance to recognize poverty and to try and do something about it? Judas, who is sometimes thought of as the group's treasurer, is represented here as emphasizing the latter viewpoint but he might just have been confused about the whole business.

IDEAS FOR EXPLORING FURTHER

Priorities   Tell the children to imagine that they have £250000 to spend. Ask them whether they would spend it on building a beautiful church (or mosque, gurdwara, mandir, synagogue, etc.) in which to worship God or give it to a charitable organization to spend on feeding the hungry. Help them to understand that people have different views about how to show love for God and how to use resources; setting priorities is not always easy. Is any compromise possible? The theme of how best to use resources could be taken up in relation to NC *Geography*. AT 5 – environmental geography; *Economic and Industrial Understanding*. How would children spend £250000 on improving their locality in order to show their care and concern for local people?

Gender Stereotyping   See notes on Story 5. See also notes on OT Story 3 – gender roles within the community. (Cf. NC *History*.)

119

26

A King on a Donkey

Mark 11: 1–11

It was morning. People were on the move. The road into Jerusalem was full of people making their way to the city. There was a feeling of excitement everywhere. Passover time was festival time.

Jesus and his disciples joined the crowd on the road. They too were going into the city. People recognized Jesus. It made them even more excited. Here was the great teacher and healer. He had not been seen for months. There were many people from Galilee in the crowd.

Jesus watched the crowd. The time had come. He had made his plans: now he must carry them out. It was dangerous, but there was no going back. It had been difficult to tell them what sort of a king he was. Now he must show them.

He called to two of his disciples. 'Go over to Bethany village,' he said. 'As you go into the village you will see a donkey tied up. Untie it and bring it here. If anybody tries to stop you, you must say, "The Lord needs it and he will return it straight away!"'

'Yes, Jesus,' said the disciples and off they went.

It was only a few minutes' walk back into Bethany. Sure enough, there was a donkey tied by a piece of rope to a ring in a wall. They went over to it and began to untie it.

'Hey,' said a voice. 'What do you think you're doing? Who said you could untie that donkey?'

A man had come out of a gate and stood looking at them. The two disciples looked at one another. What were the words Jesus had used? Ah, yes, 'The Lord'. It wasn't a title he had used before.

'The Lord needs it,' replied one of the disciples. 'And he says he will send it back as soon as he has finished with it.'

'Oh, that's all right, then,' said the man and he disappeared into the gateway.

The two men led the donkey back to Jesus. There was no saddle. The disciples took off their topcoats and put them across the donkey's back. Jesus mounted the donkey. They set off again along the road, Jesus in front on the donkey, the disciples walking behind.

At the very back walked Judas. 'Fancy coming on a donkey,' he muttered to himself. 'If he came in on a white horse people might take him seriously.'

But what was happening? At the front people were cheering. It was working. People were treating Jesus like a king.

As they got to the city gate there were crowds of people standing by the road. They had made room for Jesus' procession. The road through the gateway was covered with coats and leaves. People ran to the palm trees nearby and broke off branches. There was no 'red carpet' for their king, but this was the next best thing.

The crowd cheered and cheered. Many more people came running to see what the noise was about. The shouts told them.

'Hurrah,' called the crowd. 'David's kingdom is coming back.'

A voice called out, 'God bless the one who comes in his name.' At which the rest of the crowd took up the chant: 'God bless him. God bless him.'

Judas was still puzzled. 'What makes them cheer like this?' he asked the man next to him. 'He's only on a donkey. It looks silly.'

'You are ignorant,' came the reply. 'There's an old prophecy which says, "Your king will come to you very

121

humbly, riding upon a donkey". Jesus knows what he is doing. And the crowd knows too.'

'So do the Pharisees by the looks on their faces,' said Judas.

He was right. There at the back of the crowd were a few religious officials. They looked very angry. But there was nothing they could do. The crowd was too big.

They were now inside the city. Jesus got off the donkey. He gave it back to the two disciples who had found it for him. 'Look after it,' he said.

Jesus walked on. He went up the steps into the Temple. He looked around. It was like a street-market. There were tables everywhere. Pilgrims and tourists from other countries were changing their money for the special Temple money, used for offerings. Traders were selling all sorts of things. The disciples watched Jesus' face. It was tense with anger. What was he going to do? Anything?

Jesus turned to his disciples. 'Let's go home,' he said. 'It's getting late. We must get back to Bethany before dark. Tomorrow we will return.'

He was still angry but he had not lost his temper. They went back to Bethany in silence, tying up the donkey again as they went into the village.

ABOUT THE STORY

We now come to what is known throughout Christianity as Holy Week. One third of the Gospel Story is devoted to this one week in the life of Jesus.

The philosopher Wittgenstein once made the comment about language 'What cannot be said must be shown.' It tallies with the common-sense statement 'Actions speak louder than words.'

Little which occurs in the following incidents in Jerusalem happens by accident. Although we are not told, there has quite obviously been some very careful and secretive detailed planning behind the scenes. The donkey is available; the password is pre-arranged. Theologians make much of the use of the word 'Lord' here. In Greek it is *Kurios* and it was that word which had been used in the Septuagint, the Greek translation of the Jewish Scriptures (known to Christians as the Old Testament), as a synonym for the word 'God', which was never allowed to be spoken in Hebrew.

Jesus rides into Jerusalem on a donkey as an act of prophetic symbolism. Popular opinion at the time wanted a military Messiah but the concept which Jesus has been trying to din into his disciples is much more the message of the prophets. Zechariah, for example, had talked of Israel's king 'coming riding upon an ass'.

It is a highly dangerous game that Jesus is playing. We must imagine that the Romans have no idea what is really going on and that the religious establishment understand only too well. It is what today we might call 'coded language', although 'coded action' would be nearer the mark. Political oppressors are being hoodwinked in what might appear almost as 'playing the fool' with donkeys and palm fronds instead of chargers and red carpets, whilst the Temple high-ups are gnashing their teeth at this Galilean upstart claiming to be the embodiment of Israel's faith. The atmosphere would have been highly charged and dramatic suspense is called for in the telling of this and the following stories up to the Crucifixion (Story 33).

IDEAS FOR EXPLORING FURTHER

Heaven and Earth Joined   Through discussion, try to help children understand one of the central Christian interpretations of this story: namely, that God, through Jesus, the King of Heaven, was prepared to go to any lengths to show how much he was committed to, and wanted to be part of, what happened on Earth. Nothing was too humble for him, not even riding on a donkey – if you like, apparently making himself look ridiculous.

Jesus: King of What?   Explore meanings further by talking about what the image of Jesus riding on a donkey stands for. Could it be that using a donkey (a humble beast of burden and service) stands for: not taking the easy (showy) way out; service for others; a willingness to share the burdens of others?

Make a picture of Jesus on the road to Jerusalem. Talk about the ways in which he can be seen as a king and mark these on the scene (e.g. king of love, king of teaching, king of healing, king of listening, king of kindness, king of justice/fairness, king of looking for the good in people and nurturing it). As king in this manner, what was Jesus treading underfoot as he rode to Jerusalem? Greed? Selfishness? Violence? Cruelty? Or perhaps in the children's terms: refusing to share toys and equipment, trying to be first, rough play in the playground, calling people names?

Personal Responses Ask the children what they might have thought had they been in the crowd. Let them draw a picture of themselves carrying a palm leaf or some other item for the 'entry into Jerusalem' scene. Mark on that drawing what they think of Jesus and/or the situation before them. Some children may have comments which indicate that they disagree with others' views, that they are confused or have questions to ask. These, of course, should be respected. In any case, such was the situation at the time of the real event. The use of a word-processor for entering the written work into this scene might be most useful. (Cf. NC *Technology*: AT 5 – information technology.)

Doers, Not Watchers Discuss how important Jesus felt it was not just to say how interested he was in human beings, but actually to do something to prove it. Hence he was prepared to enter Jerusalem on a donkey and, ultimately, to die. There were those amongst the disciples and in the crowd who understood what was happening. For the time being they were watchers, but discuss whether perhaps Jesus, through his action on the donkey, was trying to encourage them also to be doers. Make a list of things that some people do to show they believe what Jesus said was important (e.g. helping, sharing, trying to put others first, raising money for charity, driving old people to and from hospital, delivering meals on wheels, visiting people in prison, being a Samaritan, acting as a volunteer for Child Line, providing music and song in church, becoming a minister or deaconess, working for Victim Support). See also Stories 9, 23, 41, 48.

27

Angry for the Sake of God

Mark 11: 15–19

Next morning Jesus was still angry. The disciples had never
seen him like that before. He strode on ahead towards
Jerusalem. Today he had hardly spoken to anybody. Something was going to happen, but what? He hadn't told anybody
his plans. He was going back to the Temple. They knew that.
But what was he going to do when he got there?

Jesus walked on through the city gates. He did not stop. The
disciples followed. A crowd had started to join them.
Through the narrow streets Jesus strode. He walked quickly,
looking straight ahead. People got out of his way, watched
him pass, and then joined the crowd behind him.

Jesus went straight to the Temple. He did not slow down.
Up the wide steps, he strode, through the arch, into the inner
courtyard. The crowd had to run to keep up with him. Jesus
stopped. The crowd behind him stopped as well.

It was just like the previous day. Everywhere there were
stalls. Everywhere people were shouting and arguing, waving
their arms in the air.

Jesus stood there and looked around him. The crowd
behind him was silent. Slowly, very slowly, the stall-holders
became aware of him and the crowd looking at them. The
shouting began to die down. People who were arguing about
money turned and looked up. They saw a tall strong figure
staring back at them with fire in his eyes.

Suddenly Jesus moved. He leapt forward to the nearest stall.

125

He took hold of it, half lifted it and threw it over. It crashed to the ground. The brass plates and copper bowls rang as they hit the stone floor. Money rolled all over the courtyard. The stall-holder fell on his hands and knees trying to pick up the coins.

Jesus moved on to the next stall and did the same thing again. There was confusion everywhere. Other stall-holders began to collect up their things and move away.

Above the noise came Jesus' voice: 'Don't the Scriptures say "God's house shall be a place of prayer"? But you,' he shouted, 'you have turned it into a robbers' den.'

The crowd behind Jesus stayed silent. The courtyard began to clear. Some women appeared carrying water jars on their heads.

'You too,' called Jesus. The women stopped. 'This is not a short cut. It is God's house. Treat it with respect and go some other way.'

They did as they were told. There was something about Jesus. Nobody dared to argue with him.

Jesus turned and pushed his way back through the crowd which had watched him. He still did not talk to anyone. As soon as he had gone, the crowd burst into excited chatter.

Across the courtyard the chief priest and some of his officials had come out to see what the fuss was all about. They were not in the least pleased or excited. 'We must get rid of this trouble-maker,' they were saying. 'But how? The crowd is all on his side.'

ABOUT THE STORY

For some reason this account of Jesus being moved to what has been portrayed as physical violence has caused problems with many people. Certainly there is anger but it is a calculated, righteous anger waged on behalf of the poor and helpless, not a sudden loss of temper. Mark's Gospel makes it perfectly clear at the end of the previous story that, having reached the Temple, Jesus looked around, took in what was happening and went home for the night.

What follows next morning is another act of carefully thought-out prophetic symbolism. Just as Jeremiah had smashed a pot to the ground to portray the coming destruction of the nation (see OT Story 34) so Jesus now turns over the money-changers' tables.

Ordinary currency was not valid in the Temple (cf. the use of chips in a casino), largely because it carried an image of a Roman Emperor. Pilgrims had to change their money in order to be able to make purchases. As tends to happen the whole world over, and not least at religious shrines, they were being ripped off. The great festival of Pesach (Passover) had become just another commercial racket.

Why was Jesus not stopped? Every teacher knows the answer. It was the power of the strong personality who has the group on his or her side. In this case Jesus may have been only one person in the middle of a large crowd but his anger was a moral anger. He was right and everyone knew it. In theory the religious establishment should have approved wholeheartedly; in practice, of course, it was they whose behaviour was totally hypocritical. There is an additional factor. If the authorities had intervened they could have had a riot on their hands.

The religious establishment is not used to being treated in this way but, because it is Israel, the fear of the prophetic voice is also very great. However, they have not only lost face (and profits). Their whole credibility as religious and moral leaders has been dealt a severe blow. The vivid picture of the action will be recalled long after mere words might have been forgotten.

Gandhi's salt march provides a modern parallel. On 12 March 1930 Gandhi set out with 78 followers to walk the 450 kilometres from his ashram at Ahmedabad to the seashore at Dandi. His purpose was to take salt from the sea and in doing so symbolically to defy a government monopoly on the production of salt which was widely seen as an unfair tax on the poor, for whom this was an essential commodity. Thousands of arrests followed as his example was widely copied. Gandhi was arrested and imprisoned but in 1931 he was released and the legislation was changed.

IDEAS FOR EXPLORING FURTHER

Non-violence to Individuals   It may be worth drawing pupils' attention to the fact that one interpretation of Jesus' display of anger centres around the fact that he did not touch anyone. His anger was directed at the physical representations of evil, namely

127

the means by which stall-holders were cheating people in the name of God. As with Zacchaeus (Story 22), where Jesus was trying to destroy the causes of hatred and not the hated person, in this incident Jesus was attempting to get rid of the instruments of evil, not the people who used them. His plan seems to have been to save people from themselves: from their own foolishness, from the evil they had stupidly created, from the consequences of their shallow respect for God which their thoughtlessness had caused.

Anger and Violence: Any Justification?　Invite children to talk about or make a list of occasions when it might be important to get/not get angry or upset, and discuss possible ways of dealing with disagreements. Older children might like to debate the subject of pacifism. Are there any occasions when it is important to be angry and to fight? Are there any causes which are worth suffering and/or dying for? History is full of battles. Explore, for example, the reasons for the Viking invasion. What were the reasons for which Britain and France went to battle during the Second World War? (Cf. NC *History*.) There is violence in many parts of the world today. Collect some newspaper reports relating to this. In which, if any, situations do the children feel war is justified? Some people say they are fighting for God. Do pupils feel this is true or do some people use God's name as an excuse to do evil? Ask children to put their comments alongside the newspaper reports.

128

28

A Widow and Two Small Coins

Mark 12: 31–44

Jesus was back in the Temple. Today he was calm and quiet. He sat on the stone bench near the entrance.

Nearby were twelve large pots. These were the collection bowls. As the pilgrims went into the main Temple to say their prayers they put their gifts into the bowls. The money they put in was Temple money. It belonged to God. It did not have Caesar's head stamped on it.

Jesus watched as people came by. There were all sorts of men and women. Some were rich, some were poor. The rich people opened their purses and tipped lots of coins into the bowls. Some did it quietly. Others made a great show of it. They held their pile of coins in both hands high over the bowls, then opened them and the money fell in with a great clatter. Some even dropped their coins in one by one. As they did so they bowed to the row of priests and scribes who stood nearby. The priests bowed back. They liked rich men.

'Look out for those people,' said Jesus quietly to those near him. 'There are always some priests and scribes who forget they are supposed to be servants. They love to dress up in fine clothes. They like people to call them "sir" and they love it when people bow to them in the streets. You will always find them sitting in the best seats or right at the front when something important is going on. Watch out for them. They don't really know very much about God.'

Just then a woman came up to the entrance of the Temple.

129

Jesus stopped talking and watched her. She was all alone. That meant she was a widow. Her dress was old and patched. She had no shoes. Her back was bent and she was very thin.

The woman had no purse. In her hand she clutched two very small coins. They were worth hardly anything, but they were all she had. She stopped by the collection bowl, where she took one of the coins and dropped it in. The other was still in her hand. She looked at it for a second or two. Then she dropped that in as well. She shuffled on past the priests, who turned up their noses at her.

'Look at that,' said Jesus to his disciples. 'That's what it is really all about. That woman has given more than all the rich people.'

'Given more?' asked Peter. 'But she had only two small copper coins.'

'Yes,' said Jesus, 'and that's all she had. She will starve again now she has given that, but the rich won't. They kept enough back for themselves. The real value of a gift is what it costs the person who gives it. That woman has given to God every-thing she owns. Follow her example, not the priests'.'

NOTES

ABOUT THE STORY

It would be easy to omit this incident from the main sequence of events in Holy Week but it carries forward a theme which has been present throughout the whole Bible Story.

Jewish wisdom literature, as represented in OT Story 50, constantly poses the questions of what and who are important in the eyes of God. It links up directly with Mary's song, the Magnificat, dealt with in Story 1. True faith in God demands a reversal of normal worldly values, exalting the humble and meek at the expense of the rich and powerful. Not surprisingly women play the key role in two out of these three accounts.

The teaching within this story would seem to be the simple but, nevertheless, profound point that the value of a gift is what it cost the giver and not the monetary value it might have for the recipient. Nor is this just a piece of religious or moral sermonizing. We all know its truth in the value of a gift from a small child or an elderly person.

The tragedy is that even in the religious life the point is often lost. Even there the rich and the powerful often seem to dominate. Poverty may have been embraced by individuals but the institutions to which they belong have often cancelled out this ideal for which they seemingly stood. (For example, compare the poverty of individual monks and nuns with the wealth of some medieval monasteries.)

Insignificant though this incident may seem to be it is of immense social and political importance, as expressed in the words of the Magnificat. Once again Jesus offends those of power and prestige. He threatens to exalt the humble and meek at the expense of bringing down the mighty from their seats. The fact that his teaching comes totally out of their own tradition serves only to make matters worse.

IDEAS FOR EXPLORING FURTHER

Valuing Gifts   Ask the children for their ideas about gifts which they could give which would cost nothing (or very little) in monetary terms but might cost them some thought and time to find/make. Ask the children whether they have received any gifts which did not cost a great deal but which they really appreciated. Discuss reasons. Is biggest always best? Cf. *The King's Flower,* by Mitsumasa Anno.

Relationships between Young and Old   Ask the children to think about the difficulties that older people might experience in daily living. What could pupils do to help? Send for some of the materials available from Help the Aged Education Department, 218 Upper Street, London N1. Find stories which highlight successful relationships between old and young (e.g. *Of Lambs and Lollipops: Stories About Young and Old* and *Book of Folk Tales,* published by Help the Aged; *My Grandma Has Black Hair,* by Mary Hoffman and Joanna Burroughes; *Grandpa's Face,* by Eloise Greenfield; *My Grandmother's Stories,* by Adele Geras; *Solomon's Secret,* by Saviour Pirotta and Helen Cooper; *My Grandpa and the Sea,* by Katherine Orr; *The River That Gave Gifts,* by Margo Humphrey; *Love You Forever,* by Robert Munsch). See also notes on Stories 11, 23.

29

Should We Pay Taxes to Caesar?

Luke 20: 19–26

The priests and some of their followers didn't know what to do. 'We've got to get rid of this man,' they said.

'How?'

'Let's arrest him for causing trouble.'

'We can't.'

'Why not?'

'Because the crowd is always with him. He's never alone. The people love him. If we arrest him we shall have a revolution on our hands. Then the Romans will blame us.'

'I know what we can do,' said a scribe.

'What?' asked the others.

'We must make him look silly in front of all the people. Let's think up some awkward questions. If we can get the people to laugh at him he's all ours. Or if we can make him say something against the Romans, they will arrest him. That's an even better idea. We shouldn't have to do anything then. They would do it all for us. Come on.'

The small group of priests and scribes went down into Jerusalem. They had no trouble finding Jesus. As usual he had a big crowd around him. They joined the crowd and found one or two of their Pharisee friends already there.

'What's happening today?' they asked. 'Is he still in a bad mood?'

'No,' came the reply, 'he's telling stories. He's just told them one about a vineyard owner. He made it sound as if he

132

were God's own son and we were trying to kill him. Some of the crowd keep giving us ugly looks. If those Roman soldiers weren't here I wouldn't feel too safe.'

'Roman soldiers, where?' asked the scribe. 'Oh, I see. Right, we shall soon sort him out.'

'Teacher,' he called out in a loud voice.

The crowd turned and looked at him. So did Jesus.

'Teacher,' he repeated in a softer voice. 'We know you're not frightened of anyone,' – he glanced towards the Roman soldiers – 'we know you will always tell us what God wants. Tell us. Should we pay taxes to Caesar and the Romans or not?'

It was a trap. If Jesus said 'Yes', some of the crowd would leave him. They hated the Romans. If he said 'No', the Romans would arrest him for trying to make the people rebel against Caesar.

The crowd waited for Jesus to reply. The scribe looked around at his friends and smiled.

Jesus spoke. 'Have you got a coin?' he asked.

'Yes,' said the scribe. He got out an ordinary coin.

'Whose head is on it?' asked Jesus.

'The head of Caesar,' said the scribe.

'Then the answer is simple,' said Jesus. 'Give back to Caesar the things that belong to him, and give back to God his own things.'

There was a pause. The crowd began to laugh. They realized what had happened. They laughed and laughed. But they were not laughing at Jesus. They were laughing at the scribe who had been beaten at his own game. They laughed even louder as the scribe and his friends left the crowd and hurried off, looking very cross.

ABOUT THE STORY

This is one of a number of questions put publicly to Jesus during Holy Week. All of them seem to have been designed as trick questions; their main purpose could well have been simply to destroy Jesus' street credibility.

We are reminded here of the Zacchaeus incident (Story 22). Paying taxes to Rome was a volatile political issue. The Romans were extremely nervous of anything which even remotely smelt of rebellion. Throughout the Empire they were deeply suspicious of all gatherings and organizations. We can be sure that Romans were at the edge of a crowd such as this, waiting to pounce on any anti-Roman rabble-rouser.

Christian theologians have made much of Jesus' answer but it could also be interpreted as not much more than a trick answer to a trick question, a matter of a quick-witted response which turns the tables on those trying to catch him out and makes them rather than him look foolish in public. In that case it would simply be akin to the answer given at the dispatch box by a government minister wanting to avoid saying anything incriminating, with more attention focusing on the person than on the answer.

Early Christian theology about attitudes to the State was to undergo significant change during the first fifty or sixty years of the Church's existence. In his early letter to the Church in Rome (written before the Gospels) Paul makes, in Chapter 12, a strong point of the need to support the State and he calls for loyalty to magistrates and civil government. By the time Revelation, the last book in the New Testament, was written things had changed dramatically. The Church was being openly persecuted and the writer of that book, again in Chapter 12, sees the need to stand against the State.

IDEAS FOR EXPLORING FURTHER

Caesar   Find out more about Roman Emperors and their power (cf. `NC` *History:* CSU 1 – invaders and settlers), especially the first Emperor, Caesar Augustus (also called Octavian, great nephew and adopted son of Julius Caesar), who lived from 63 B.C.E. to 14 C.E.; Tiberias, Augustus' adopted son (42 B.C.E.–37 C.E.), who was Emperor at the time of this story; Nero (37–68 C.E.), who used the fire which destroyed much of Rome in 64 C.E. as an excuse to persecute many of the early Christians.

Materialism   Look at coins of the realm and those of other countries. What symbols or words do they carry and what is their significance? What seem to be the principal messages carried on the coins? Does this story suggest that God is not interested in material things, power or social status? If God were to ask for a coin to be made to reflect what he values most and to provide an important message, what might appear on his coin? Ask the children to devise appropriate symbols and words for such a coin. Challenge the children to make a free-standing coin with two sides to view, one relating to Caesar's opinion of what is important and the other to God's. (Cf. `NC` *Technology*.)

Getting People into Trouble   Talk to children about how God might view those who, like the scribe, try to get other people into trouble. See Matthew 18: 6; Mark 9: 42; Luke 17: 2. In what different ways can this occur? Discuss how some older children or adults try to introduce children to harmful substances such as alcohol, cigarettes and drugs. (Cf. NC *Health Education.*) Invite the children to create a poster warning people about this problem. (Cf. NC *Technology.*)

Taxation   Talk about why we pay taxes. Why has poll-tax been so unpopular over the centuries? (E.g. in 1381, Wat Tyler led the Peasants' Revolt in protest against the poll-tax and the labour legislation passed by the government of Richard II.) Are there occasions when it is justifiable to withhold tax payments? Consider local government structures: who decides how money should be spent in the locality? Invite a member of local government to talk to the children. In theory, the money should be spent in the best interests of local people. Who decides what 'best' means and who sets the priorities? Ask the children to consider their local area and to brainstorm how it could be improved using local tax income. Let them decide on priorities. Perhaps send their opinions to local government officers. (Cf. NC *Geography:* AT 5 – environmental geography; *Citizenship.*)

30

A Last Supper

Mark 14: 12–26

'Where are we going to have our Passover feast?' asked Peter. Jesus and his disciples were once again in Bethany. At first Jesus did not answer. He looked around and then took Peter and John outside.

'Listen,' he said in a very quiet voice. 'I have made some plans. Do exactly what I tell you. Go down into the city. At the gate you will see a man holding a water jar. When he sees you he will walk away. Follow him and make sure no one follows you. He will lead you to a house. Say to the owner of the house, "The Teacher says, 'Where is the room where I am to eat with my disciples?'" He will take you upstairs to a room built on to the roof of his house. Go in and get the meal ready. We will come this evening.'

Jesus turned and went back indoors.

Peter and John looked at each other. 'What's the secret for?' asked Peter. 'Why doesn't he just tell us the address?'

'I don't know,' answered John. 'But come on. I expect he has a reason.'

The two men set off up the hill. 'At least we can't miss a man with a water jar,' said John. 'Only women carry water.'

'Let's hope he's there,' replied Peter, 'or we shan't know which way to go.'

They came to the city gate. Sure enough, just inside stood a man with a water pot on his head. They went towards him. He saw them coming. Before they could speak he turned and moved away through the crowd. Peter and John followed.

136

The man turned off the main street into a small alley. The disciples went after him. John turned and looked back. No one was following them.

'Come on,' called Peter, 'we shall lose him.'

They hurried to catch up. The man walked quickly. He turned to the left and then to the right. Peter and John had never been in this part of the city before. They were lost.

Suddenly the man disappeared.

'Where's he gone?' asked Peter.

'There,' said John, 'that door.'

The door of a house was open. The man had gone inside. Another man appeared in the doorway. Peter and John stopped in front of him.

'What do you want?' the man asked.

Peter spoke. 'The Teacher says, "Where is the room where I am to eat with my disciples?"'

The man nodded to the steps at the side of the house. Peter and John went up. They heard the door of the house close behind them. Just as Jesus had said, at the top of the steps, instead of a flat roof, was another room. They opened the door and went in. The two men began to get the meal ready.

A short distance away Judas Iscariot was in a room at the Temple. A small group of priests and Pharisees were with him.

'I know he will be in the city after dark,' Judas was saying, 'but I don't know where.'

'Why not?' asked one of the priests.

'Because he has not told anyone where we are having the feast. As soon as I know I will come and get you.'

'Make sure you do,' said the priest. 'It is our only chance and we will pay you well.'

'If I am too late,' said Judas, 'I can tell you this. He will go home by the footpath through the olive woods.'

Jesus and the other disciples arrived in the evening. They sat on cushions around a small table. It was a simple meal.

Each man took a lump of bread and dipped it into the

central bowl of meat soup. They talked. Judas sat at the end near the door.

Suddenly Jesus said, 'One of you is going to betray me.' The talking stopped.

'Betray you?' gasped Peter. 'Who? I shall kill him first.'

'It will be one of you,' was all Jesus would say. 'One of you who is dipping into the dish with me.'

The disciples were silent. They looked at one another.

Jesus spoke again. He had picked up the long loaf of bread. 'This is my body,' he said. He broke pieces off the loaf. 'It is broken for you,' he added as he passed the pieces round.

Then he took a large cup full of wine and said, 'This is my blood which is shed for you. Drink it, all of it.'

He passed the cup round. They all drank from it.

There was silence. Judas moved towards the door. 'Excuse me a minute,' he said.

Jesus replied, 'Be quick', and Judas had gone.

They started to sing. Then Jesus said, 'Let's go.'

Quite suddenly the feast was over. They moved through the dark narrow streets towards the gate.

The owner of the house was in bed. Suddenly there was a lot of noise. Men were running up the stairs above him. Fire torches shone in the night.

'They've gone. They've gone,' someone shouted. More footsteps. Men came running down the stairs.

'John, John,' called the man to his son. 'Quickly, get up.'

Young John rubbed his eyes and got out of bed. 'What's up?' he said. He reached for his clothes.

'No time,' shouted his father. 'Quick, run. They are after Jesus. As fast as you can. Run to the olive wood. You might get there first. Warn Jesus.'

Dressed only in a loincloth, John Mark ran out of the house. He ran off into the night chasing after the men who were following Jesus. The streets were empty. It was late at night. No one was about.

ABOUT THE STORY

This is a crucially important story, faithfully recorded in all four Gospels, and the basis of the central act of Christian worship variously known as Mass, the Eucharist, Communion or, simply, the Lord's Supper.

Bible scholars argue about whether or not historically this was actually the Pesach (Passover) meal of the Jews but, whatever the historical timing, there can be little doubt about what the event immediately came to mean.

At the Jewish Pesach meal the basic ingredient is the lamb, which in the Exodus story (see OT Story 13) was killed and its blood used as a means of protection or salvation from death. Jews use wine as a symbol of blood at their Pesach meal and splash ten drops from the goblet to represent the ten plagues.

At this meal, which occurs at Pesach time, but appears simpler, it is the bread which becomes the first focal point. As in most of the world the basic meal seems to consist of bread (or rice or mealie meal) dipped into a central dish of relish or stew. The host might well break or cut up the bread and pass it round. As Jesus does this he utters the words 'This is my body, broken for you'. In the same way he passes round the wine with the words 'This is my blood, shed for you'. The disciples are baffled. Later it makes sense and they understand the significance of what happened. Jesus himself has taken the place of the lamb. Some Christians see Communion as a re-enactment of Jesus' sacrifice. For others it is enough continually to remember what the faith is all about by repeating the breaking and the pouring.

Two small details of the wider story have been woven into this telling. It is always difficult to imagine how Judas escaped the attention of the others after Jesus' prediction and children often ask, 'Why didn't they stop him?' Is it too crude to suggest that it was just like a child asking to 'be excused'?

Secondly, there is the young man in the loincloth. He is the seventeen-year-old son of the owner of the house, who is an unknown secret disciple. But he is also John Mark, who was to accompany Paul on a dangerous missionary journey and was, in later life, to be the author of Mark's Gospel, the first record the world possesses of the Christian Story.

IDEAS FOR EXPLORING FURTHER

Meals/Symbols   See notes on Story 18. Ask whether any of the pupils have been to a church service involving bread and wine and, if so, invite their description/comments. Ask a church leader to visit the class to show/tell the children what (s)he thinks a Communion service/Eucharist/Mass/Lord's Supper is all about. This would link well with work on Elizabeth I because she attempted to unite Protestants and Catholics by re-establishing the Church of England (1559) and reforming the Communion service, using a good deal of language which could be interpreted in different ways. (Cf. **NC** *History*: CSU 2 – Tudor and Stuart times.)

Choices   See notes on Story 15, OT Stories 3, 28.

Temptation   It might have been that Judas could not resist the temptation to get rich quick. Ask the children: 'If you were promised £1000 to spend on anything you liked in return for telling a lie about your best friend, would you be tempted to do it?' What reasons do children have for their response? Discuss with pupils the times when they have been tempted to do foolish things and talk about the outcomes. Explore these ideas through poetry (e.g. Hilaire Belloc's 'Mathilda', who was tempted to tell lies) and through fiction (e.g. *The Balaclava Story*, by George Layton; *A Pack of Liars*, by Anne Fine). Talk to pupils about the way some people believe in a very strong spiritual force of evil (sometimes called Satan, or the Devil) in the same way as they believe in a spiritual force of good, embodied in the idea of God. The notion of the Devil actively working to get people on his side sits alongside this. It has been clearly demonstrated in *The Screwtape Letters*, by C. S. Lewis, and the German legend about Faust, who made a pact with the Devil, surrendering his soul in return for youth, knowledge and magical power. The latter inspired Berlioz to write an opera called 'Faust' in 1846, and Marlowe, Goethe and Liszt to make use of the tale too. It was the fear of witchcraft and the Devil that caused so many women to be executed as witches in Tudor times. (Cf. **NC** *History*: CSU 2 – Tudor and Stuart times.) See also OT Story 49.

31

Arrest at Midnight

Mark 14: 27–52

The night was dark. Jesus and his disciples went out of Jerusalem and down the hill. They crossed the stream at the bottom. In front of them was the Mount of Olives covered in trees. The wood looked very black.

Jesus stopped. They were standing in a small open space, like a garden. Nobody spoke. Jesus appeared very sad. He looked round at the disciples. Suddenly he broke the silence. 'You will all run away from me,' he said.

'I won't,' said Peter, without stopping to think.

'Yes, you will, you all will,' replied Jesus, 'like sheep when the shepherd is knocked over.'

'I don't know about the others,' said Peter, 'but I tell you this. I shall stay whatever happens.'

'And I shall tell you this,' Jesus replied sadly. 'Before the cock crows in the morning you will have said three times that you have never heard of me.'

'I'll die first,' said Peter.

Jesus did not answer. They were all silent again. Then Jesus said, 'Stay here. I want to pray.'

Most of the disciples sat down. They were very tired. Peter, James and John went on with Jesus.

Jesus stopped again. 'Wait here,' he said to the three men. 'I want to be alone for a few minutes. Keep watch.'

They were at the edge of the wood. Jesus went on a little

farther. The three men sat on the grass. One by one they lay down. In a few minutes they were all asleep.

Some time later Jesus came back. His footsteps woke Peter, who sat up.

'Were you sleeping?' said Jesus. 'Couldn't you even keep awake for that long? Keep watch. Pray hard.' Jesus went off into the trees again. He had his own prayers to say. He did not want to die, but he did not want to run away either. 'Tell me, God, what should I do?' was what he was saying, over and over again.

Jesus came back. This time the disciples were all fast asleep. They did not even hear him coming. 'Asleep again?' said Jesus. They sat up. They didn't know what to say. They had let him down again.

For a third time Jesus went off. For a third time the disciples fell asleep.

Down near the stream there were lights. Men with torches were hurrying down the hill opposite. Jesus came back to Peter, James and John. 'Still asleep,' he said. 'Never mind. It doesn't matter any more. I have been betrayed. Here they come.'

There were shouts from down the hill. Men were running. Shadows and flaming torches were moving through the trees. Cries of 'Look out', 'Run', 'Don't let him get away' and 'Where's the leader?' could be heard as the mob found the main group of disciples. One or two crashed past Jesus in the darkness. They did not stop. Jesus did not move. The mob with torches came close.

'Which is Jesus? Is he here?' shouted a voice.

One man with the group broke away. He ran over to Jesus, put his arm round his neck, kissed him on the cheek and in a loud voice said, 'Master'. It was Judas.

Jesus stood still. He was surrounded now by men with swords. They were waiting for him to fight or run. Instead he looked at them and said, 'Are you looking for a thief with all

142

those weapons? You've seen me in the Temple every day for this last week. Why didn't you catch me there?' He was very calm. Everybody else was excited.

A little way away Peter was still shouting and waving his own sword around. Just then out of the trees ran a young man of about seventeen. All he had on was a loincloth. He stopped. He could see that Jesus was already captured. He was too late. One of the soldiers took a grab at him. He caught hold of the loincloth. The boy twisted and the cloth came away in the soldier's hand. Before he could do anything the boy had run off down the hill as fast as he could. He had nothing on at all.

'Leave him,' said a voice. 'This is the one we want.'

In all the excitement James and John and Peter had slipped off into the woods. Jesus was alone. The soldiers tied his hands behind his back. They pushed him back down the hill towards the city of Jerusalem.

Peter was still watching. He had hidden in the trees. He kept in the shadows and followed the mob which had taken Jesus. It was midnight.

NOTES

ABOUT THE STORY

What exactly had Judas done? We must surmise that he had sneaked away to tell the High Priest where Jesus could be located inside the city after dark when the crowds had gone. Because of all the secrecy he himself had not known where the supper was going to be until he was taken there with the others. On returning and finding they had already left, he still knew where they were headed and by which route.

Why, though, did Jesus not make a run for it? We do not know. He could perhaps have got back over the hill to Bethany. Then what? There could only have been some sort of violent struggle in which a lot of people would have got hurt or killed – maybe even Mary and Martha. A certain inevitability creeps into the story. There is no escape. Morale among the disciples collapses and tiredness overtakes them.

The detail given about Peter and John Mark, on the edge of the skirmish, has some interest. It is as if this is the authors' signature to the book. What we are reading is almost certainly the account written by John Mark some twenty or more years later on, acting as Peter's scribe. By then Mark would have been in his forties and Peter, considerably older, near to dying. We are told by another source that 'John Mark wrote down accurately but not in order those things which Peter had told him'.

143

There had been much time for such telling. This encounter on the Mount of Olives could well have been the first joint experience of two men who were to share many future dangers while preaching the Gospel of the Christ they were to feel they had let down on this night. It is worth noting that, although they wrote this account themselves, they do not appear in a good light within the story. It would have been easy to have made themselves out to have been hero figures. The fact that they did not adds to the authenticity of the narrative.

IDEAS FOR EXPLORING FURTHER

Traitors Just the word 'traitor' arouses strong emotions in many people. If the children were going to draw a traitor, what would they put into that picture? Explore the concept of a traitor by looking at fairy tales and other fiction, by considering so-called traitors of the past (e.g. Anne Boleyn, Mary Queen of Scots, Lady Jane Grey, Guy Fawkes, collaborators during the Second World War, spies like Anthony Blunt). (Cf. NC *History*.) What about industrial espionage? Are all traitors the same? Mount pictures (or names) of a number of so-called traitors in the middle of large sheets of paper. Write around the outside of each picture/name the deeds or qualities which earned that person the title of traitor. Which of the traitors known to children seems to have committed the greatest crime? Ask children to give their reasons.

Betrayal This story shows that there are at least two kinds of betrayal:

(i) that committed through a specific action intended to do harm, as demonstrated by Judas;

(ii) that committed through inaction, as demonstrated by Peter, James and John falling asleep. The loyalty of the disciples was undermined by their physical and mental weakness. If they had been on watch, as Jesus asked, would Judas and the soldiers have come upon him so suddenly?

Today, do we, like Judas, through a specific action, sometimes betray people's friendship by telling tales and getting them into trouble? Do we hurt them by setting them aside roughly in favour of someone else, or a new toy/activity?

Likewise, how many times do we pay lip-service to an ideal and then do nothing about it? Do we, for example, say we do not like bullying but then watch someone being ill treated? Do we say we want to help people, or share, but always make an excuse when there is an opportunity to do these things? Do we claim to be committed to recycling materials but never take things to recycling points? Do we complain about people who drop litter and then not clear up properly after a picnic ourselves? Do we make promises but then break them? Do we do all this because we are in too much of a hurry, too busy, too lazy or too tired? See Stories 4, 15, 30.

Combatting Stereotypes See Stories 3, 7, 14, 24, 45, OT Stories 11, 18, 36, 40, 41.

32

Peter – Half a Hero

Mark 14: 15–72

It was a cold night. A fire burned in the middle of the court-yard. A few servants and one or two soldiers sat round it. It was hard to see their faces properly. Peter crept into the yard. He was alone. The others had all run away. He kept in the shadows. One room of the house was lit. Through the window Peter could see Jesus standing. He had soldiers at his side. Facing him was the High Priest. Peter could see that the High Priest was talking. He could not hear what was being said.

Peter moved closer. Now he was near the fire. Its light shone on his face. Peter sat down on the stones in the court-yard. He pretended to be warming himself. Perhaps he could find out from the servants what was happening.

He looked up at the window again. Now the High Priest was on his feet. He was shouting at Jesus. Jesus seemed to be just standing there, saying nothing.

Peter was trying to catch what was being said. Suddenly he realized that somebody was very close to him. He took his eyes from the window and saw a young girl standing in front of him. She was one of the servants.

'Hullo,' she said. 'Who are you?'

Peter did not answer.

The girl bent down and looked closer. 'You were with him, weren't you?' she went on. 'With that Jesus of Nazareth they've got in there.' She nodded towards the windows.

Peter felt very frightened. 'What are you talking about?' he said. 'Jesus of Nazareth? I've never heard of him.'

'Huh!' said the girl. She moved over to the small group of servants sitting nearby.

Peter glanced up at the window again. What he saw filled him with horror. Fists were flying now. Somebody had put a blindfold on Jesus. He was being pushed about by the servants. From time to time one of them hit him across the face or punched him in the stomach. The fire was warm but Peter shivered with fear.

He suddenly realized that the little group of servants were all looking at him. The girl who had spoken to him was saying to her friends 'He's one of them'.

Peter heard. He spoke up. 'Take no notice of her,' he said. 'She doesn't know what she's talking about.'

He tried to say it quietly, but it was no good. Other people in the dark courtyard had stopped talking. They were all looking at him. One or two of the men started to walk over towards Peter. They stood near him. Peter got to his feet.

'You've got a northern accent,' said one of the men. 'You obviously come from Galilee. I think the girl's right. You are one of them. Perhaps they'd like to ask you some questions too.'

Peter swore. Then he said, 'Jesus? I've never had anything to do with that man. I don't know what you're talking about.'

Just at that moment the main door of the house opened. A voice called out of the darkness, 'Escort wanted. Take the prisoner to Governor Pilate.'

The men who were near Peter moved quickly. They ran over to where they had been sitting, picked up their swords and coats and went over to the door. The white figure of Jesus appeared in the doorway. His hands were tied. The soldiers marched away with him out of the gateway.

All was quiet again in the courtyard. Peter looked up. The first rays of daylight could be seen in the sky. Dawn was breaking. Away in the distance a cock crowed. Suddenly Peter remembered almost the last thing Jesus had said to him:

146

'Before the cock crows in the morning you will have said three times that you have never heard of me.' The tears ran down Peter's cheeks. He turned and ran out of the gate. Behind him he heard the laugh of the servant girl.

NOTES

ABOUT THE STORY

What follows now is a routine which, sadly, does not seem to have changed over two thousand years and has become all too frequent in our own time. Arrest at midnight is followed by interrogation in the small hours, a summary trial and execution before the outside world has a chance to realize what is happening.

This story would appear to have been written, as much as anything, to show the fulfilment of Jesus' prophecy about Peter's behaviour. Peter is overcome with remorse because he, a strong Galilean fisherman, makes his denials to a mocking servant girl. Nevertheless, what could he have done? Equally important, where were the other disciples? Peter actually shows great courage in being there at all but he remains a helpless bystander. The account, which, we need to remind ourselves, was almost certainly related to Mark by him, presents him as a coward.

The religious authorities have been angered by Jesus' religious teaching. They see him as a heretic and worse. He is a trouble-maker who has ridiculed them in public, making them lose face and status. However, even here they have little real power. The country is under Roman rule and the Romans are strong on the Rule of Law. All the High Priest's strong-arm men can do to Jesus is to 'rough him up' and 'give him a going over', unless they can find a charge which will make the Romans themselves want to sit up and take notice.

We see in the following story how, even two thousand years ago, words could be twisted for purposes of what today we would call propaganda.

IDEAS FOR EXPLORING FURTHER

Denying Jesus   Peter may have denied knowing Jesus, but where were the other ten disciples? Discuss what they might have been thinking or doing. Is fear, shock, or tiredness any excuse for their actions? Ask the children to imagine they are one of the disciples and to write down in bold print on large paper one excuse for what they did. Ask the pupils to discuss these excuses and to decide which, if any, might be the most valid. Would any one excuse actually be a sufficient explanation for one of the disciples' behaviour? Emphasize the fact that people have many complicated motives for their actions and that it is not easy to discern them. How might God have viewed the disciples' behaviour? Would we have acted differently? Does this story point to the cowardice of ten individuals or to the weakness of human nature in general?

How easy is it for present-day Christians to say that they would never deny Jesus? Is it true that people who say they love Jesus and want to follow his teaching and yet let him down by behaving in a way which he would not appreciate are, in fact, denying him? (Cf. Alleged English football fans who say they support the English team and England yet disgrace both by violent behaviour.) When Christians behave badly, is it as if they were saying to Jesus, 'I don't know you'?

Draw a cartoon of, act out informally, or write a script for a play about a situation in which Christians might (later) feel they were denying Jesus through their behaviour. (Cf. NC *English*.)

Loyalty   Read some myths, legends or stories from different cultures and faith traditions to help children explore further the concept of loyalty between friends. Reading extracts from *Charlotte's Web*, by E. White, and *The Wind in the Willows*, by Kenneth Graeme, might also be helpful. Central characters in these books show how to rally to a friend's aid, even if that friend is a little unusual or foolish.

Bullying   Talk about different forms of bullying inside school and outside. What are the reasons and results? Is doing nothing about bullying the same as condoning it? Help pupils to draw up a charter for how they wish all people to be treated (e.g. no name-calling, no cold-shouldering). Are adults being bullies when they mug or murder people? Is it a case of bullying when one country uses force to take over another and enslaves its people? (NC *History*: CSU 3 – Empire and slavery, CSU 6 – exploration and encounters.) Most nations around the world have pluralist communities. If people do not have equal rights to land, homes and jobs, is that a form of bullying? (NC *Geography*: AT 2; *Citizenship*.) Read extracts from *The Heartstone Odyssey*, by Arvan Kumar.

148

33

Our King Must Die

Luke 23: 1–49

Pilate was in a bad mood. He did not like the High Priest and his followers at any time. At six o'clock in the morning it was all too much. Here they were with a prisoner, and they had brought a small noisy crowd which filled his courtyard.

'Sort it out yourselves,' Pilate said to the High Priest. 'I don't want to be bothered with your little affairs at this hour of the morning.'

'But you are the Roman Governor,' answered the High Priest, 'and only the Romans can give the death penalty.'

'Death penalty?' echoed Pilate. 'You want this man put to death? Why? What's he supposed to have done?'

'He claims he is a king,' came the answer.

Pilate turned to Jesus. 'Is that true?' he asked. 'Are you King of the Jews?'

'The words are yours, not mine,' answered Jesus. He knew he could not begin to explain what sort of a king he was. The priests and the crowd did not want to listen to him.

Pilate turned back to the priests. 'There is nothing wrong with this man,' he said. 'He is not guilty.'

'You cannot let him go,' screamed the High Priest. 'He has been stirring up trouble everywhere from Galilee, where he comes from, right down to Jerusalem.'

'Oh, he comes from Galilee, does he?' said Pilate. 'Good, well take him off to Herod, then. He's supposed to be in charge of Galilee. I shall not condemn him to death.' He got up and went back into his palace.

Herod was a very fat man. He thought he was very witty. He had heard all about Jesus but until now he had never met him.

Jesus stood quietly in front of Herod. Herod walked all round him, jabbing him with a fat finger.

'King,' said Herod. 'You don't look like a king, do you?' He laughed. 'Let's make him a king,' he said.

Herod sent his soldiers off. They came back with a purple robe. Herod put it around Jesus' shoulders. It covered his torn and muddy white cloak.

'A crown,' called Herod. 'A king must have a crown. Get one that will fit tightly.'

The soldiers ran off into the garden. A few minutes later they returned carrying some thin branches off a thorn bush. One of them twisted the twigs into a circle. He scratched his hands as he did so. Then he carefully took the rough crown and lifted it over Jesus' head.

'Hail, King of the Jews,' Herod shouted.

The soldier brought the crown down hard on Jesus' head. The thorns dug in. Blood began to trickle down Jesus' face. He did not make a sound.

That annoyed Herod. 'Salute the king,' he shouted and gave Jesus a push. Before Jesus could fall a soldier behind pushed him back. They all joined in pushing and shoving. Still Jesus did not say a word.

'Take him away,' snarled Herod. 'Take him back to Pilate. I don't know what to do with him.'

Jesus stood in front of Pilate again.

'So, Herod can't find anything wrong with you either,' said Pilate. He took Jesus outside to the courtyard. 'There is nothing wrong with this man,' said Pilate. 'Today is a feast day. It is my custom to let a prisoner go free on such a day. . . .'

Before he could finish speaking a voice in the crowd called out, 'Free Barabbas. We want Barabbas.'

'Barabbas?' gasped Pilate. 'But he is the biggest thief and murderer in town.'

The crowd in the courtyard began to chant, 'We want Barabbas. We want Barabbas. We want Barabbas.'

Pilate looked around. At his shoulder the High Priest whispered, 'You're going to have a revolution if you're not careful. I don't think Caesar in Rome would like that. Especially if it's all over a man who claims to be king.'

Pilate suddenly felt frightened. He held up his hand. 'All right, all right,' he said as the shouting stopped. 'I shall set Barabbas free.' The crowd cheered. 'But what shall I do then with this man Jesus?'

'Hang him,' called a voice. 'Hang him on a cross.' The mob started to chant again, 'Hang him, hang him on a cross.'

Pilate tried again. 'Why?' he called out. 'What has he done wrong?'

Nobody answered. The crowd went on chanting, 'Hang him, hang him on a cross. Hang him, hang him on a cross.'

Pilate whispered to a soldier. The soldier went away. He came back with a towel and a bowl of water.

'Look,' called Pilate, 'I wash my hands of this man Jesus. Do with him what you want.' He turned and walked away. He could not look Jesus in the face.

By nine o'clock in the morning the pilgrims were pouring through the gates of Jerusalem in their hundreds. Outside on a small hillside stood three crosses.

'Poor devils,' said one man to another. 'The Romans are very cruel. I wonder what they've done.'

Few of them realized that Jesus whom they had cheered all week was one of them. When they found out, it was too late.

Jesus hung there in the sun. Roman guards stood near the cross. One or two of his disciples stood nearby. There was nothing they could do.

151

At three o'clock in the afternoon Jesus died. People were in tears. 'He was a good man,' they said. 'He never did anything but good to anybody.'

'Well, that's it,' muttered one of Jesus' followers. 'It's all over now.'

Little did he know. It was not all over. The most exciting thing of all was just about to happen.

NOTES

ABOUT THE STORY

The main trials and crucifixion are run together here as one continuous incident as, indeed, they were. There is no gap between judgement and punishment. Earlier collections of Bible stories for children have often omitted the crucifixion but the cross is the central symbol of Christianity and the Christian Story is seriously altered without it. The staggering walk down the street now called the Via Dolorosa under the weight of the cross has been left out only because of length. It could well be added.

Jesus has claimed, through his actions, more than through his words, to be Messiah or Christ. One of the poetic images for Messiah was 'King' ('Your king will come to you riding upon an ass'). With a few notable exceptions (see Story 14) the Romans neither understand nor care about the Jews' beliefs, let alone the metaphors and symbols through which they express them. However, if those metaphors could be made to sound literal, then perhaps those in real power could be persuaded that this Galilean carpenter is a genuine threat to the mighty Roman Empire itself.

Everything in Jesus' trial hinges on the image of 'king'. We are reminded again of the problem encountered in Story 19, about words and what they can be made to mean. Pilate is a busy man and impatient with Jewish leaders. He seems to sense instinctively that this is a put-up job but he cannot be bothered to go into all the rigmarole of religious fanaticism. In his own estimation he simply has more important things to do, decides that it is a Jewish problem and passes the buck to Herod. By this act he indicates that no really serious crime has occurred.

In fact it means that Jesus gets the worst of all worlds. Herod is only a puppet king with no real power but he is a bully and his insecurity allows him to humiliate what he sees laughingly as a pretender to his own position. The mock coronation is an all too familiar case of gang violence.

Back in front of Pilate organized mob rule takes over. This time the High Priest's aides are better prepared. Pilate has recently had local rebelliousness to deal with.

Questions are being asked in Rome about his abilities. The threat to tell Caesar that he is soft on political agitators gets through. The crowd is almost certainly the local 'rent-a-mob', not the natural crowd of pilgrims who have been cheering Jesus all week. They would be drifting back into the city later in the day. By that time the executions would be well under way.

Crucifixion was a particularly cruel form of execution. The victim was simply tied or nailed up and left. Death could take days. Asphyxiation through muscular failure to draw breath was probably the most common cause of death. Heat and thirst were major factors. In Roman Palestine it was an all too familiar sight. Tragically, as Amnesty International have discovered, it has not been eliminated even from our modern world. Sometimes it might be a good thing if the Bible *were* out of date!

IDEAS FOR EXPLORING FURTHER

Justice   Find out more about the Police and the legal system, whose purpose is to ensure that justice is done, although cases arise where this is brought into doubt. Older children could discuss how easy or difficult it might be to collect evidence today, what could be done to stop people giving false information, what it might be like to be wrongfully imprisoned, or the feelings of families who have had a relative executed in error. This could lead to a debate on capital punishment. Talk about rights and responsibilities of being a citizen. (Cf. NC *Citizenship.*) Consider crime and punishment in the past. (Cf. NC *History.*) How concerned were people in the past to determine the truth of a case? By what methods was evidence obtained then?

Gang Pressure   Talk about the temptation to follow the crowd and the possible outcomes of this. *The Balaclava Story*, by George Layton, illustrates this well. Discuss the need to think for oneself as an individual in order to avoid the consequences of gang action which has not been thought through at all. See notes on Story 32 – bullying. See also Stories 41, 47 – behaviour towards others.

Haste   Pilate was bound up in his own life and was in too much of a hurry to listen to other people's problems. He brushed aside the whole affair. Do we sometimes hurt people by being too hasty or too busy? Talk to the children about the importance of taking time to listen to people and, if necessary, to their problems. Over a period of time, help them to listen to each other and to make thoughtful replies. If appropriate, focus on listening skills by playing listening games. See also Stories 39, 47.

34

Resurrection: Not Here but Everywhere

Luke 24: 1–11; John 20: 1–10

It was Sunday morning. Jesus had been dead for two days.

Mary Magdalene got up very early. It was still dark. She could not sleep. She was still very upset at what had happened to Jesus. There was nothing she could do, but she did not want just to sit around feeling miserable. She decided she would go down to the cave where the body of Jesus had been put. She would take spices and herbs and anoint Jesus' body for the last time.

Mary left the house and walked out of the village. She was glad to be alone. It was a long walk to the graveyard outside Jerusalem. Suddenly she stopped. What a fool she was! It had taken three men to roll the huge boulder into the mouth of the tomb. How could she possibly push it aside on her own? No. She was nearly at the graveyard. Better to go on and just sit in the garden than to go back to a house where everybody was miserable and sad.

The first rays of light were just creeping into the eastern sky when she got to the tomb. Mary shivered. It was cold. It was also rather frightening. She stood in front of the tomb. Suddenly a look of horror came into her eyes. She could not believe what she saw. The entrance was wide open, a huge hole in the darkness in front of her. The stone she knew she could not move had gone.

Mary crept forward. She peered into the darkness of the cave. On the left was a rough stone slab. That was where

Jesus' body had been placed. It was empty. The body had gone.

Mary's hand flew to her mouth. She stopped the scream as it came into her throat. She turned and ran. On and on into the first light of morning she ran, all the way back to the village.

When she came to the house she looked a dreadful sight. She was out of breath. Her dress was covered in dust. The sweat poured down her face. She stood in the doorway leaning against the doorpost.

Peter and John, who were sitting inside, leapt to their feet.

'Mary, what's the matter? Where have you been?'

'He's gone,' she gasped. 'He's not there. Somebody has taken him.'

'Who?' demanded Peter. 'What are you talking about?'

'Jesus,' sobbed Mary. 'I've been to the tomb. It's empty. He's not there.'

John was out of the house in a flash. He bounded down the slope. Peter was hard on his heels. John was still ahead when they got to the tomb. He stopped at the entrance. Peter crashed past him, straight into the cave.

It was daylight now. They could see. The stone slab was not quite empty. There were some white linen cloths on it. They were the sheets in which the body had been wrapped. It was as if the body had just melted away in the middle of them.

The two men looked at each other. They said nothing. They were both thinking the same thing. 'On the third day I will rise again.' Jesus had said that many times. Could it really be?

There was nothing they could do here. They turned and made their way back to the village. They needed time to think.

Meanwhile Mary had followed them back to the tomb. She had walked slowly this time. She sat on a stone crying quietly to herself. Through the tears she looked up into the empty tomb. What was that? Two figures could be seen inside the cave, sitting where the body had been. One of them spoke. 'Why are you crying?' he asked.

155

'Because someone has taken away my Lord and I don't know where they have put him,' replied Mary.

She turned away. There was another figure in white standing just behind her. He asked the same question: 'Why are you crying? Who is it you are looking for?'

Mary thought it was the gardener. 'Tell me, sir,' she sobbed. 'Tell me. If you have taken him away, tell me where you've put him.'

In reply the tall figure said one word – 'Mary'.

Mary could not believe her ears. Only one person ever spoke her name like that. For a moment her heart almost stopped beating, and then she whirled round to face the speaker. 'Rabboni,' she gasped. 'Rabboni, great teacher, how can it be?' She moved towards him, arms outstretched.

The figure backed away and put out his hand. 'No, Mary, don't touch me, not yet. Just go back to the others. Tell them I have risen. Tell them that soon I shall go back to God but I am not dead.'

At that the figure disappeared.

Mary stood there alone. Then for the second time that morning she ran back home. Nearly all the disciples were there now. John and Peter were excited. The others looked frightened. Mary's face shone. She looked quite different from the way she had an hour ago. She was calm and very, very happy, whereas a little while before she had been sobbing and crying. The men were quick to see the difference.

'What is it, Mary?' asked John quietly.

'I have seen the Lord,' said Mary. And she told them what had happened in the garden.

John listened. He believed her. So did Peter. But the others shook their heads and looked at one another. Was Mary all right? Or was she so upset that she was going slightly mad?

ABOUT THE STORY

The Resurrection is the great central tenet of the Christian faith. 'Christ is risen' is the proclamation which has come ringing down the centuries bringing hope to millions in times of despair. But what does it mean? Is it literal? Is it the same as 'Jesus is risen'? Above all, is it true? What sort of evidence would be needed to 'prove' it?

The possible 'evidence' we have consists of the stories of the resurrection appearances (Stories 34–37) and all that followed from them. What they show is how certain individuals became convinced one by one. That conviction went so deep that their creation – the Christian Church – is to be found in every country in the world with the possible exception of Tibet. Those who founded it often suffered terribly in the process but there is no evidence of any of them going back on their conviction.

Attempts at understanding exactly what happened are probably futile. The TV cameras were not there and it is purely speculative to ask what exactly they might have recorded if they had been.

There is deep mystery within each of the stories of the resurrection appearances. There is the appearance of a physical body and yet it is somehow no longer human. It comes and goes, sometimes immediately recognizable, sometimes not.

The resurrection appearances begin with Mary Magdalene. Late on the Friday Jesus' body had been placed in a cave-tomb. Shabbat (Sabbath) began at dusk and it would have been utterly unthinkable to do anything over the following thirty-six hours. On the Sunday morning (the third day) Mary sets off just before first light intent on anointing the body, an act which should have been done straight away. What follows can have come only from her description, given to Peter who, with John, was involved immediately afterwards. Mary assumes a tomb robbery until she hears the voice, intangible but, for her, unmistakable.

Note The word 'Easter' comes from the name of a European fertility goddess, Eostre. Early Christian missionaries converted pagan festivals of Spring. The symbolism is close – the return of life to a dead world. The Christian stories, however, add an altogether new dimension.

IDEAS FOR EXPLORING FURTHER

Seeing Things in a New Way For the early Christians, the Easter story meant that they saw death and life in a new way – as if with new eyes or through new spectacles. They realized that what seemed ordinary was not. Death was not what it appeared. Life was to be viewed and lived in a new way, putting God and others first, in response to God's great love for the world and its people. In this way, the familiar became unfamiliar: full of new meaning.

Help the children to choose some familiar aspect of the world around them to look at in greater detail with a view to gaining new understanding/insights. Ask the children to draw what they think they know about their chosen focus of attention. Help them to talk together, to examine, compare, reflect with a view to being able to say 'I never knew/noticed before, but …' (Cf. the work of surrealist artists, who sometimes placed apparently unrelated objects next to one another, or put objects in abnormal contexts in order to encourage new insights and awareness. Cf. NC *Art*: AT 2.) For example, look at the school garden as a whole, or focus on particular items; take a walk in the locality with a view to seeing it differently as a whole, or becoming aware of new detail (cf. NC *History*, *Geography*: local study); make a collection of things which are of a particular colour or shape; look again at any resources used for project work; find out about a local playgroup, disabled children, the elderly; focus on one or more jobs done in the community; find out more about a group of people in the community who tend to be ignored or forgotten (cf. NC *Citizenship; Careers and the World of Work*); go to the local park or woods and undertake an Earthwalk – listening and feeling blindfolded, creating an aroma cocktail out of natural things mixed with a little water, etc. (cf. NC *Geography*: AT 5 – environmental geography; see also *Sharing Nature with Children* and *Sharing the Joy of Nature*, by Joseph Cornell).

Alternatively, ask the children to think of someone they would like to know more about, to draw up a questionnaire and to interview that person in order to make new discoveries about them. How well do children think they know their parents, siblings, other relatives? Are they so familiar and so taken for granted that they seem to 'fade into the wallpaper'? Do they have needs, concerns? Should we put these people first sometimes?

Following their investigations, ask children to design and make a display, perhaps incorporating the shape of eyes or glasses (e.g. one eye or lens showing how the children used to see the person or subject, the other reflecting their new view). Help the children to evaluate the display afterwards. (Cf. NC *Technology*.)

Destroying Life Totally Focus on an area in the school grounds or in the locality. Suppose one wanted to destroy life totally in that area, so that nothing would ever, ever grow there again nor would it be repopulated by animals or people. What would one have to do? Talk about the volcanic explosion of Mt St Helens in 1980. The eruption devasted all wildlife, but within a few years, plants were growing again and animal life was observed there. It is true that, in many ways, the 'life force' is extremely persistent? Speculate also about nuclear disasters. Do the children feel that regeneration might occur? How long might it take? Discuss the effects of nuclear accidents such as those at Three Mile Island in the U.S.A. and Chernobyl in the Commonwealth of Independent States (ex U.S.S.R.).

Festivals of Spring Help the children to find out more about the pagan festival of Eostre and to discover how different people around the world celebrate the arrival of Spring. Point out that not all countries have four seasons and, accordingly, may have different types of festival. (Cf. NC *Science*: AT 4 – physical processes; *Geography*: AT 2 – knowledge and understanding of places.) See *Festivals*, by Jean Gilbert; *Easter*, by Norma Fairbairn and Jack Priestley (Living Festivals series).

158

35

A Stranger on the Emmaus Road

Luke 24: 13–33

Emmaus was a little village about eleven kilometres from Jerusalem. Two weary people walked along the dusty road towards it. Their heads were low and they dragged their feet. They were going home.

'What did you think of Mary's story, Cleopas?' muttered one of them.

'She was imagining things,' said Cleopas. 'You know what some people are like. They get all excited and start seeing things.'

'Yes, I'm afraid you're right,' replied his companion. 'It's sad though. Jesus was such a splendid person. How could it all happen to him? Why did they do it?' The voice became more and more tearful.

'Forget it,' said Cleopas sharply. 'We followed him. We had high hopes and they came to nothing. There's nothing we can do except go home and get back to normal.'

While the two were talking, another traveller had caught up with them. He slowed down and walked alongside Cleopas. He gave the normal Jewish greeting. 'Shalom', he said. 'Peace be with you.'

'Shalom,' replied Cleopas, not even bothering to look up.

The three trudged along in silence for a while. Then the stranger spoke again. 'I could not help hearing you talking just now,' he said. 'What was it all about?'

Cleopas and his companion stopped. 'For goodness' sake,' said Cleopas, 'don't tell me you're the only person who doesn't know what has been going on these last few days.'

'What things?' asked the stranger.

Cleopas groaned. How could anybody be so ignorant?

'The things about Jesus of Nazareth,' answered Cleopas as they continued walking. 'He was a great teacher. A lot of us followed him. We thought he was the Messiah who was going to save us all. But the priests and the Pharisees all ganged up on him. They got the Romans to crucify him last Friday. Do you mean to say you haven't heard all this? Where have you been these last few days?'

The stranger did not answer straight away. Then he said, 'And that was the end of it, was it – last Friday? I thought I heard you talking about something happening this morning.'

'Oh, that was just one of his followers,' replied Cleopas. 'She went off to the tomb early today. They couldn't find the body and she came running back with a story about angels and Jesus' being still alive. It upset everybody. You know what some people are like.'

'But I thought you said you all believed this Jesus was the Messiah,' said the stranger.

'Well, what of it?' asked Cleopas. He wished this man would go away. He made him feel uncomfortable.

'If he was Messiah,' said the stranger, 'he had to die and then come back. It's what the Scriptures say. Listen.' The man started talking about Moses and Elijah and all the prophets.

He went on and on and on: Cleopas only half listened. He was tired and sad and angry. Still the stranger talked. Let him, they were nearly there.

It was almost dark. The three entered the village of Emmaus. Where was the stranger going? He had not said.

'Come and eat with us,' said Cleopas. 'It's nearly dark. You can't continue your journey at night.' He rather hoped the man would say 'No' but he replied, 'Thank you.'

They went indoors. A meal was made. The three sat together at the table.

Before Cleopas could do anything the stranger reached out and took the long loaf of bread. He held it in his hands and broke it. He offered the pieces to Cleopas and his companion. Nothing was said. There was a moment of perfect quiet.

'Jesus,' gasped Cleopas. He looked down at the bread in his hand. The two looked at one another. Both looked across the table at the stranger. He had gone. There was nothing there but an empty seat.

'Am I imagining things?' gasped Cleopas.

'No, the bread is real enough. And we have listened to him talk all afternoon. Mary was right – that's what he said. It was him all the time.'

'No one will believe us,' cried Cleopas, still clutching the bread.

'They must,' answered his companion, jumping up and reaching for a cloak. 'Come on.'

'Where are we going?' asked Cleopas.

'Back to Jerusalem,' came the answer.

'But it's already dark,' said Cleopas.

'Who cares? We've seen a light tonight which will last for ever. I'm going to tell the others. Are you coming?'

The two went out into the night. Their heads were high and they no longer dragged their feet through the dust. They hurried back to Jerusalem as fast as their legs would carry them.

NOTES

ABOUT THE STORY

How was it possible for two people to walk for some miles in the company of a third person and not to recognize who he was when he had been uppermost in their minds? This is the most difficult question about this story. Were the two travellers so engrossed in their own depression that they could not recognize the familiar voice which Mary had immediately identified? How close had they been to Jesus during his lifetime? They were not members of the twelve. Cleopas may be the same person as the Clopas mentioned in John 19: 25 but that does not get us very far. We do not even know the gender of his companion. It is usually assumed that it was another man but it could equally have been his wife.

What does seem to be emphasized in this lack of recognition is that the two travellers have no expectation whatsoever of Jesus being alive. They know that he is dead and buried and that the whole excitement he has generated for a week in Jerusalem is over and finished.

It is the symbolic breaking of the bread which reveals Jesus' identity. He disappears: the bread remains broken on the table. 'This is my body' (Story 30) are the words which immediately come to mind. Two more people are convinced of what is happening. Will anybody believe them?

IDEAS FOR EXPLORING FURTHER

Personal Identity   Blindfold one of the children then ask that person to feel gently the face, hair and clothing of one of the other children (who remains silent) in order to try and recognize them. Talk about how people recognize each other. Obviously, the physical features of a person help a great deal. But what about other factors such as voice, footsteps, mannerisms? Do outward features tell us everything there is to know about a person? Can they be misleading? When children are scruffy or dirty on the outside after a vigorous game of sport, does this mean that the inside person is scruffy and dirty? How easy is it to misjudge 'the down and outs', or people who look or behave differently to ourselves? (Cf. Stories 14, 20, 24, 45, OT Story 18.)

Each human being is unique. Even identical twins usually have some small distinguishing features. Ask each child to find a partner. Their task is to interview each other to discover more about their partner's 'inner self', for example to find out:

- three things their partner finds really beautiful;
- two things they enjoy doing outside school;
- something of which they are afraid;
- two things they find really annoying;
- two things they really hate to do;
- two things they hope to do in the future;
- their favourite story relating to a religious tradition (and why);
- what they would like to change in the world.

Younger children could make simple responses to one or more of this type of question. With older children, the interview questions could be determined by the class in advance or partners could draw up their own interview schedule. (Someone could even interview the school staff!)

If the questions are printed on paper with a space left after each one, partners could cooperate to make notes or rough sketches to serve as quick reminders of the answers given by the child responding to the questionnaire. (Alternatively, a tape recording of the interview could be made.) The child interviewed could then be invited to use these responses to make a symbol/badge/shield/poster for his/her bedroom door to provide information 'for visitors' about the identity of the person whose room it is. (Cf. NC *Technology; English.*) Children could display their finished items and, if names are recorded on the back only, other class members, etc., could try and guess which representation of personal identity belongs to which child.

36

Behind Closed Doors

John 20: 19–30

There was a loud knocking on the door. Inside the room the men looked at one another. Their faces were white with fear. They held their breath and said nothing.

The knocking started again.

'Open the door. Open the door,' called a voice.

No one moved. The knocking went on.

'They will break the door down,' whispered Peter. 'What are we going to do? We shall have to let them in.'

The others nodded. This was really the end, then. The priests and Pharisees had killed Jesus. Now they had found his disciples. Would they all be killed as well?

'Open up. Open up,' called the voice again.

Peter broke the silence. 'Who is it?' he called.

'Cleopas,' came the answer. 'Let me in. Quickly.'

There was a sigh of relief. Men rushed towards the door. Hands pulled back the heavy wooden bar. Cleopas and his companion almost fell into the room. The door was shut again. The bar was pushed back in its place.

'What's the matter?' asked Peter. 'We thought you had gone back to Emmaus. It's nearly midnight. What are you doing back here? Have you been followed?'

'We've seen him, we've seen him,' gasped Cleopas. 'We saw him in Emmaus and we've almost run all the way back to tell you.'

'Seen who?' said Peter impatiently.

'Jesus!' Cleopas almost shouted. 'We have seen Jesus! Mary was right. He is not dead. We have seen him. We have talked to him.'

Then they sat down and slowly Cleopas told the other disciples all that had happened on the way home to Emmaus.

When he stopped Peter interrupted. 'And you say he talked to you all that time and you didn't know who he was?' he asked. 'How is that possible?'

'I don't know,' said Cleopas. 'He is the same and yet he is different. I can't explain it. It was only when he broke the bread and handed it to us that we realized who he was.'

The room was very still. No one said anything. No one moved. The silence seemed to grow. They were all looking at Cleopas when suddenly a voice from behind them said very quietly, 'Shalom. Peace be with you.' The men whirled round and stood, eyes and mouths wide open in amazement. There stood Jesus. Behind him the door still had the bar across. Nobody moved.

'What is the matter?' asked Jesus quietly. 'Why are you worried? I told you it would be like this. Touch me if you like. See my hands and side just as they were wounded on the cross.' He held up his hands. 'I'm more than just a ghost,' said Jesus. 'Have you anything to eat?'

All that was left on the table was a bit of boiled fish. Peter held it out. Jesus took it and ate it and then – as quietly and suddenly as he had come – he was gone. There were just the disciples in the room.

They looked at one another. Nobody could speak. Then there was another noise at the door, a gentle tapping this time.

'Who's there?' called Peter.

'Thomas,' came a whispered reply. 'Let me in.'

Peter slid back the bar and Thomas stood in the doorway. He looked at the disciples. Nobody spoke.

'It's all right,' said Thomas cheerfully, 'it's only me. Goodness, you all look as if you've seen a ghost.'

Nobody thought that was funny.

'He was here a minute ago,' gasped Peter. 'Jesus was here.'

'Jesus?' echoed Thomas. 'Here?'

'Yes,' said Peter, 'standing right where you are now.'

'You must be crazy,' laughed Thomas, 'I've just come up the stairs and nobody passed me.' He looked around at the others and shrugged his shoulders. 'You're as bad as the women,' he muttered. He looked at the table. 'Haven't you left me anything to eat?' he asked angrily.

'Yes,' replied Peter, 'we left you some fish – only,' he paused, 'we gave it to him. He was hungry.'

The plate stood empty. There had been some fish there. Cleopas looked down. In his hand he still clutched the small piece of bread Jesus had given him. He had been the same but he had been different. The bread and the fish were real enough, though.

Thomas was still talking. 'You're all going mad,' he was saying. 'Fish or no fish I'll only believe when I can put my fingers against the holes in his hands. Seeing is believing, that's what I say. It's late. I'm going to sleep. You should do the same. You'll feel better in the morning.'

A week later the men were still living in the same house. They did not know what to do. The door was still bolted, although it seemed the priests had forgotten about them. They sat around talking.

Suddenly it all happened again.

'Shalom,' said a voice and there he was. Jesus stood in the middle of the room. He looked straight at Thomas. Thomas looked back.

'See,' said Jesus. 'Here are my hands. Put your fingers into the holes where the nails went. I want you to believe.'

Thomas did not move for a second. Then he fell to his knees on the floor. 'My Lord and my God,' he sobbed.

Jesus spoke again. 'You have believed because you have seen me with your eyes,' he said. 'I am happy for all those who will believe without seeing me like that.'

Again he disappeared as silently as he had come. The disciples sat down and began to talk.

165

'There's nothing else we can do here,' said Peter. 'I am going back home to Galilee.'

The other fishermen agreed. Next morning they set off for home.

NOTES

ABOUT THE STORY

Two resurrection stories have here been run into one. There is the appearance to the main body of the disciples in the upper room and the separate appearance to Thomas.

As with the other resurrection stories it may be helpful to look back again to what was said in the Introduction about truth and story. In this narrative the bulk of the disciples become convinced of the risen Christ. The only possible evidence is the evidence of those who were there. Thomas represents all those down the centuries who have demanded some form of empirical evidence. He receives it but, of course, he cannot reproduce it for others. People may believe or not according to their own disposition. Like falling in love, proof is available only for the person concerned. Telling others is, by comparison, feeble. Perhaps all personal convictions are like that.

As with the other resurrection stories it is the smallest details which seem to leave the largest impression and the greatest air of mystery. The voice is real, as is the broken bread and the empty plate where the fish had been. How true is this of our own real-life experiences?

Traditionally Thomas is credited with having travelled east while the main focus of the history of the Christian Church has been on the westward route around the Roman Empire. It is certainly the case that European Christian missionaries found a very ancient Church already existing in southern India just as they found an equally ancient Church in Ethiopia. We are again reminded of the one hard fact underlying all these stories. If these disciples were making it all up they lived out a lie for the rest of their lives after going their separate ways, often amidst great suffering, hardship and even martyrdom. That too takes some believing. We can never know exactly what happened and exactly what depth of experiences lies within these stories but that something happened, which changed the future of whole continents and civilizations, is historical fact.

166

IDEAS FOR EXPLORING FURTHER

Doubt   Thomas is reported here as being the chief doubter. But before Jesus' arrival, several of the disciples were unsure of the truth of Mary Magdalene's story of the empty tomb and the risen Lord.

All the disciples must have had questions in their minds both before Jesus' arrival and afterwards. Ask the children what questions they would have liked to have asked Jesus. Would they also have said, 'I'm not sure about …'? Children's ideas could be recorded on paper question marks or exclamation marks for display. Are there other questions children would like to ask concerning what they know of the life and work of Jesus? Invite the children to evaluate whether some questions are more important than others and to discuss their decisions.

Help the children to understand that everyone's questions and doubts should be respected. Older children could discuss the meaning of the words 'atheist', a person who denies the existence of God, and 'agnostic', a person who believes that nothing can be known about the existence or nature of God.

Seeking Answers   Talk to the children about some of the major questions people have asked in the past and still ask today. For example:

- How was the universe and the earth created?
- Why are we here?
- How should we behave while we are here?
- What will happen to us when we die?
- Is there a God?
- If there is a supreme power, what is it like?
- What kind of relationship can we have with God?
- How can we show our beliefs in action?

Explain how the faith traditions help people to explore these questions, and report on answers offered in the past through religious texts and stories. Younger children might focus on stories from different faiths which tell of the creation of the world or raise issues concerning behaviour: service to others, the dangers of pride, jealousy, anger, greed, the importance of wisdom, sharing, etc. (See Appendix 1: Useful Resources.)

167

37

Come and Have Some Breakfast before Going to Work

John 21: 1–14

'I am going fishing,' said Peter. He looked round at the group of men near him. There were James and John, Thomas, Nathaniel and two other men. They had all been followers of Jesus. Now they were back home again in Galilee.

The sun was just going down. The lake was calm. It would be a good night for fishing.

'I am going fishing,' Peter repeated. 'Is anybody else coming?'

'Yes,' answered the others. 'We will come with you.'

They dragged the boat into the water and climbed in. The nets were already in the boat. They rowed away from the shore. It was dark by now. They cast the net at the side of the boat, waited and then pulled it in. Nothing. They tried again on the other side. Nothing there either. They rowed on a little and threw the net out once more. Again, nothing.

All night long they kept trying. The men were all fishermen. They knew just where the fish could be found, but on this night it was as if the lake had been emptied of fish. It was hot, hard work throwing the net out, pulling it back into the boat again. Although it was night Peter was so hot he had stripped off nearly all his clothes.

At last daylight began to come. The boat was nearly back by the shore, but still they had no fish.

'One last try,' said Peter as he stood up in the boat and threw the net out on the left-hand side of the boat. He waited. He began to pull in the net. It was very light. He knew it was empty long before he had got it into the boat.

Suddenly a voice came across the water from the shore. 'Have you got any fish, lads?'

The men looked round. There on the beach stood a lonely figure. In the half-light they could not see who it was.

'No!' they shouted together.

'Try casting the net on the right-hand side of the boat,' came the reply.

Peter shrugged his shoulders and looked at the others. They nodded. Why not? One more try wouldn't hurt anybody. Peter turned. The sweat on his huge shoulders shone in the early morning sun as he swung the net again. It landed on the sea. The ripples spread. The net sank slowly under the water.

Peter waited. Then he grasped hold of the net to pull it in. It would not come. Perhaps it was caught on a rock. He bent down and pulled harder. The whole boat tipped on its side. Out in the water where the net was came a flash of silver. The net was so full of fish that Peter could not pull it in. It would sink the boat if he were to do so.

John had turned round. He was looking again at the figure on the shore. 'It's the Lord,' he gasped.

'What?' shouted Peter.

Before anyone could stop him Peter had grabbed his clothes and jumped into the water. It was quite shallow. The water came up to his shoulders. He started to wade towards the beach.

The other fishermen took the oars. They rowed slowly to the shore, pulling the heavy net behind them. As the boat touched the stones they jumped out. Sure enough it was Jesus standing there.

Nearby there was a fire burning on the beach. On the hot stones fish were cooking and bread was toasting.

'Bring some more fish from your catch,' said Jesus.

Peter jumped into the boat and hauled the net on to the beach. It was packed tight with fish. (Later on Peter counted them and found there were one hundred and fifty-three altogether.)

'Come on,' called Jesus, 'come and have breakfast.'

They sat round the fire, a group of weary but very happy men. Jesus took the bread and the fish and handed it to them. It was just like old times. As the sun rose in the sky they ate breakfast together. It was more than a new day: it was the beginning of a new life.

What was it Jesus had said to them at the start of the story? 'Let's go fishing for people.' As Jesus left them they knew that that was what they were going to do. Now they knew for certain. Things were different. Their world had changed. Nothing could ever be the same again. They had work to do.

Once again they pulled their boats up the shore, hung up their nets, said goodbye to their families and set off.

NOTES

ABOUT THE STORY

There are strong similarities between this story and Story 9, probably for good reason.

The disciples have returned to Galilee, where originally they came from. Their wheel has come full circle. Once again they are fishing and once more their work is ineffective until the shadowy figure on the shore tells them where to cast their nets. Again it is Peter who leaves the boat and wades ashore. They are where they started but they are not the same people. One is reminded immediately of T. S. Eliot's lines from 'Little Gidding' in *The Four Quartets:*

> We shall not cease from exploration
> And the end of all our exploring
> Will be to arrive where we started
> And to know the place for the first time

He goes on, later in the same passage, with other words which catch something of the mood of this story and its place between what has happened and what is about to take place:

> A condition of complete simplicity
> (Costing not less than everything)
> And all shall be well and
> All manner of things shall be well

This final appearance is a very gentle and peaceful story – a group of men who have been through traumatic experiences sit together on a lake shore and share a simple meal. No doubt years later it stuck in the mind as one of the most memorable of occasions, like moments in a family holiday which seem casual and incidental at the time but which, in fact, form the most vivid memories in later years.

This incident is both an end and a beginning. It rounds off the Gospel Story but does so in a cyclical way which makes for a perfect literary balance. The birth stories proclaim the idea of incarnation (coming in the flesh). This story, along with the more traditional Ascension Day story in Acts 1, forms the balancing function of 'ex-carnation' (a word not used in Christian theology but perhaps one which ought to be). God who came in the flesh has now altogether left the flesh. But the disciples have no doubts about what it is they have experienced. In the calmness of this incident their depression has totally gone. They are changed people who will have a mission to change the world. In life every ending is a new beginning but for the moment that lies in the future. For the present they are at peace.

IDEAS FOR EXPLORING FURTHER

Story-telling through Dance   Explore the different moods of this story through dance. Exaggerate all movements to create a more vivid effect.

(i) Emphasize the rhythmic nature of the fishermen's work at the beginning of the story. Ask the children to identify some working actions of fishermen in a boat (e.g. lifting, throwing, hauling, dumping the nets, scanning the surface of the sea for signs of fish, while moving from side to side). Ask individual children to demonstrate their ideas. Children should then choose two of these movements (e.g. hauling/lifting, lifting/ throwing, hauling/dumping). Each one of these actions is to be repeated rhythmically, and the two actions are to be linked by steps and turns (e.g. haul, step(s), turn, dump).

Repeat the dance sequence several times. Choose music with a strong rhythmic beat.

(ii) Slow down the movements performed in (i) to indicate feelings of tiredness and depression. Choose slow, languid music.

(iii) Freeze – to show shock at the sound of Jesus' voice. Keep still for a counted 5 seconds.

(iv) Choose some vigorous music with a strong beat and ask the children what actions would indicate haste and desire to see Jesus. Ask individuals to demonstrate (e.g. large finger pointing movements; large arm waving movements; strong pushing movements with arms, forwards or sideways, to get rid of encumbrances; large wading steps, using arms to help push water back).

Choose two or more movements (depending on the age of the children). Link the movements with a chosen number of leaps, turns, and small steps. Combine the chosen movements into a dance sequence which is repeated over and over again and performed vigorously, but not necessarily quickly. With some children, it may be helpful to define the number of times each movement should be performed, depending on the beat of the music (e.g. waving movements x 4, leaps x 4, wading steps x 4, full turns x 4, stepping on the spot x 4; repeat).

The dance can be performed anywhere in the room. Upon a signal from the teacher, children can repeat their dance sequence along a pathway to reach the spot where Jesus is designated to be standing. Then they should just do the arm movements, turning and stepping on the spot until the whole class forms a sea of people pushing things aside, waving and turning, etc., in excitement.

(v) Upon a signal from the teacher, the children should freeze at the end of the last piece of music to form a still tableau. Hold for a counted 10 seconds.

At the end of the session, brainstorm for words to describe different parts of the dance. If the teacher acts as scribe and records these, they can be used later in class, group or individual poems. See also notes on OT Story 25.

Miracles   See Stories 11, 12, 14, 17, 34, OT Story 30.

38

Rushing Winds and Glowing Fires

Acts 2: 1–47

The disciples were back in Jerusalem. Jesus had left them. They knew they would never see him again. But he was not dead: his spirit was still there. If only they could feel it.

They sat and looked at one another. Outside in the street there was the noise of people talking and singing. It was the Day of First Fruits. The wheat harvest had been gathered in and it was a holiday. It was also called the Day of Pentecost.

Peter looked out from the window. All those people! He glanced back into the room. Just a handful of men! What could they do? They were not even powerful men. They were fishermen, tax-collectors, ordinary workers. Outside were priests, Pharisees, civil servants, rich business men and the rest. So many of them were clever; some had lots of money. When Jesus had been here Peter had felt strong. Now he suddenly felt very weak. He turned back to the others.

And then it happened. The room was dull and quiet. The only light came from the tiny windows; the only sound was the crowd in the street outside. Suddenly it was all changed. There seemed to be a rumbling sound and a movement in the air. It felt as if a strong wind were beating through the house. The disciples looked up. Across the room they gazed at one another. They glowed. There was no other word for it. It was as if they were on fire. A minute ago they had been gloomy. Now each of them suddenly felt more alive than he had ever felt before. They started to talk and shout. Most of the words didn't seem to make any sense but it didn't matter.

The wind stopped and the light faded. But the fires inside them went on burning.

Peter, as always, was the first to move. 'Come on,' he shouted. 'Let's go.' He opened the door and rushed out into the street.

The others followed. They were still all very excited, talking in loud voices. People in the street stopped and stared at them. Who were these strange men rushing about shouting at everybody? They seemed to be talking every language in the world except their own.

'Are they mad?' someone asked.

'I think they're drunk,' said another.

The crowd had got bigger. People started to laugh. 'That's it. They're drunk. Come on. Leave them to make fools of themselves.'

It was Peter who got things under control. He jumped up on to a wall. He held up his hands and shouted out. The talking stopped. The other disciples came over and stood near him. Everyone went quiet.

'Listen to me,' said Peter. 'These men are not drunk. It is only nine o'clock in the morning. They are like this because something great has just happened to them. Do you remember what the prophet Joel said God would do? What was it?

'"I will pour out my Spirit upon all men.
Your young men shall see visions
Your old men shall dream dreams
I will pour out my Spirit and they shall speak out."

'That's what's happened,' Peter went on. 'It is Jesus from Nazareth who was put to death here eight weeks ago. We are his followers. He came back from the dead. Then he left us. This morning his Spirit has come into all of us. That's why we are excited.'

Peter went on and on. But the crowd listened. He seemed to

174

know what he was talking about. The crowd grew bigger and bigger.

Still Peter talked, first in one part of the city and then another.

At nine o'clock that morning there were just a few Christians – the disciples and a few women like Mary Magdalene. By nine o'clock that night there were several hundred.

It was the birthday of the Church. Day after day it went on getting bigger and bigger.

NOTES

ABOUT THE STORY

The whole point of the Christian Story or the Christ Story is that it does not end with the physical life of its founder. He is present in all that follows in the continuing story of what is known as the Church, sometimes called by Christians 'The Body of Christ'. (Note the use of a capital to distinguish 'Church' in this sense from 'church' meaning a building or one denomination of the Church.)

In the Bible the book usually known as 'The Acts of the Apostles' is where we get the fullest detail of how the story continues. In the Greek, however, there are no definite articles so it would be more appropriate to call it 'Acts of Apostles' or, more accurately, 'Some of the Acts of Some of the Apostles'.

This first story is really about the birthday of the Church. It takes place on the Jewish festival of Pentecost or Shavuot. Pentecost (from the Greek word meaning fifty) is fifty days after the Feast of Unleavened Bread. In other words seven weeks have passed between the crucifixion and the incident recorded here. Today the Christian festival celebrating this event is also known as Pentecost or, in Britain, as Whit Sunday, from the custom of confirmations and processions in which the main participants dressed in white. A Pentecostalist is a member of a group of churches which put great emphasis on the coming of the Spirit as in this story.

The disciples (or most of them) are back in Jerusalem. They lack direction. Again the incident apparently takes place in the upper room. Fire and rushing wind are the main images used to explain an overwhelming sense not only of Christ being with them but of Christ's presence, as it were, taking them over. Paul, a later convert (see Story 43), describes this basic Christian experience as 'I in Christ and Christ in me'. The main sense is one of power (the Greek word is *dynamis*, from which we get 'dynamic' and 'dynamite'). The disciples are taken over. They cease to be afraid: they manage to communicate their enthusiasm (a word itself derived from words meaning 'in God' or 'God in') to people speaking a range of different languages.

175

This has given rise to 'glossolalia', or speaking in tongues, which Pentecostalists practise. In many modern black churches this has acquired a close-harmony musical form: a highly controlled expression of emotional enthusiasm through sound, like humming, which does not communicate direct meaning. It raises, however, the fascinating question of how music communicates and why it sometimes does so more effectively than words.

Christ returns not as Jesus but as the Holy Spirit. The disciples recognize this as the same thing, which brings us to the Christian idea of Trinity. Just as water, ice and steam are all manifestations of the one substance H_2O, so the same God is experienced as Father, Son and Spirit.

IDEAS FOR EXPLORING FURTHER

Christianity as a World Religion   Once convinced, the disciples spread the Gospel to the world. Talk about the way the Christian faith has been spread across the world by other people convinced of the importance of Jesus' life, death and resurrection. Sometimes they brought tremendous help, healing and hope to people as faith was turned into action. Consider the lives of different saints and famous philanthropists in many parts of the world (e.g. those mentioned in the Faith in Action series). Sometimes, too, however, those trying to spread the Christian faith brought with them incredible violence and the destruction of whole cultures. (Cf. NC *History*: CSU 2 – Tudor and Stuart times, the Spanish Inquisition, CSU 6 – exploration and encounters.) What about religious strife today?

Collect pictures relating to ways in which Christianity is expressed around the world. (See, for example, the CEM pack *When Christians Meet*.) Make comparisons concerning the way in which ideas are expressed and also artistic styles, media used, etc. (Cf. NC *Art*: AT 2 – knowledge and understanding.) Look for religious songs or hymns used in different countries or by people emanating from a variety of ethnic origins. Enjoy the differences in style of music, rhythm, wording, instruments used, etc. (Cf. NC *Music*: AT 2 – listening and appraising.) See also Story 42.

Christian Denominations   Think about churches in the local area which represent different denominations. Mark them on a map and talk about different routes for reaching them. (Cf. NC *Geography*: AT 1 – geographical skills.) If possible, visit some. Discuss similarities and differences between the denominations under headings such as: type of place of worship; Holy Communion; vestments; artefacts and symbols used; written materials for services; ways of celebrating Holy Week; expressions of faith (e.g. important ideas central to the way believers express their faith). Relate these to Martin Luther and the rise of Protestantism from 1517; to Henry VIII's break with Rome and the founding of the English Church (1534); to the re-establishment of the Church of England by Elizabeth I in 1559 in an attempt to unite Roman Catholics and Protestants (cf. NC *History*: CSU 2 – Tudor and Stuart times); to the work of John and Charles Wesley from 1789, and to other influential church leaders. (Cf. NC *History*: SSU on houses and places of worship.)

39

Give Us Strength, Lord

Acts 3: 1 – 4: 31

'Alms, masters, alms! Can you spare money for a poor lame man?'

The beggar called out to Peter and John. They were going into the Temple. Two friends of the beggar were just putting him down on the steps by the gate.

'Alms, masters, alms! Help a poor lame man.'

Peter stopped. He looked at John. John shrugged his shoulders. He had no money either. Peter found he was shaking. He knew what Jesus would have done. But had he got the power to do it? He drew a big breath and spoke out. 'Look at us,' he ordered in a firm voice.

The beggar looked up. Usually he sat staring at the ground. Peter looked back straight into the man's eyes. He was sure. This beggar was not pretending. He was really poor and ill.

'Listen,' said Peter. 'I have no money, no silver, no gold. But I am going to give you what I do have. In the name of Jesus of Nazareth get up and walk!'

The beggar suddenly looked frightened. He looked away. But Peter could not stop now. He put out his hand, took hold of the beggar's arm and pulled him to his feet.

For a moment it looked as if the man would fall. He swayed from one side to the other. And then all at once he was standing up. He started to put one foot in front of the other. First he walked one way and then back again. He could not believe it. A crowd started to gather. The man began to jump up and down.

Seeing the crowd, Peter turned round and started to preach again. He never missed a chance. The crowd was all over the Temple steps. Nobody could get in or out.

Peter was still talking when a rough voice suddenly called out, 'All right, enough of this. Take both of them.'

It was the Temple police. Peter and John were arrested. They spent the night in prison.

Next day they were taken to court. Peter could hardly believe his eyes. The High Priest himself was the chief judge and every important person in Jerusalem seemed to be there. Suddenly he realized he wasn't afraid any more. What a change! He remembered when he had been scared of a servant girl.

Annas, the High Priest, spoke. 'You've healed a lame man,' he said. 'Where did you get the power from?'

Peter did not hesitate. 'From Jesus of Nazareth,' he replied. 'The man you put to death. He is alive again. He made this man well. Jesus is the Messiah, the Christ.'

Annas was taken by surprise. Usually people were frightened of him. He signalled to the other judges. They got together in a group.

'What shall we do with them?' he asked. 'The lame man is walking. He is here and everybody knows him. He has been sitting by that gate for years and years.'

'Let them go, but give them a warning,' said his advisers.

Annas went back to his seat. He spoke to Peter and John. 'We are going to let you go,' he said. 'But this must not happen again. Do you understand? We cannot have all this talk about this Jesus coming back to life.'

'We can't help it,' replied Peter. 'That is what happened. We know. We met him and we know he is with us now.'

'Enough,' shouted Annas. 'I am warning you. Stop it!' He got up and stormed out of the court. He was very angry.

The people in the court were all cheering. The man who had been lame was there as well.

Peter and John pushed their way through the crowd and made their way back to the house. All the other disciples were there. They celebrated and prayed to God. 'Make us strong, Lord Jesus,' they said. Once again they felt power go through them just as it had on the Day of Pentecost.

Peter knew he was going to preach again. He had never felt like this before. Nothing could stop them now.

NOTES

ABOUT THE STORY

It was inevitable that the disciples should quickly run foul of the religious authorities, some of whom had been responsible for getting Jesus put to death.

This incident takes place at one of the gates leading into the Temple courtyard, a scene rather like that encountered on entering a cathedral close such as that at Salisbury. Such an entrance would have been a spot frequented by beggars much as today it might attract buskers.

The feature of this miracle which has been brought out is the new confidence and courage of the two main characters. The Peter who a few weeks before had given way before the banter of a servant girl in the garden of the High Priest's residence is now seen preaching and proclaiming back in the Temple area where Jesus himself had drawn anger upon himself. There is also the courage to take on the situation of the beggar who is unable to walk.

As with all the miracles we can never ascertain exactly what happened. All we can know historically is that something occurred which invoked the wrath of the authorities.

Annas decides to try and defuse the situation. He wants no more martyrs but at the end of this story he has failed in his main aim, which is to frighten the two men off. The execution of Jesus has not achieved anything. Killing people rarely leads to the death of an idea or a movement. What people are prepared to suffer and die for usually prevails over what people are ready to kill for.

IDEAS FOR EXPLORING FURTHER

Opinions Vary   Talk about the story with the whole class, concentrating on the range of opinions held by the lame man, the lame man's friends, the disciples, people in the crowd, Annas the High Priest, and the Temple police. Debate whether or not Annas was a wicked man. Was he wrong to be worried about law and order? Are the Temple police to be viewed as 'baddies'? Emphasize the complexity of deciding whether people are good or bad. Act out the story informally over a period of time, giving children a chance to play more than one role and to voice more than one set of opinions. Older children could work at this in groups of eight to ten and give informal presentations to the class. Younger children could take turns to play parts, with the teacher acting as narrator and giving the children their cues. See also notes on OT Story 4.

Listening to Points of View   Imagine that Annas decided to take this matter to a higher court and that everyone involved in this story had to be heard there. Either as a class with one person acting as scribe, or with children working in small groups and concentrating on one category of people in the story, draw up questions which might be put to each of these by someone who really wanted to get at the truth or at least understand what had been going on. Encourage some children to act as interviewers and to put the questions to other children playing the various roles. Class members who are not directly involved in interviewing can be subdivided to form a group of supporters to shout encouraging comments to Annas and the Temple police, or to act as members of the crowd who support the lame man and the disciples. The interviews could be taped to form a presentation for assembly. (Cf. NC *English*: AT 1 – speaking and listening.) Alternatively, reports could be written either on a scroll or as an anachronistic 'special supplement' for a newspaper commenting on the miracle. A word-processing package or software designed to make a newspaper would be useful here. (Cf. NC *Technology*: AT 5 – information technology.) See also notes on Story 47.

40

We Can't Fight God

Acts 5: 12–42

Peter was in prison again. This time the other disciples were with him. It was the middle of the night and pitch dark. The prison floor was hard. Peter could not sleep. Something told him to get up. Slowly he got to his feet. Thoughts were racing through his head.

What would happen tomorrow? he wondered. Would it always be like this? It didn't matter now. He wasn't afraid to die if they wanted to kill him. Things had changed.

He moved over towards the door and leaned against it. Then he jumped back. The door had moved. It was not locked. Very quietly and carefully he pulled the door open. There was no one there. The prison was quiet.

Without making a noise Peter shook the others. Together they tiptoed out of the prison and into the street. It would soon be daybreak.

Peter made his way towards the Temple. He was not going to run away. As soon as the sun rose, there he was in the Temple courtyard preaching about Jesus to the first people awake.

Annas had called the High Court, the Council of Seventy together. 'Bring those prisoners out of the jail,' he ordered the Temple police.

A few minutes later the officer was back. He looked very frightened. 'They're not there,' he stammered.

181

'What!' shouted Annas.

'The prison was all locked up. The sentries are on guard outside but the prison is empty,' explained the officer.

Annas was furious. He started to scream at the officer. 'They've escaped. Go and find them. Search the country. I want them found.'

Suddenly he was interrupted. A Pharisee in the court said quietly, 'Please, I think they are outside.'

Annas stopped what he was saying. 'Outside,' he echoed. 'What do you mean?'

'They are in the Temple court where they always are. They have been preaching there since early this morning.'

The Pharisees smiled. They did not like the priests very much. Pharisees and Saducees were not friendly to one another.

'Bring them here,' shouted Annas.

The officer rushed outside. Annas sat down. How could he stop these people?

The police brought Peter and the others into the court-room.

Annas spoke. 'I thought we had told you to stop this preaching,' he said. 'We warned you but you have gone on. Half of the city is talking about nothing else. They are beginning to blame us for the death of Jesus. What are you trying to do? You are nothing but a load of trouble-makers trying to get the people to turn against their rulers.'

Peter answered back. It was the same message. 'You killed Jesus,' he said. 'God brought him back to life again and now he is giving his Spirit to those who believe that Jesus is our proper Messiah and Saviour.'

'That's enough,' shouted Annas. 'You don't show any signs of being sorry for what is happening.' Annas turned to the other priests. 'We shall have to get rid of these people,' he muttered. 'It is the only way.'

They all nodded.

'Wait a minute.'

Annas turned round. It was the voice of Gamaliel. Gamaliel

was a Pharisee. He was very well known and almost everybody liked him.

'Will you clear the court,' asked Gamaliel, 'so that we can talk?'

Annas agreed and the prisoners were taken outside.

Gamaliel talked for a long time. 'Let's not do anything stupid,' he said. 'We have seen people getting all excited before. Then nothing has happened. It has all died down again. These men have done some good. They have healed people. They are always in the Temple. What if they are right? If we kill them we might just make things worse. If what they say is wrong, their new Church will just die out. But if they are right, nothing we can do will stop them. We should be fighting God himself.'

Annas did not like it but he had to admit that Gamaliel was wise. He could not kill Peter and the others now.

'Take them away and beat them with whips,' he ordered the police. 'That at least will teach them a lesson. Then let them go.' He knew that tomorrow they would be back preaching outside the Temple.

And they were.

NOTES

ABOUT THE STORY

'Court of the Seventy' is a translation of the Greek word 'Sanhedrin'. This was presided over by the High Priest and, in fact, probably numbered seventy-one. It was made up of two parties.

First, there were the Sadducees, the party of the priests. For generations only a man who was the son of a priest could himself become one. They had, therefore, at least in their own eyes, become something of an aristocracy. (Cf. the Brahmin caste of traditional Hinduism.) The Sadducees had lost touch with the people. They were deeply conservative, or, as has been said of them, 'They lay under the curse which rests upon all aristocracies, the inability to realize that the best things must grow.'

Secondly, the Sanhedrin contained the party of the Pharisees. Generally in the New Testament Pharisees get what we might term 'a bad press'. Jesus ran into some untypical ones. The Pharisee movement had grown up during the long period of occupation to defend the faith but its members did this on the basis of constant interpretation of Torah (Tradition or Law) rather than of unchanging authoritative pronouncements. As in all such movements, there were always some who felt they had to hold on to what an earlier generation had said rather than the principle they were evoking. (Similarly, defenders of the Authorized Version of the English Bible overlook the fact that Tyndale, on whose work it was based, put the Bible into English so that it could be understood even by 'the boy who drives the plough'. In other words he stood for the tradition of modern translations, not for holding on to ancient ones.) The Pharisees believed in education for all and they were seen as being of the ordinary people.

Gamaliel was well known as one of the most liberal of the Pharisees as well as being recognized as amongst the greatest scholars of his time. His interpretation is simple. If these men are wrong their movement will die out: if they are right we should not be opposing the truth. This has become known simply as 'the wisdom of Gamaliel', as rarely applied now as then.

Annas could not, legally, apply the death penalty but accidents could easily happen and blind eyes be turned, as the next story shows.

IDEAS FOR EXPLORING FURTHER

Bravery   Explore the concept of bravery at a deeper level. Are there different kinds of bravery? In what way was Peter brave? Read stories from different cultures which illustrate a variety of aspects of bravery: standing up for what you believe in; facing physical danger in order to defend someone else; facing a long illness or disability with little complaint; putting forward an unpopular opinion (like Gamaliel); admitting when you have made a mistake; persistently applying for new jobs in the face of redundancy, etc. Do heroines tend to get ignored? Talk about these (e.g. Grace Darling, who, with her father, rowed out to the *Forfarshire*, wrecked off the Farne Islands on 7 September 1838; Mary Seacole, a black nurse who served alongside Florence Nightingale in the Crimean War; the suffragette Emmeline Pankhurst, 1858–1928). (Cf. NC *History*: CSU 3 – Victorian Britain.) Read also *Grace*, by Jill Paton Walsh, *Afro-Bets Book of Black Heroes* (including women), by Wade Hudson and Valerie Wilson-Wesley, *Equiano's Travels*, edited by Paul Edwards, and *Woman in the Moon – Tales of Forgotten Heroines*, compiled by James Riordan. What about the present-day heroes and heroines often talked about on news programmes and in newspapers? Is one type of bravery superior to another? Can the class decide upon a 'Top Ten' of the bravest people they know? By what criteria will the candidates be judged? Make a display to record the opinions and feelings of the class. Perhaps design part of the display as a general-knowledge quiz. (See also Stories 41, 43, 45, 48, 50.)

41

Stone Him until He's Dead

Acts 6: 1 – 8: 1

Stephen was the first to be killed.

The Church had got too big for the disciples to look after on their own. They called all the Christians together for a meeting.

'We need more leaders,' said Peter. 'We can't do everything by ourselves. Our job is to be apostles – preachers who knew Jesus. We have to make new Christians. There must be other leaders to look after those who are already Christians.'

They chose seven men. Stephen was one of them. They were called deacons or helpers.

Stephen worked very hard. All day long he worked as a deacon. He visited the sick and did all he could to help the poor. He tried to be a good Christian and a good Jew at the same time.

Every sabbath Stephen went to the synagogue. After the service he always started arguing with the elders. He wanted them all to become Christians as well. The elders did not like it, because Stephen kept winning the arguments. Other members of the synagogue started to join in.

'He is leading people astray,' said one of the elders one day. 'He is attacking our religion. People don't respect us any more. We must report him to the High Priest and the Council.'

The others agreed. They would teach Stephen a lesson.

Stephen was arrested. He was put on trial just like Peter and

185

John had been. Witnesses were called in. They said, 'Yes, we have heard him say that Jesus will destroy the Temple and that Christians will change our customs.'

Stephen was given a chance to defend himself. Instead he gave a long speech. He tried to tell the High Priest how all the stories in the Old Testament pointed towards Jesus. Then he said, 'Look at all the bad things our ancestors did. When good prophets came they hurt them because they thought they were bad men. Now we know the prophets were telling the truth.' Stephen pointed straight at the High Priest and said, 'And you are doing just the same. You can't tell the difference between a good man and a bad one. Jesus of Nazareth was the best man there ever was and you had him put to death.'

The court went very quiet. The High Priest was a very powerful man. But suddenly Stephen stopped talking. Into his eyes came a far-away look. He wasn't looking at the judges any more. He turned his head upwards. 'Look,' he said, in a strange voice. 'Look, I can see right into heaven and there he is. There's Jesus sitting next to God himself.'

'Stop! Stop!' screamed the priests. They held their hands over their ears. They could not listen to any more. They jumped up and rushed at Stephen. 'Kill him,' they shouted. 'Stone him! Stone him until he's dead.'

They grabbed hold of Stephen and dragged him outside into the yard. Then they took off their coats and started throwing stones at him.

Stephen knelt in the middle of the courtyard and prayed aloud. 'Lord Jesus,' they heard him say, 'receive my spirit. And do not blame them for what they are doing.'

The stones went on hitting Stephen. He fell over and lay on the ground. The stoning went on until he was dead.

At the side of the courtyard, watching, was another young man. He was looking after the coats of the men throwing stones. His name was Saul. He was glad Stephen was being killed. He hated Christians and wanted to see an end to them all.

NOTES

ABOUT THE STORY

Stephen becomes the first Christian martyr. He was to be the first of many right up to our own time. We see in this story too different forms of Christian ministry beginning to emerge. The original disciples (followers) start to become known as apostles (teachers of special authority because they have had direct first-hand experience of Jesus and especially of the resurrection appearances) and then, as numbers grow, choose deacons (helpers) to look after the members while they themselves move on. In some churches deacons have become the lowest order of ordained ministers under priests and bishops: in others they are elders, appointed to help run the affairs of the church, but they are not ordained.

Stephen's task was that of counsellor or pastoral assistant – to be available to those in need. We need to remember that at this stage all Christians were also Jews. No new religion had been created. The Christians were all synagogue attenders on the Sabbath (Saturday) but they were intent on persuading their fellow worshippers that Messiah had arrived. Stephen was no exception; indeed he started to become a leading advocate or trouble-maker depending on which side people stood.

The charge brought against Stephen again revolves around the use of language. Was 'destroying the Temple and raising it in three days' (Acts 6: 13–14) ever meant to be a literal statement? Or was it always picture language for a new foundation of faith which would automatically change the basis of authority? In the same way many early Christians were to be persecuted as cannibals because of the words used at the Last Supper: 'This is my body/blood; eat/drink all of it'.

Stephen's real crime, however, becomes that of blasphemy. Like other visionaries (cf. Joan of Arc) he suddenly claims a vivid insight which his accusers find totally unacceptable. Legally the death penalty could not be handed down by this court but here mob rule takes over in the emotionally charged atmosphere. No doubt the Romans did not always pay too much attention. Stephen would have been of no interest to them. Lynchings have happened in many countries, including Northern Ireland and the Southern States of the U.S.A., which even modern governments have been powerless to prevent. In this story we come, for the first time, across the person who was to become a key figure in the spread of Christianity. An up-and-coming Pharisee, he is here the young man who takes care of the garments of the stone-throwers.

IDEAS FOR EXPLORING FURTHER

Martyrdom   Talk about the way some people are prepared to die for what they believe in – people from different faith traditions and others. Several of the apostles were executed for their beliefs (e.g. Paul and Peter). Discuss whether the early Christians would have been willing to suffer like this for saying they believed in the Resurrection if they had known the story to be a lie. (See Appendix 2: Extracts from Roman Writings, concerning the treatment of early Christians in Rome.) Many saints were also martyrs.

With older children, discuss the wider meaning of martyrdom. People throughout the ages have been killed because of their religious, political, social beliefs or principles. For example, the following might be mentioned and further information sought: the Polish priest Jerzy Popieluszko, murdered in 1984 for his anti-government preaching; Oscar Romero, Archbishop of El Salvador, murdered in 1980 for criticizing the government and the terrorist death squads; the Sikh Banda Singh Bahadur, killed for his tolerant beliefs in 1716; Joan of Arc, burnt as a heretic in 1430; John Fisher and Thomas More (1535), executed for refusing to acknowledge Henry VIII as supreme head of the Church in England; Nicholas Ridley (1555), Hugh Latimer (1555) and Thomas Cranmer (1556), burnt as Protestant heretics by Catholic Mary I (cf. **NC** *History*: CSU 2); Mahatma Gandhi, assassinated in 1948 for advocating policies of non-violence and religious tolerance; Martin Luther King, an American clergyman, leader of the non-violent struggle for racial equality, assassinated in 1968; women in the suffragette movement, campaigning for votes for women in the early twentieth century, prepared to die for their beliefs; people involved in wars, willing to die for the freedom of their country (e.g. French resistance fighters, people willing to hide Jews like Anne Frank from Nazi persecution). (Cf. **NC** *History*: CSU 4 – Second World War.)

Behaviour Towards Others   Talk to children about how there are many ways in which people can be hurt by us, and that it is important to think about this – even if our actions do not actually result in someone being killed. A discussion of life at school may raise issues such as: calling people nasty names; refusing to share; being rude; rushing to be first; stealing; cheating at games; playing roughly; not helping to tidy up; being impatient and pushing in queues; standing by while others are being hurt/upset. (See also *Tyrone, the Dirty, Rotten Cheat,* by H. Wilhelm.)

Following this discussion, ask the children to cut a sheet of paper into a stone shape and to draw and write on it something concerning one of the types of behaviour which it is important to try to avoid. Then, using each 'stone' as a focal point, talk to children about what it would be preferable to do in order to help make people feel better in that instance. Encourage children to write one sentence as a speech bubble to show this (e.g. 'I like the model you made today' might represent not calling people nasty names but complimenting them on something they have done). Make some large pictures to show the stones being ceremonially buried, thrown over a cliff, or otherwise got rid of in some way, by people who have pleasant and supportive things to say to each other, as shown by the speech bubbles.

Gang Pressure   See notes on Story 33.

42

Magic and Mission

Acts 8: 5–39

All the apostles were in danger now. Some of them left Jerusalem and went off in different directions.

One of them, Philip, went north to the old city of Samaria. There he started telling people about Jesus and all that he had done. A lot of them believed what he was saying and became Christians. Then, just like Peter, Philip found that he could cure some people. News spread and there was a lot of excitement.

Back in Jerusalem Peter and John heard what was happening in Samaria. They decided to go and have a look for themselves, to see if they could help.

One of the best-known people in Samaria was a man called Simon. He was better known in the city as the Great Magician. He was supposed to be able to do lots of tricks. For years he had been famous.

All that changed. What Philip was doing seemed even better. Simon did not like being ignored, and he had to admit that Philip was doing good things. Simon got himself baptized and became a Christian like lots of others. He watched as Peter, John and Philip put their hands on people's heads to pass on the spirit and power of Jesus. He thought it was a new magic trick, one he didn't know.

Simon went home and collected a bag of gold pieces. Then he went back to find Peter. 'Here,' he said, 'show me that trick – the one where you put your hands on people and they get this new power. I know it will cost me a lot but take this.' He held out the bag of money.

Peter had never been more angry. 'Your money will take you to hell,' he said sharply. 'Do you really think you can buy God's gift with gold pieces? You haven't even begun to understand what it is all about. You haven't changed one little bit. To be a Christian you have to change the way you live and think.'

Simon could see how angry he was. He wanted to be like these apostles but he had a lot to learn. 'Pray for me,' he said, 'so that I won't go towards hell.'

Philip left Samaria. He turned south, went back right past Jerusalem and on towards Egypt. He was near the desert road which goes from Jerusalem to Gaza when something told him to run over to the road itself.

Coming towards him in a great cloud of dust was a carriage pulled by horses. Philip ran out on to the road and the driver pulled up. The carriage was like a large open chariot. Sitting in the back was an African, very richly dressed. Seeing Philip he invited him to ride in the carriage with him.

The African was a tall, dignified, dark-skinned man. He looked very important. He was reading a book. Philip could see that it was the Book of Isaiah.

'Does it make any sense to you?' asked Philip.

'Not really,' said the African. 'I need someone to explain it to me.'

The words he was reading were all about a suffering servant of God.

'Who is he talking about?' asked the African. 'That's what I want to know. Who is this suffering servant? He doesn't say what his name is.'

That gave Philip a chance. He explained how for hundreds of years the Jews had waited for a Messiah, a Saviour. Then he went on to tell the man how Jesus had been just like this suffering servant that the words were all about.

190

All this time they had been travelling along, and now Philip was telling the African how people who became Christians had to be baptized.

'Look,' said the African suddenly, 'there is some water over there. What is to stop me becoming a Christian here and now?' He told his driver to stop.

They walked into the water and Philip baptized the African.

Philip and the African said goodbye. The African continued on his journey. He was going home to Ethiopia, where he was treasurer to the Queen. When he got back he would tell the Queen about the religion of Jesus. Then he would start a Church there.

─────────────────────── NOTES ───────────────────────

ABOUT THE STORY

These two stories are about Philip, one of the lesser-known apostles. They serve to show that it was not just Peter, John and, later, Paul who were involved in the early spread of Christianity.

From the first of these stories, about Simon the Sorcerer, the word 'simony' was coined to describe what was originally regarded as a terrible sin, namely the attempt to purchase a position within the Church. Sadly, at some stages of the Church's history, not least in England, it became an all too frequent occurrence. What this story also shows, however, is that the apostles demonstrated some sort of power, which others found threatening and misinterpreted as superior magic.

The second incident gives us the evidence for the very early appearance of Christianity in Africa, centuries before Europeans ventured south of the Sahara. There had been links between Israel and Ethiopia ever since King Solomon's time (see OT Story 27). The 1989 refugee flight of the Falasha Jews to modern Israel to escape persecution in Ethiopia brought home this ancient link. Similarly, nineteenth-century Western missionaries discovered the Ethiopian Coptic Church, which owed absolutely nothing to European influence. It had been there many centuries before they arrived. Modern Rastafarianism, based on the concept of Emperor Haile Salassie as 'The Lion of Judah', is an offshoot of that tradition which has now penetrated the West.

This record reminds us that, as with the Thomist Church of Southern India (see Story 36), there is danger in Eurocentric assumptions about the spread of Christianity. Whilst being recognizably of the same basic faith the Ethiopian Copic Church owes nothing to European culture. It may well have started with the events of this story.

191

IDEAS FOR EXPLORING FURTHER

Christianity as a World Religion   See notes on Story 38.

Explaining the Bible   Divide children into groups and ask them to work together to produce a sequenced comic-strip version of a chosen Bible story for a younger child. Emphasize that, although the language used and the layout of the work can be simple, the ideas, meaning and importance of the story should be kept. Each child can work on one part of the story – drawing the picture and writing the words. The parts may then be assembled to form a comic or a book. Children could work on making giant-sized books for group-reading, using a word-processor or very neat handwriting to produce the text in large letters. Each comic or book could have an introduction in which the children explain why they have chosen this particular story. The whole venture should be carefully designed and executed so that the books are worth keeping in the class or school library. They could even be used by local Sunday-school groups or play groups. (Cf. NC *English*: AT 3; *Technology*.)

Jesus: the Suffering Servant   See notes on Story 26 – Jesus: King of What?

192

43

The Road to Damascus

Acts 9: 1–18; 22: 1–21

The Christians were spreading everywhere. Now news came that they were in Damascus. Saul went to see the High Priest.

'Give me a letter,' said Saul, 'so that people will know that I am doing it for you. Then I shall go to Damascus with some men, arrest all the Christians there and bring them back for trial in Jerusalem.'

'Well done!' said the High Priest. 'We could do with more young men like you around. We must wipe out these Christians.'

It was a long way to Damascus. Day after day Saul and his men walked on and on through the desert heat. At last the white walls of Damascus came into sight on the distant horizon. Not long now, thought Saul.

Suddenly the light changed. It became brighter, like the glare of a powerful torch. Saul glanced upwards. As he did so he screamed and fell to the ground, holding his eyes. As the others rushed to help him they heard him shout 'Who are you? Who are you, Lord?'

They pulled Saul to his feet. He was shaking all over. Worse still, he was blind. He could not see a thing. His friends had to take hold of his hands and lead him into the city. For three days and nights he was so ill he could not eat or drink.

On the other side of the city lived a man called Ananias. He was a Christian, one of those Saul was coming to arrest.

Without any warning Ananias had a vivid dream. He heard his name being called.

'Ananias, Ananias!'

Ananias sat up. 'Yes, Lord. What is it?'

'Get up and go down to Straight Street. Knock on the door of a house belonging to a man called Judas. Then ask to see Saul of Tarsus. He will be expecting you.'

'Saul of Tarsus!' gasped Ananias. 'I can't go to see him. He has come here to get me killed.'

'Do as I say,' said the voice. 'Saul is going to be one of my messengers.'

Ananias got up and went out into the street. He was still frightened. He made his way across the city. In Straight Street he found the house. It was just as he had been told. Saul was there. He was still blind.

'What happened?' asked Ananias.

'There was a blinding light,' Saul began. 'It seemed to knock me over. As I lay on the ground I heard a voice. It kept saying, "Saul, Saul, why do you keep on persecuting me?" I kept asking, "Who are you? Who are you?" In the end the voice said, "I am Jesus of Nazareth, the one you keep trying to destroy." '

'Is this true?' Ananias asked the other people in the room.

They nodded. 'We did not hear the voice,' they said, 'but we saw the light and we heard Saul shouting out just as he has said.'

Ananias put out his hands and touched Saul's eyes with his fingers. 'Brother Saul,' he said, 'the Lord Jesus has sent me to help you to see properly again. You have felt his spirit upon you. Now you are to be one of his followers.'

Light came back into Saul's eyes. He could see again. He got up and left the house with Ananias.

Saul's men left Damascus and hurried back down the road to Jerusalem. The High Priest would have to be told what had happened. He would be mad with rage. Saul himself had become a Christian.

ABOUT THE STORY

Despite Gamaliel's advice open persecution of Christians soon began. Because of their long history of invasion, persecution and deportation Jewish communities were to be found, even two thousand years ago, scattered all over the Mediterranean region. This is known as the Dispersion (sometimes the Greek word 'Diaspora' is used). It had begun some six hundred years before (see OT Story 35). Immediately after the period we are dealing with – in the year 120 to be precise – the Romans finally lost patience and banned all Jews from Palestine. That total dispersion, in which they had no country of their own, lasted until 1947 when the modern State of Israel was created after the Nazi Holocaust. Old Testament Stories 37 and 38 tell a tale very similar to the clashes between returning Jews and the 'people of the land' in modern Palestine.

It was the Dispersion which was to be the main vehicle for the spread of Christianity around the Mediterranean world. The apostles showed enormous vigour in setting off in all directions but always they were travelling to Jewish communities in far-away places. Those pursuing them also knew where to go.

Saul himself was a child of the Dispersion, coming from Tarsus in Asia Minor (Turkey). He was not from a priestly family but was to describe himself later as having been a 'Pharisee of the Pharisees', an extreme Puritan. He was obviously seen as an up-and-coming person of some importance – on the fast track, as we might say today. He first entered the story as a bystander at Stephen's death. He would have been eager to impress on his way to a high position.

Had Stephen's martyrdom affected him? We cannot know for certain but it is obviously more than a possibility. His vision on the Damascus road was clearly a dramatic event and resulted in a total and permanent change in his orientation. He never went back on it. It remained real and vivid to him up to his own execution in Rome many years later.

Ananias shows enormous courage in this story. Saul's reputation and mission have gone before him. Ananias is somewhat in the position of a European Jew in the 1940s who is told to go and welcome a leading Nazi Jew-hunter. His is a remarkable act of faith and completes this most significant conversion. Saul himself, of course, now joins the 'most wanted' list.

IDEAS FOR EXPLORING FURTHER

Conversion Talk to the children about the different stages in Saul's thinking and explore what he might have been feeling. Did he go through something like the following?

(i) Initially Saul was ambitious for power and respect and wanted to show himself in a good light as far as the authorities were concerned; his avowed intent was to get rid of these troublesome Christians, one of whom he had just witnessed being killed (Story 41).

(ii) Saul had time on the journey to think about what he was going to do. He had probably been in two minds about the Christians and their story for some while, but his ambition had pushed his rising sympathy for and interest in them to the back of his mind. Now he had to face some hard questions. Had Jesus really deserved to die? Had Stephen deserved his treatment? What kind of person was he, Saul, if he could stand by and let another human being be murdered?

(iii) Saul underwent a sudden intense realization – like a blinding light – that his plan to destroy all Christians was wrong. He knew in his heart that the story of Jesus and what he stood for was true – and more than that – he wanted to be part of it. This realization was a tremendous shock.

(iv) Saul was in turmoil inside. He who had been a chief persecutor of Christians was going to become a Christian himself! How was this going to be explained to the High Priest? What would become of him? Talk about Saul's bravery in this context. (See notes on Story 40.)

(v) The mental struggle and turmoil made Saul ill. Talk about how worry and stress can make people ill. (Cf. NC *Health Education*.) This is fully recognized by many groups of people throughout the world who make every effort to treat patients from the spiritual as well as the physical point of view.

(vi) Because Saul was aware of the harm he had done in the past he was even more eager to serve Jesus in the future to make up for it.

See also notes on Story 20 – sudden realizations. For additional material on dreams, visions, reality and the question 'What is truth?', see the Introduction and OT Stories 5, 8, 9, 35, 41, 45.

Diaspora   Invite some children to write to a rabbi or other people who know about Jewish affairs to find out some of the countries to which the Jews were dispersed. Help the children to mark these on a world map. (Cf. NC *Geography*: AT 1 – geographical skills.) Older children might like to find out the contribution of the Jews to different countries.

44

Escape by Night

Acts 9: 22–25

There was a knock at the door, a gentle tapping noise. Ananias moved quickly across the room. He opened the door. A young man slipped into the house from the dark street. He had been running. He was out of breath.

'Well?' asked Ananias.

'It's no good,' gasped the young man, 'still there. I've been to every gate. Always the same. Two or three of them just standing around.' He saw the look on Ananias' face. 'Don't worry. I wasn't followed.'

Ananias was worried. 'We've got to get him out somehow,' he muttered. He looked round the room. A small oil lamp flickered from its shelf in the wall. Its weak light showed up the faces of the small group of men seated round the table. Most of them looked worried too. Only one seemed calm. He smiled at Ananias. It was Saul.

How he had changed! He had come to Damascus to arrest Christians. Now he was one himself. He had even changed the name he used. 'Don't call me Saul,' he had said on the day he was baptized. 'From now on call me by my Roman name, Paul.'

Paul had come to Damascus to hunt down the Christians. Now other men had come to the city to hunt down Paul. His enemies were everywhere. Day and night they watched the gates. There was no escape.

Ananias sat down with the others. What could they do?

There was silence in the room. It was Paul who broke it. He said just one word: 'Rahab'.

The others looked up. Paul was smiling. 'Rahab,' he said again, louder this time. He saw the others looking at him. They looked puzzled.

'Remember Rahab,' he explained. 'She was hiding two of Joshua's spies in the city of Jericho. They couldn't escape because the gates were being watched.'

'Of course,' said Ananias as he jumped to his feet. 'Tomorrow I can arrange it. One of our members lives in a house by the city wall. Let's pray we are not found before then.'

It was another dark night. There was no moon. The small group of men crept silently up the staircase on the outside of a small house. Ananias came last. He carried a large basket, the sort vegetables were kept in. It would have been better to go through the window but it was too small. Up here on the roof they might be seen. And the rope might be too short. That was why he had brought the basket. It would be terrible if Paul fell off the end of the rope and broke a leg.

The flat roof was part of the top of the city wall. Ananias walked to the edge. He looked down. The side of the wall went down into darkness. He could not see the ground below. He looked right and left. Nothing moved. It was time to go.

Ananias pushed the rope through the top of the basket and tied it tight. 'Climb in,' he whispered to Paul.

Paul was only a little man but he filled the basket. 'This started with my thinking about Rahab,' he said. 'Now I feel like Moses in the bulrushes.'

Hands reached out and touched Paul for the last time. Then they lifted the basket, took the strain on the rope, and gently lowered the basket over the wall.

In the silence of the night the scraping sound of the basket on the wall seemed loud enough to waken the whole city. There was no other sound. Slowly the men let out the rope. Down and down went the basket. They were coming to the end of the rope.

Suddenly the rope went slack. The basket had touched the ground. For a few seconds they waited. Then there was a short tug on the rope. Quickly they pulled up the basket.

Paul had gone. By dawn he would be far away. His enemies at the gates would have a long wait. He was free – free to wander about the world and to tell the good news about Jesus to anyone who would listen.

──────────────── **NOTES** ────────────────

ABOUT THE STORY

This story should be told with all the suspense of a spy thriller. Its context is that of the awaited night-time knock on the door. The enclosed, high-walled city would have been difficult to enter or leave when the gates, which were shut at night anyway, were being watched. A systematic search within the city would also have been relatively straightforward, especially as the Jewish community would have been known and readily identifiable, probably living together within a Jewish quarter.

The references to Rahab (see OT Story 16) are purely imaginary but the practical problems of escape are similar.

Saul's change of name has often been likened to the selection of a new name by those entering a religious order. It could have had that significance. Equally it could have been an attempt to disguise identity. In fact Saul almost certainly possessed both names anyway. Saul was his Jewish name, after the first king of Israel, who had come from his own small tribe of Benjamin (see OT Story 21). But he was also a Roman citizen with all the privileges that that bestowed, and as such he would have had three Roman names, a *praenomen* and a *nomen*, which we do not know, and a *cognomen*, which was Paul. It was the Jews who were hunting him, not the Romans, and he could identify equally with either.

Even as a young man Paul must have been marked out for his high intelligence and leadership qualities. Those pursuing him realized his importance and they were to be proved right. He was to become not only a tireless messenger of the Christian cause but also one of its most influential formulators. Space does not permit us to give a full account of the research of the last two centuries into the authorship and dating of the New Testament books but we can state with a high degree of certainty that most of the Christian Scriptures, outside the Gospels, were almost certainly written by him, including some of the very earliest, which existed before the Gospels were written in the form in which they have come down to us. Millions of people have read his words and continue to do so.

IDEAS FOR EXPLORING FURTHER

God's Help   Many Christians would say that God helped Paul through his friends to get out of the city; that if human beings make an effort and trust in God, then he will give them wisdom, power and strength beyond that which they might normally possess. Draw out children's responses to this tense and dramatic story which demonstrates one solution to a very difficult problem: how to get Paul out of the city. Ask the children to act out the story, putting as much suspense into it as possible. Invite them to work in pairs or small groups to devise different methods for helping Paul to escape. In what other ways could Paul's friends have got him past the guards at the gate? Consider the consequences of Paul not being able to trust his friends and of betrayal. Incorporate ideas into story-writing and poetry.

What's In a Name?   Provide information about the origin and meaning of names of people and places. (Parents can often give valuable information to supplement reference books.) Read *Boy Without a Name*, by Penelope Lively. A survey may reveal factors about name-giving. Let pupils choose a new name for themselves or someone else. Ask for reasons behind decisions. Look at newspaper births columns to see popular names for children at present. Contrast these with names from gravestones entered into a data base. (NC *Technology*: AT 5 – information technology.) Older pupils could consider why some names are more common than others. Discuss the 99 names of Allah and compare with names for God used by other religious traditions.

45

A Dangerous New Idea

Acts 10: 1–48

Peter climbed up the staircase to the flat roof of the house. It was quiet there. Joppa was a busy port. From the top of his friend's house Peter could look down on the busy harbour.

It was midday. Peter was getting hungry. Soon there would be a meal. The women were getting it ready. He sat down and thought. What was going to happen? Would all the Jews become Christians? Or would the High Priest have them killed if they tried?

Peter looked out towards the sea. He had never been outside Palestine. Somewhere out there was Rome, the centre of the Empire. Could the Romans ever become Christians? He had never thought of that before.

The sun was hot. Peter was hungry. How much longer would he have to wait? He felt quite weak and drowsy. His head nodded. He was almost asleep.

It came down out of the sky – a huge sheet like a giant table-cloth. At first Peter could not see what was on it. It looked like food. A voice called out, 'Peter, come and eat.' At last!

And then he could see. It was a terrible shock. The cloth was full of all the things that a Jew could never eat – pork and rabbit and certain other meats. Peter felt sick. He shuddered. 'Never,' he said. 'Not in a million years. I'll die first. It's against my religion.'

Three times the cloth came down. Three times the voice

told Peter to eat. And the last time the voice added, 'How can you call something unclean when God has cleaned it?' It was a real nightmare.

Suddenly Peter was wide awake. He was sweating all over. What had woken him? There was a lot of movement downstairs.

'Peter, Peter. Where are you?'

'Up here,' he replied, fully awake by now.

'Some visitors to see you.'

Peter came downstairs. He was surprised when he saw the visitors. They were not Jews; they were Romans, sent by Cornelius who was Captain of the famous regiment stationed up the coast at Caesarea.

'Can you come to Caesarea?' said one of the soldiers. 'Our master wishes to see you straight away.'

It was a day's journey to Caesarea. 'We will go tomorrow,' said Peter.

Next morning they set off. When they got to Caesarea Captain Cornelius came out of his large house. To Peter's amazement he knelt down in front of him.

'Please stand up,' said Peter. 'I'm only a human being, you know.'

Cornelius got to his feet. 'Come inside,' he said, moving towards the house.

Peter hesitated. How could he? All his life, from the time he was a small boy, he had been told that Jews did not mix with people from other races. He could not enter a Roman's house. Or could he? Was that what his dream was all about? Hadn't he just said he was only a human being? Did being a Christian make a difference?

All these thoughts went through Peter's mind in a flash. Suddenly he knew what he must do. 'All right,' he said and he followed Cornelius into the house. His friends who had travelled with him looked at one another in amazement. Then they followed him in.

Inside, Cornelius had got lots of his friends together. 'I asked you to come,' said Cornelius, 'because we wanted someone to tell us all about this Jesus of Nazareth we keep hearing about.'

Peter began to talk. The Romans listened. By the time Peter had finished, Cornelius and some of the others had decided to become Christians.

Peter made the long journey home in silence. He had a lot to think about. This new faith meant more than he had thought. Jews like Peter had always believed they were a chosen race. Now he knew they weren't any more. The Christian Church was taking its place. Anyone could become a Christian. It was like making a new race of people out of all the other races.

It was an exciting new idea. It was also a very dangerous one.

NOTES

ABOUT THE STORY

Peter, as we already know, was a very different sort of person from Paul. Nevertheless, in his influence upon the growth of Christianity he ranks as highly. A Galilean fisherman with no more than an elementary Jewish education at the synagogue school, we almost certainly owe Mark's Gospel to him. A very early source tells us that Mark wrote down, although not in order, all those things which Peter told him. In this story we also come to a conversion of huge significance in terms of the future religious and cultural development first of the Roman Empire and later of all Western Europe.

The dream, with the coincidental arrival (if it is coincidence) of the messengers from Cornelius, is demanding of Peter that he abandons some of the strongest elements in his cultural upbringing and changes his identity. It is not easy to find comparisons but perhaps the decision by leading white South Africans in 1989 to release Nelson Mandela and his decision to try to work in harmony with them contains at least some of the same elements, as might the decision of some leading Northern Ireland Protestants to talk with Sinn Fein.

The Romans were in, by far, the most superior position politically. They did not make a habit of socializing with Jews, let alone go seeking their counsel. At the same time most Jews at this time would have held themselves morally and religiously aloof – as the Chosen People – and would have regarded socializing with Gentiles as tantamount to betrayal of their faith. To do what Peter was commanded to do in terms of food prohibitions has been enough to bring on extreme physical nausea even in the starvation conditions of the Nazi death camps. The divide which Peter was asked to bridge here was equivalent to apartheid and, in some respects, even wider. At the same time there had long existed within Judaism a universalist streak although it had rarely enjoyed a dominant position. (See notes on OT Stories 40 – Ruth, 41 – Jonah.)

This dream and its subsequent outcome mark the door by which Christianity was to become more than a Jewish sect and to break out into the non-Jewish world. From this tiny incident comes the possibility of a sweeping change of religion and culture over whole continents.

IDEAS FOR EXPLORING FURTHER

Change   Talk to the children about the way they feel about change. Propose some fairly major change to classroom seating, procedures or work. Ask children for their reaction. What is threatening/exciting about change? How often does change occur? What would happen if nothing ever changed? Collect information about a variety of possible changes in the children's world (e.g. growing, advancing their learning, moving house, losing a relative, friend or pet, changing school, friends moving away, seasons, new fashions in, say, toys and books). Consider change over a fairly long period of time (e.g. in housing, transport, clothes). (NC *History.*) Look for similarities and differences and discuss reasons for these. Who finds it easier to adapt to change: younger or older people? What reasons can be given? What changes can children suggest to improve their local, national and international world? See also OT Story 42.

Britain as a Pluralist Society   Make an initial display of items to show the significant contribution which a variety of cultures have made to life in Britain. Ask children to extend the display and to write labels for exhibits stating why they are interesting, etc. Celebrate in particular the richness of poetry and story, art, music, song, food, sports personalities and festivals. Help the children to appreciate that a great deal of mathematical, scientific and medical knowledge was developed outside Britain. (Cf. NC *History:* CSU 6 – Ancient Greece, SSU on Ancient Egypt.) Discuss with older children tensions caused by apartheid, anti-Semitism, and other racial and religious divisions. What do they feel would be best for Britain? See also Stories 3, 7, OT Stories 11, 18, 36, 40, 41.

46

In Gaol at Midnight

Acts 15: 1 – 16: 40

'We must go across the sea and tell all the world. The story of Jesus is for everyone, not just for the Jews.'

All round the room came nods of agreement. It must be true. First Peter had said it. Now Paul was saying the same thing. They should know. They had travelled to many places. The Council agreed. The meeting came to an end.

Paul was setting off again. He never seemed to stop. This time he was taking Silas with him.

Paul and Silas went across the sea. They visited many towns, walking from place to place. At last they came to the land of Greece. There another man called Luke joined them. All three went on together until they came to a city called Philippi.

Philippi was a beautiful city. They made lots of friends there and started a church. Things were going well. There was just one thing that seemed to spoil it.

Everywhere Paul and Silas went they were followed by a girl. She was a slave and she seemed to be mad. Some men owned her and they used her to make money for them. She was supposed to be able to tell fortunes.

She would not leave Paul alone. Every time he went down the street she followed him. At the top of her voice she kept shouting out, 'These men are servants of the Most High God. They have come here to tell us how we can be set free.'

One day Paul could stand it no longer. He turned round and faced the girl. In a loud voice he shouted, 'In the name of Jesus Christ come out of her.' He spoke as if he were talking to someone inside the girl.

It worked. The girl suddenly went all quiet and peaceful. She wasn't mad any more. But she could not tell fortunes any more either.

Her owners were very angry. They got hold of Paul and Silas and dragged them into the market-place. 'These men are trouble-makers,' they shouted. 'They are foreigners who have come to upset our town.'

Paul tried to speak but the rest of the crowd started to hit and kick him and Silas. The magistrate came out to see what all the trouble was about. He listened to the girl's owners and then said, 'Flog them and put them in prison for the night.'

Before Paul could say anything he and Silas were beaten with sticks and dragged to the prison. Their backs were sore and bleeding. They were covered in bruises. The prison was a filthy place. There were lots of other prisoners there.

It became dark. There were no lights in the prison. And it was then that it happened.

About midnight Paul and Silas started singing hymns. At first the sound they made was very soft. Then they sang louder and louder. The other prisoners joined in. No one had heard singing coming from the prison before.

They were still singing when the earthquake came. The ground shook. There were screams as walls moved and started to crack. Then it was all over as quickly as it had started. But the prison doors were hanging open.

The open doors were the first thing the gaoler noticed when he came rushing down. They have all escaped, he thought, I shall be blamed.

He took out his sword and was about to kill himself when out of the darkness a voice called out 'Stop! We are all here'.

It was Paul. He had all the other prisoners with him. The gaoler could not believe his eyes. Why were these prisoners so different from all the other ones he had ever had? He stopped

206

to talk with Paul and Silas. Before the night was over he had become a Christian.

Next morning the magistrate sent a messenger to the prison. 'You can go now,' he said to Paul.

'No, thank you,' said Paul.

'But you're free,' said the messenger.

'Free,' exclaimed Paul. 'Yes, I was born free – a freeman of the Roman Empire.'

The messenger's face went white.

'Your masters have broken the law of Rome,' Paul went on. 'They have beaten a freeman in public and without a proper trial. Tell them I want to see them.'

The man ran off. In a very short time he was back with the magistrates. They looked frightened. Paul could complain to the Roman Governor. Then they would really be in trouble.

'Why did you not tell us you were a freeman?' asked one of the magistrates.

'You didn't give me a chance, did you?' replied Paul. 'Every time I tried to speak, someone hit me.'

It was true and they knew it.

'We have come to apologize,' said the magistrates. 'We are very sorry. But please, will you leave our city before there is any more trouble?'

'We accept your apology,' said Paul, 'but as for leaving the city, we will do that when we have had time to see our friends again.'

ABOUT THE STORY

This story begins with what is known as the Council of Jerusalem. It was here at a meeting involving both Peter and Paul, together with others, that the crucial decision was formally made that the Christian message was directly open to anyone. Gentiles did not have to convert to Judaism first before they could become Christians. It was an historic moment and prevented a split in the movement.

Paul had already made one missionary journey, crossing by sea to the south coast of Turkey and then travelling inland on foot. John Mark had accompanied him but had then turned back at the coast. Paul refused to take him again. On this second missionary journey Paul, fresh from the decision taken at the Council, sets off for Greece, accompanied by Silas. Greece, despite having been conquered by the Romans, was still regarded as the cultural centre of the Mediterranean world and it still provided the main language. The Christian Scriptures were to be written in Greek, not in Latin or even Aramaic, which is likely to have been Jesus' own first language. Alone among the world's religions Christianity, therefore, was in a translated form from the very beginning. It has never regarded any language as sacred in the way in which Jews revere Hebrew or Muslims Arabic.

We know very little about Silas. He could have been both a leading Jewish Christian and a Roman citizen. This is speculation but there can be no doubt that it would have been a distinct advantage in allowing access to the Gentile world. It is on this journey that Luke, a Greek physician, is converted and joins the group. Another highly educated person, he would seem immediately to have begun collecting the evidence which would form the basis of his Gospel narrative. It is one of those small but exciting discoveries of literary criticism that he suddenly changes from the third person plural to the first person plural at the point in Acts (20: 6) where he is said to join the story.

Roman citizens possessed a number of civil privileges denied to others. They had a right to trial by Romans. In the mob rule which takes over in this incident the question is not asked but Paul, in any case, leaves it until next day before drawing attention to the matter. He was not above winning moral victories but the new morality is shown in the Christians' refusal to take advantage of others' misfortunes even in the extreme conditions of harsh imprisonment. There is no evidence that Paul was a full pacifist but the principle of suffering evil and thereby exposing it, rather than physically resisting, seems to have been understood by him from the beginning.

IDEAS FOR EXPLORING FURTHER

Community and Citizenship   Talk with the children about the rights and responsibilities of belonging to any community: family, school, club, nation. What can people expect as a right? What must they be prepared to give in return? With older children, talk about how local services are provided. Discuss the value of legal, health and education services. Do ethnic-minority groups have equal access to rights and services? What happens in South Africa, where the black population is far larger than the white, yet the whites have many more advantages? What about land conflict in many economically developing countries, where much of the land is owned by a tiny minority of the population? (NC *Geography.* AT 2 – knowledge and understanding of places.) See Story 2.

Speakers' Corner Talk about the idea of Britain as a 'free country'. In what ways is it 'free' and 'not free'? Discuss the value of Speakers' Corner. What changes would children like to propose for any of the communities to which they belong? What would they like to see more of/less of? Invite children to discuss in small groups, to consider alternatives and to nominate a spokesperson. Invite children to run their own Speakers' Corner, where they air their opinions and the reasons for them. Some interesting debates could ensue. Children could be challenged to handle controversial issues and differences of opinion in a balanced, non-aggressive manner. (NC *Citizenship.*) See Stories 2, 6, 39, 47, 48.

Prisons Find out about prison conditions of the past, about crime, punishment and justice. (Cf. NC *History.*) See also Stories 33, 50.

47

The Riot of the Silversmiths

Acts 19: 21 – 20: 1

It was Demetrius who started it. Demetrius was the leader of the silversmiths who worked in the town of Ephesus. The silversmiths did a good trade. In Ephesus was the main temple of a goddess called Artemis. All the tourists liked to buy little silver models of her.

Then Paul and Silas arrived. When they had been in Ephesus a few weeks Demetrius came to realize that he was not selling as many models as he used to. He found out that the other silversmiths were complaining too. He called a meeting.

'Men,' said Demetrius, 'you know how we make our money. And you know why our trade has gone down. This man Paul is preaching a new religion. He is making everyone Christians. If this goes on we shall be ruined. Are we going to sit here and do nothing about it?'

'No, no, no!' shouted the silversmiths. 'Down with the Christians! Throw them out! Come on, let's get them!'

They rushed out into the street. Demetrius could not control them any more. All through the city they marched. As they went along they chanted 'Great is Artemis of the Ephesians, Great is Artemis of the Ephesians!'

The crowd grew in number as they went through the streets. All through the city the chant could be heard, 'Great is Artemis of the Ephesians'.

The crowd started to make its way towards the stadium. Suddenly someone shouted, 'There they are! Grab them!'

Two of Paul's followers, Gaius and Aristarchus, were chased through the streets and caught. They were beaten up and dragged into the stadium.

The stadium filled up. The chanting became louder and louder. It seemed to go on for hours.

In the house where he was staying Paul did not know what to do. 'Let me go,' he said. 'Let me go into the stadium and rescue Gaius and Aristarchus.'

He began to move towards the door but his friends pulled him back. 'Sit down,' they said, pushing him into a chair. 'There's nothing you can do. If you go in there they will kill you. What good will that do?'

Paul sat down. He knew they were right.

In the stadium the shouting went on. They didn't seem to do anything except keep chanting 'Great is Artemis of the Ephesians'. A Jew called Alexander tried to stand up and take control, but it was no good.

In the end the Town Clerk himself had to go into the stadium. 'What is this all about?' he shouted. 'Do you want the Roman soldiers sent in here to put down a riot?'

For the first time the chanting died down.

'Listen to me,' said the Town Clerk. 'The courts are open. If you think anyone has done anything wrong go there and the judges will decide.'

Demetrius said nothing. He knew that Paul had not broken the law. The riot stopped. People started to go home.

A few days later Paul, Silas and Luke left the city as well. There were lots of Christians now in Ephesus. It was time to move on and start work somewhere else.

NOTES

ABOUT THE STORY

In this story, as in Stories 42 and 46, trouble arises as soon as profits are affected. Here it appears to be the tourist trade which suffers.

In many translations the goddess referred to in this story is called Diana of the Ephesians. This is a mistake which goes back a long way. The goddess in question was Artemis. Unfortunately there were two goddesses of that name in Greek mythology. One was simply a parallel of the Roman goddess Diana, sister of Apollo. She was a hunter and usually depicted with bow and arrows.

A totally different Artemis was worshipped at Ephesus. This one was a fertility goddess depicted as many breasted. Consequently what was at stake here was probably not just a fall-off in the sales of effigies like plastic pixies in Killarney. It was rather the whole trade based on pornography and sexual licence.

Not only the silversmiths made money out of Artemis. The rich bought silver effigies but the less well off would purchase the same thing in terracotta or marble. Hundreds of such artefacts have been unearthed at Ephesus. It would seem that when the temple got overcrowded with them they were simply thrown out in piles; the silver ones were no doubt melted down for handsome profits.

Paul's message amounted to a lively attack on the whole trade which went on in the name of religion but was really about sensual gratification and money. His teaching affected jobs – always a strong and emotive argument whether the issue in question is the one here or a topic such as armaments or pollutants. Christian protest has early origins and a long pedigree.

IDEAS FOR EXPLORING FURTHER

Exploring Alternatives   Did the violence of the silversmiths lead to any lasting positive outcome? Did they really address the root of the problem? After all, there were a lot of Christians in Ephesus to spread the Gospel. Getting rid of Paul and Silas solved nothing in the long term. Ask the children to work in small groups and to suggest alternative courses of action which the silversmiths could have followed. Do the groups have any suggestions in common? Which of the suggestions offered seems 'best' and why? (What does 'best' mean?)

Are there any problems at school or in the local community for which alternative strategies could be sought? See also Stories 33 and 41. Consider figures in history who have had to weigh up alternatives, and discuss reasons for and consequences of their actions. (Cf. NC *History*: e.g. CSU 2 – Tudor and Stuart times: Elizabeth I had to consider alternatives concerning whether or not to marry. She had to choose between playing her various suitors off against each other, thereby remaining single and retaining power in her own hands, and possibly keeping England English, or agreeing to marry, losing a great deal of power, and possibly having England taken over permanently by another country.)

Employment   Many people agree that the environment should be protected. However, politicians and others sometimes stop short of carrying out measures to ensure this because jobs might be lost. Debate this, perhaps taking the Brazilian rainforest as a focus. Here, the forest is being destroyed at a tremendous rate, but if logging and ranching is stopped, many people will be put out of work, which will cause extreme hardship to families. Similarly, should the ivory trade be banned? Should the fur trade cease? Should the sale of exotic birds stop? Whaling and sardine fishing, which often causes dolphins to be harmed, are other controversial issues. Could any jobs be described as unethical? What about people who earn a living by shoplifting or stealing, who sell drugs or arms, who exploit tourists, who scare people into buying insurance? (Cf. NC *Geography:* AT 2 – knowledge and understanding of places, AT 5 – environmental geography; *Environmental Education; Economic and Industrial Understanding; Careers and the World of Work.*) See also Stories 6, 22, 25, 29.

Listening to Points of View   Were the silversmiths justified in being angry about falling profits? It might be assumed that they were just being selfish, but maybe they were thinking about their families' well-being. Is this a satisfactory excuse for violence? Is any riot justified? Does the size of their profits have any bearing on the case? Emphasize the complexity of judging the 'rights' and 'wrongs' of a case. Ask older children to discuss a controversial issue currently in the news. (See also notes on Story 39.)

Community and Citizenship   See Stories 46, 48.

213

48

Take Me to Caesar, the Emperor of Rome

Acts 20: 22 – 25: 12

'I must go back to Jerusalem,' Paul said to his friends one day.

'But you can't. They will kill you.'

'I must go back. I must show them that Jesus is for Jews as well. He is their Messiah if only they will believe it.'

Paul's friends argued and argued; but it was no good, he had made up his mind. They set off in fear and trembling.

For a few days everything was all right. Nobody recognized Paul. He had been away for so long that most people had forgotten all about him.

Then one day in the Temple courtyard the trouble started. Some Jews from Asia were visiting the Temple. One of them looked at Paul closely and then shouted, 'Look, that's him. That's the man we were telling you about. He came to our synagogue saying that Jesus of Nazareth was our Messiah.'

There was a lot of shouting and pushing. Paul was grabbed and pulled out of the Temple. He was punched and kicked. Somebody started shouting 'Kill him, kill him'.

It was the shouts which brought the Roman guards racing to the scene. With drawn swords they pushed the crowd back. They pulled Paul to his feet and took him away with them.

Just as they were entering the barracks Paul spoke to the officer. 'Would you let me talk to the people?' he said.

The crowd had gone quiet now so the officer agreed.

Paul stood on the steps and started to tell the people how he had once hated Christians. He told them how he had had a vision on the road to Damascus. The crowd listened quietly. It was only when he started to tell them how Jesus was for the whole world and not just for the Jews that all the noise started again. 'Kill him,' shouted some. 'Traitor,' shrieked others. They started to throw dust up in the air.

'Quick, get him inside,' ordered the officer.

Paul was pushed up the steps and the doors of the Roman barracks banged shut behind him.

'String him up,' said the officer. 'Get the whips. We will soon get the truth out of him and find what this is all about.'

Soldiers seized Paul's hands and tied them to rings in the wall. As the whips were being brought Paul shouted out, 'Are you going to whip a freeman of Rome?'

'What?' gasped the officer. 'Are you a freeman? How could you afford it? It cost me a lot of money.'

'I was born a freeman,' replied Paul. 'I have been one all my life.'

'Cut him down,' commanded the officer. 'We cannot do this to him.'

Paul was a special prisoner. The Jews in Jerusalem swore that they would kill him. He had to be moved. Two hundred foot soldiers, two hundred spearmen and seventy horsemen marched Paul to the Roman town of Caesarea. The Jews were very angry. The Romans were far too strong for them.

For two years Paul was a prisoner in Caesarea. The Romans did not know what to do with him. And then a new Governor came. The Jews tried again. They told Festus, the new Governor, that Paul should be killed.

Festus was a very fair man. He sent for Paul and had him brought from the prison. He even invited King Agrippa to be there as well.

Paul told Festus and Agrippa all about how he had become a Christian and why it was important. They thought he was a bit mad. But they had to admit that he had not broken the law. Paul thought they were going to send him back to Jerusalem. There was one last thing he could do.

'I am a Jew,' he said, 'but I am also a freeman of Rome. I

have done nothing wrong, but if you send me back to my fellow Jews they will kill me. They will not give me a fair trial. I appeal to Caesar. Take me to Caesar, the Emperor of Rome. It is my right.'

Festus was surprised. He had been going to set Paul free. But Paul had claimed his right as a freeman. It had to be done.

'Very well,' said Festus. 'It is your right. You have asked to go to Caesar in Rome. To Caesar you shall go.'

NOTES

ABOUT THE STORY

Just like Jesus before him Paul decides that he must 'set his face towards Jerusalem'. He must realize the dangers but perhaps he has some deep hope that he might yet be able to show the religious establishment the error of their ways and get them to recognize that Jesus is their long-expected Christ.

It is an impossible and unrealistic hope. Ironically it is pilgrims from the Dispersion who recognize him and give away his presence. Even more ironically it is the Roman occupiers who save him from a certain lynching.

We see here the full force of the privileges of Roman citizenship. Once it is known Paul is protected at all costs. For two whole years he is guarded in the Roman sea-port fortress of Caesarea rather than Jewish-dominated Jerusalem. The Romans had their laws and their commitment to the Rule of Law was very strong whatever individuals may have thought of Paul's behaviour. In some ways the position was not altogether unlike that of Salmon Rushdie when faced with an Islamic *fatwah*.

Did the Romans finally tire of holding Paul? Did they really think the Jewish leaders would have forgotten? Paul himself knows that he cannot escape on his own but does he want to? The story is written on the lines of 'if not Jerusalem then why not Rome?' Whatever the judgement of the Governor a direct appeal to Caesar was paramount. The irony here is that the Governor is prepared to release Paul as innocent. It is against that decision that Paul appeals and makes himself once again an escorted prisoner in order that he might get right to the centre of the Empire itself.

IDEAS FOR EXPLORING FURTHER

Importance of the Gospel Message   Paul felt that his message about Jesus being the Messiah (and the freedom necessary to deliver it) was so important that he wanted to speak to the Emperor of Rome himself. Compare this with the idea of ourselves having something so important to say that we decide to claim an audience with the Queen or Prime Minister, or demand to speak before the council of the United Nations in New York.

Explore further ideas relating to what we value. Ask the children to draw what is the most important thing in the world to them. (This may need to be discussed in small groups first.) In what ways do the children show that they really value this? Talk about whether any monetary value is involved. Ask the children to imagine that what they most value is going to be taken away from them. Let them speak before the rest of the class. Make a recorded message or write a letter to an influential person explaining why they would like to keep their particular item. The teacher could 'test' the children's case by offering to give them something else which s/he thinks they may value more to see whether they will change their mind about their original choice. Make a display of drawings and writing related to what is most valued by class members.

Community and Citizenship   See notes on Stories 2, 6, 39, 46, 47. Debate issues relating to pacifism and the rights of conscientious objectors, the desire of many people to protest against the poll-tax (or community charge), the commitment of some to non-violence through the use of passive resistance (e.g. the women who camped outside the American air base at Greenham Common to protest against nuclear weapons and the way in which common land was being used). Talk about the importance of elections and universal suffrage. When do citizens have the right to speak out against a government and openly to rebel (e.g. Nazi Germany, Iraq, Yugoslavia, Cambodia, China)? Why is this sometimes very difficult to do?

Martyrdom   Many Christians were martyred in Rome. See Appendix 2 concerning what the Roman historian Tacitus and the Roman man of letters Pliny the Younger had to say about Christians.

49

Shipwreck

Acts 27: 1–44

The wind howled over the stern of the ship. Four men struggled with all their strength to hold the steering oar. The gale tore through their hair and clothes. They were soaking wet from the spray. All the time the wind seemed to want to push the boat sideways. If that happened the huge waves might roll it over on its side. Grimly they held on.

The movement of the ship was frightening. One minute its bow rose steeply into the air as it mounted a wave. The next it plunged steeply downwards so that the men at the stern felt they were in mid-air.

In one corner of the deck a small group of men sat huddled together. They were prisoners. Among them sat Paul and his friend Luke who had asked to travel with him. Like the sailors they were soaking wet. They knew that the Roman soldiers who were in charge of them were just as uncomfortable.

'Why did they not listen to me?' Paul asked. 'I said it was too late in the year to leave the port. We should have stayed there for the winter.'

'Because you are a prisoner,' Luke replied. 'No one takes any notice of prisoners. They thought you were saying it just to avoid going to Rome.'

'But I want to get to Rome,' protested Paul. 'I want to go there more than anything else.'

'I know that,' said Luke, 'but they don't.'

Paul shook his head. 'Anyway,' he said, 'I know we shan't drown. We shall get there safely, whatever happens.'

'I doubt if they will believe that at the moment, either.'

Sadly they watched an island disappear on the horizon. A few miles over there people were living in houses, safe and dry. If only they could turn the ship. It was impossible. All they could do was let it run in front of the wind.

The wind grew even stronger; the waves got steeper. There was a crash against the stern of the ship. 'Watch the life-raft,' the captain shouted. The waves had begun to knock it against the ship. It might make a hole. Sailors leaned over the side to grab the rope. Waves swept over them. Slowly and with great strength they pulled the little boat on to the deck.

Water had started to come in. The rough sea was forcing the planks apart. The sailors who had pulled the life-raft on board had no time to rest.

The captain's voice rose above the noise of the storm again. 'Secure the ship,' he called.

Sailors ran to the bow of the ship carrying ropes. They lowered the middle of each rope over the bow. Then, with one sailor holding each end, the rope was pulled back along the length of the ship and tied. Each rope ran right under the ship holding it together.

A day and a night passed. The storm was as bad as ever. The ship was sinking lower and lower in the water. The sea was coming in faster than they could bale it out. Finally the captain ordered, 'Throw the cargo overboard.'

The prisoners and the crew worked together. Sack after sack was brought on deck from down below. They were thrown into the sea. It was a long and tiring job. The sacks were soaking wet and very heavy.

Slowly the boat lifted higher in the water. Another day and night passed. Still the wind raged. The boat started to settle again. 'Throw away the gear' was the captain's last order.

Everything went overboard, tables, seats, pulleys, ropes, bunks, even passengers' luggage. There was nothing left except the people and the things necessary to sail the ship.

'We shall be next. We shall all drown,' said a voice.

'Nobody will drown,' came the reply. It was Paul.

'What makes you so sure?'

'God wants me in Rome. I know we shall all be safe in his hands.'

On and on the ship sailed. It was now two weeks since they had set sail. At last in the middle of the night the movement of the ship seemed to change. The sailors looked at one another. One ran to the bow and lowered a line with a lead weight on it. He pulled it up. 'Twenty fathoms,' he called. A minute later he did the same thing again. 'Fifteen fathoms,' he called.

There was panic. The ship was being driven into shore – fast.

'Stop them!' shouted Paul.

Julius, the Roman officer in charge, looked round. The sailors had put the life-raft overboard. They were starting to leave the ship. Julius moved quickly. There was a sharp order. Two Roman soldiers drew their swords. They slashed at the rope and the life-raft drifted away into the night. No one was on it.

The sailors were angry but they could do nothing other than wait. Four anchors were thrown out from the stern of the ship. The ship pulled them along but was slowed down by them. They were still floating when dawn came.

Now they could see the land. There were sandy beaches, but there were also hundreds of rocks between the boat and the land.

'Cut the anchor ropes. Hoist the sail,' shouted the captain.

The boat surged forward. They were going to run on to the beach.

Then suddenly there was a crash. The whole ship shook. There was a splintering sound. The ship had hit a rock. It was breaking up and sinking.

'Keep calm,' said a voice. 'We shall all be saved.' It was Paul.

But then another voice could be heard. It was that of one of the Roman soldiers. He stood with sword in hand. 'Shall we kill the prisoners, sir, before they can escape?' he asked.

The few seconds before the officer replied seemed endless. 'No,' he said at last, 'we shall have to trust them. Swim, those of you who can,' he shouted. 'The rest of you grab hold of planks!'

Men jumped into the waves all around the ship, to be washed in towards the shore.

On the beach Paul stood up and looked around. Men were staggering to their feet. They looked exhausted, but there were no dead bodies. Everyone was safe. He heard a shout and looked up. Men and women were running towards them from the island. Help was coming. They were safe. They had landed on the island of Malta.

NOTES

ABOUT THE STORY

The ship on which Paul travelled was probably a wheat vessel bound for Puteoli (modern Pozzuoli), near Naples. This port was a storage centre for wheat imports, mostly from Alexandria, from where this boat may have come before calling in at Caesarea.

These grain ships were quite large vessels. The Bible narrative records that there were 276 people on board and there are no grounds for thinking this was an exaggeration. Luke, who wrote Acts, liked to supply this sort of detail and we need to remember that, while he would have had to research the early narrative and his first volume (Luke's Gospel), from the point of Paul's entry into Greece on his second journey (Story 46) Luke was writing at first hand. He was on this voyage himself. Other historians of the time support the facts. Lucian records that one of these ships was driven into Piraeus (the port for Athens) and his measurements come out at about 60 metres by 15 metres. Josephus records being wrecked on a ship carrying 600 people.

The vessel would have had a large square sail with a long yard-arm attached to a central mast. There would also have been a small mast set diagonally from the bow, holding a small foresail. We know these details from coin inscriptions of the period.

Although such vessels were square rigged we now know that, like Viking ships, they could sail closer to the wind than was once thought. This vessel was obviously blown off course but the hazards of winter sailing were not just storms. At least as serious would have been prolonged cloud, which prevented the taking of bearings at sea.

Paul's presence on board dominates the mood. He appears utterly convinced that he has a destiny to fulfil and that nothing is going to prevent him from reaching his destination. As in the prison at Philippi it is his trustworthiness which is accepted and prevents the execution of all the prisoners.

221

Malta provided a winter refuge and became the setting for one of the earliest Christian churches. When Paul finally reached Puteoli it was to find that there was already a Christian church there. The final stage of the journey would have been completed on foot entering Rome by the Appian Way.

IDEAS FOR EXPLORING FURTHER

The Roman World Find out more about the power of the Roman Emperor, Roman life and trade. How did the Roman masters of the Jews live at home? What would Paul have seen as he entered Rome? Wheat, oil, wine, precious stones, and cloth would have crossed the sea. In what kind of ship? From where to where, by what routes and by which compass bearings? In what ways would the goods have been sold? (Cf. NC *Economic and Industrial Understanding*.) Where exactly is Malta? What routes would people have taken to travel from Malta to Puteoli and Rome? Map work can be incorporated into a board game using co-ordinates. (NC *Geography*: AT 1 – geographical skills.) Talk about Roman ships and seafarers as part of a project on that subject. (NC *History*: SSU on ships and seafarers, CSU 1 – invaders and settlers.) See also Story 29.

Talk about how we gain evidence of the past through writings, archaeology, coins, oral tradition, etc. Discuss how the Gospels were written down some years after Jesus' death by people who had either been an eyewitness or heard the story from eyewitnesses. Talk about how Jesus' death is mentioned by the Roman historian Publius Cornelius Tacitus (55–120) in his *Annals*, covering most of the period 14–68, and how early Christians are discussed in letters written by the Roman author and administrator Gaius Plinius Caecilius Secundus (*c. 62–c.* 114), known as Pliny the Younger, to the Emperor Trajan (53–117). See Appendix 2. Children could also discuss the Gospels as historical evidence. Look at stories which are found in more than one Gospel and compare the different versions. What about the letters in the New Testament? (NC *History*: CSU 1, AT 3 – use of historical sources.)

Metaphor/Picture Language Compare images of a ship sailing on stormy seas, the storm getting worse, final shipwreck and landing safely on the shore to how life can be for everyone at times: problems arise, things seem to get worse so we take frenetic action, disaster occurs, but somehow we survive. Perhaps write a story together as a class about the events leading up to and including a road accident, being late for school, losing something or forgetting to do something. Perhaps make a collage of the story of Paul's shipwreck and superimpose upon it the class story. Children can also work at this in pairs and small groups, of course. Talk about how stories can convey several layers of deeper meanings. See the Introduction, Stories 16, 21, 24, OT Stories 8, 9, 35, 41, 45.

50

A Runaway Slave

Paul's Letter to Philemon

Paul was busy. At last he was in Rome. He was still a prisoner but because he had not run away when he had had the chance, he was trusted. He lived in a house. A Roman soldier was stationed there too. But Paul could have as many visitors as he liked.

He was busy writing letters. He wanted to write to many of the churches which he had helped to start. Travellers from all over the world came to Rome. Sometimes they took the letters back with them.

But who could take this letter to the church at Colossae? Nobody seemed to be going there. Then he remembered. Of course, there was 'Useful'.

Paul smiled as he thought about it. It was a funny name even for a slave. In this case it was even funnier. Useful had been completely useless because he had run away. He had come to Rome. Then he had become a Christian. That was how he had come to meet Paul. When Useful came to see him again Paul said, 'I have a job for you. Would you do something for me?'

'Of course,' Useful replied. 'You know I would do anything for you.'

'Will you take this letter and carry it to Colossae where you used to live?'

Useful's face fell. 'Anything else,' he said, 'but I can't do that. Everyone in Colossae would recognize me, especially in the church. My old master Philemon is one of the members. I

223

am his runaway slave. He could have me beaten or put to death. If he didn't kill me he'd be bound to make me a slave again.'

'But you are a Christian now,' said Paul. 'Jesus told us to love one another. If you are a Christian and Philemon is a Christian everything is different. Christians can't go round making slaves of one another and killing one another, can they?'

Useful thought. When Paul put it like that it sounded good. But did Philemon think like that? Useful still wasn't very happy with the idea of seeing him again. In fact he felt miserable about it. 'That's all very well,' he said, 'but there is a lot to learn about being a Christian. They don't all do what they should do.'

Paul could see he was very unhappy. 'Come and see me again tomorrow,' he said.

When Useful had gone Paul sat down, took out another sheet of paper and started to write one more letter. It was a very short letter, not much more than a note. He was writing not to a church but just to Philemon himself.

'Dear Philemon,' he wrote, 'Your old slave Useful is carrying a message to your church for me. I know he has been pretty useless to you but he has been very useful to me while I have been a prisoner. I can't force you to do so, but I should like you to treat him like a brother and not as a slave. Please treat him as you would treat me. And have a room ready for me. I might come and visit you one day myself if I am set free.'

Next day when Useful came back, Paul showed him the letter. Useful was still frightened. It was a big test, but he agreed to go to see Philemon in Colossae.

He never saw Paul again. Paul died in Rome and never visited Philemon. But Philemon kept the little letter. It was very precious to him to have a letter all of his own from Paul himself.

What happened to Useful? Nobody really knows. But if Philemon kept the letter it seems certain he did as Paul asked and made Useful free again.

The letter to Philemon still exists. It is part of the New Testament. Paul died. The other apostles died. But the Church went on living. The story of Jesus was spreading everywhere. It had started to change the world.

NOTES

ABOUT THE STORY

The letters of Paul make up a substantial part of the Christian Scriptures. However, in the main they do not lend themselves to story form.

The brief letter to Philemon, the shortest book in the Bible, is something of an exception and it gives us a rare insight into Paul as a person. It accompanies the longer letter known as Colossians and is little more than a note about the bearer. In this case, however, the bearer is a runaway slave who has become a Christian but had escaped from Philemon, to whom the letter to the church at Colossae is to be delivered.

It would be a mistake to read into this letter a whole Christian theological view of slavery, which was an integral part of life throughout the Roman Empire and elsewhere. Nevertheless, Paul's assumption is that being a Christian does make a difference. Whether Onesimus (Useful) was as convinced we can never know. It was to be many centuries before Christian campaigns against slavery in general terms really got under way. In Britain the great anti-slave campaign of the early nineteenth century was led by the evangelical William Wilberforce. At the same time it has to be recalled that one of the first ships to ply the West African slave trade on the triangular route out of Bristol was the good ship *Jesus*!

Tradition has it that Paul finally met a martyr's death somewhere around the year 65. In that case he suffered under the persecution of Christians by Nero, who himself died in 68. Luke remained with Paul until the end then appears to have left Rome and produced his Gospel a few years later. By that time, despite persecutions the Church was established in hundreds of places. Now it exists in many more, in every village, town and city throughout Europe and still growing rapidly in other parts of the world, particularly in Africa.

IDEAS FOR EXPLORING FURTHER

Achievement Despite Hardship   Paul kept his courage high and achieved a great deal even though he was a prisoner. Ask the children to imagine they are hostages. In groups, ask them to decide how they would keep themselves cheerful. What would they do, think about, try to remember first thing in the morning, and throughout each day to keep their morale high? The teacher can designate what few items the prisoners have access to (e.g. small stones on the floor, paper and pencil).

Emphasize the difficulty of fending off boredom, of feeling sorry for oneself, of losing hope. Incorporate these ideas into a story about how the children were taken hostage and what happened to them; or use the ideas to compile diary extracts or to write poems. (Cf. NC *English*: AT 3 – writing.)

Read extracts from *Pilgrim's Progress*, the first part of which was written by John Bunyan (1678) while he was imprisoned in Bedford jail for preaching without a licence. (The second part was written in 1685.) For many years the book was (and, for some, still is) a most influential work. (Cf. NC *History*: CSU 2 – Tudor and Stuart times.) Find out about Douglas Bader, the flying ace who had both legs amputated. Older children may be interested by extracts from *The Diary of Anne Frank*, written while she was in hiding from the Nazis, or by the exploits of the men held in Colditz Castle during the 1940s, as described by Commander Reid in his book *Colditz*. (NC *History*: CSU 4 – Second World War.) See also Story 24.

Bravery How brave did Useful have to be to return to his old master? Discuss his hopes and fears and talk about the matter from the master's point of view. Having 'prepared' the part, the teacher could assume the role of the master (or the master's wife if preferred). Ask the children to imagine that Useful has just had an interview with the master/mistress of the house and has been sent to the kitchen for food. The pupils, acting as other members of the household, have met the master/mistress in the courtyard and ask about past events concerning Useful, what plans s/he had first had upon the return of the runaway slave and what s/he had finally done in light of receiving Paul's letter. See also Stories 40, 41, 43, 45, 48.

Slavery Find out more about slavery at different periods of time (e.g. read *The Future-Telling Lady*, by James Berry, which includes a story about the slave trade). (Cf. NC *History*: CSU 1 – invaders and settlers (Romans), CSU 2 – Tudor and Stuart times, the beginning of the slave trade in the sixteenth century, CSU 3 – Victorian Britain, the contribution of slave labour and exploitation of people as cheap labour in other countries and at home to the wealth of Britain, the American Civil War (1861–1865), the abolition of slavery, CSU 4 – Britain since 1930, the contribution of people from many countries who helped to get Britain back on her feet after the Second World War, often working for low wages, CSU 5 – exploration and encounters 1450–1550, Cortes making slaves of the native indians in Mexico, CSU 6 – Ancient Greece.) Consider also current exploitation of cheap labour. Look at how many toys and clothes are made in Taiwan, Hong Kong, Korea. (Cf. NC *Economic and Industrial Understanding; Citizenship*.) See *Staying Power: The History of Black People in Britain*, by P. Fryer.

Seeing Things in a New Way See notes on Story 34.

Prisons See notes on Stories 21, 33, 46.

226

Appendix 1: Useful Resources

Anno, M.   *The King's Flower*, Macmillan.
Ashley, B.   *Boat Girl*, Julia MacRae.
Batchelor, M. & Brown, K.   *Buddhism and Ecology*, Cassell. (T)
Belloc, H.   'Mathilda', in *Cautionary Verses*, Cape.
Berry, J.   *The Future-Telling Lady* (includes a story about the slave trade), Hamish Hamilton.
Breuilly, E. & Palmer, M.   *Christianity and Ecology*, Cassell. (T)
Bunyan, J.   *Pilgrim's Progress*, Penguin.
Clarke, B.   *Tales of Courage: Fighting for Their Faith*, Cherrytree Press.
Cooney, B.   *The Little Juggler*, Longman.
Cornell, J.   *Sharing Nature with Children* and *Sharing the Joy of Nature*, Exley. (T)
Crane, W.   *Beauty and the Beast and Other Tales*, Thames & Hudson.
Do It Justice!: Ideas for Introducing Education in Human Rights, Development Education Centre, Birmingham. (T)
Edwards, P.   *Equiano's Travels*, African Writers Series, Heinemann. (T)
Emmerich, E. & Hull, R.   *My Childhood in Nazi Germany*, Wayland.
Faith in Action series, RMEP.
File, N. & Powers, C.   *Black Settlers in Britain 1555–1958*, Heinemann. (T)
Fine, A.   *A Pack of Liars*, Hamish Hamilton.
Frank, A.   *The Diary of Anne Frank*, Puffin.
Fryer, P.   *Staying Power: The History of Black People in Britain*, Pluto Press. (T)
Fynn   *Mr God This Is Anna*, Collins.
Gallico, P.   *The Small Miracle*, Michael Joseph.
Geras, A.   *My Grandmother's Stories*, Letterbox Library.
Gifts and Giftbringers, CEM. (T)
Gilbert, J.   *Festivals*, Oxford University Press.
Gillham, B.   *My Mum's a Window Cleaner*, Methuen.
Graeme, K.   *The Wind in the Willows*, Armada.
Greenfield, E.   *Grandpa's Face*, Letterbox Library.
Grunsell, A.   *Bullying*, Franklin Watts. (T)
Hastings, S.   *Sir Gawain and the Loathly Lady*, Walker.
Havill, J.   *Jamaica Tag-Along*, Letterbox Library.
Hearn, E.   *Franny and the Music Girl* (wheelchair dancing), Letterbox Library.
Hodges, M.   *St George and the Dragon*, Little, Brown.
Hoffman, M. & Burroughes, J.   *My Grandma Has Black Hair*, Letterbox Library.
Hudson, W. & Wilson-Wesley, V.   *Afro-Bets Book of Black Heroes* (includes women), Letterbox Library.
Hughes, P.   *Gender Issues in the Primary Classroom*, Scholastic. (T)
Humphrey, M.   *The River That Gave Gifts*, Letterbox Library.
Igus, T.   *Great Women in the Struggle* (about black women's achievements), Letterbox Library. (T)
Jackson, R. & Starkings, D. (eds)   *The Junior RE Handbook*, Stanley Thornes. (T)
Johnson, P.   *The Boy Toy*, Letterbox Library.
Journeys, CEM. (T)
Judaism through the Eyes of Jewish Children (video), Chansitor.
Keats, E.   *The Little Drummer Boy*, Bodley Head.

Keller, H. *The Best Present*, Julia MacRae.
Khalid, F. & O'Brien, J. *Islam and Ecology*, Cassell. (T)
Khattab, H. *Stories from the Muslim World*, Macdonald/Simon & Schuster.
Kumar, A. *The Heartstone Odyssey*, Allied Mouse, Longden Court, Spring Gardens, Buxton, Derbyshire SK17 6BZ.
Lawrie, R. *Katy's Kit Car*, Letterbox Library.
Layton, G. *A Northern Childhood: The Balaclava Story and Other Stories*, Longman.
Lively, P. *Boy Without a Name*, Heinemann.
Living Festivals series, RMEP.
Masheder, M. *Let's Play Together*, Letterbox Library.
Me and My Communities, CEM. (T)
Miller, B. & Miller, T. *That's Not Fair! A Resource for Exploring Moral Issues in Primary and Middle Schools*, RMEP. (T)
Munsch, R. *Love You Forever*, Letterbox Library.
Norris, O. *Legends of Journeys*, Cambridge University Press.
Ormerod, J. *The Frog Prince*, Walker.
Orr, K. *My Grandpa and the Sea*, Letterbox Library.
Paola, T. de *The Clown of God*, Methuen.
Paola, T. de *Oliver Button is a Sissy*, Letterbox Library.
Parker, S. *The History of Medicine*, Belitha Press.
Paton-Walsh, J. *Grace*, Viking.
Pavlac, L. *Jewish Tales*, Beehive.
Pirotta, S. & Cooper H. *Solomon's Secret*, Letterbox Library.
Places of Worship, CEM. (T)
Prime, R. *Hinduism and Ecology*, Cassell. (T)
Project Pack on the UN Convention on the Rights of the Child for 8–13 Year Olds, Save the Children Fund. (T)
Rankin, J. *et al.* *Religious Education Topics for the Primary School*, Longman. (T)
Refugees Pack for Primary Schools, Save the Children Fund. (T)
Reid, P. *The Colditz Story*, Hodder & Stoughton.
Riordan, J. *Women in the Moon – Tales of Forgotten Heroines*, Letterbox Library.
Roots of Racism, Commission for Racial Equality. (T)
Rose, A. (ed.) *Judaism and Ecology*, Cassell. (T)
Ross, C. & Ryan, A. *Can I Stay In Today Miss?*, Letterbox Library.
Rowlands, A. *Fergus Travels South*, Hillside Publishing.
Schoop, J. *Boys Don't Knit*, Women's Press, available from Letterbox Library.
Smith, P. & Thompson, D. *Practical Approaches to Bullying*, David Fulton. (T)
Southgate, V. *The Enormous Turnip*, Ladybird.
Steig, W. *Brave Irene*, Gollancz.
Tatum, D. & Lane, D. *Bullying in Schools*, Trentham Books. (T)
When Christians Meet, CEM. (T)
White, E. *Charlotte's Web*, Puffin.
Wilde, O. *The Star Child*, Evans. Out of print: try libraries.
Wilhelm, H. *Tyrone, the Dirty, Rotten Cheat*, Hippo Books.
Wood, A. *Faith Stories for Today*, BBC/Longman.
Working Now: Photographs and Activities for Exploring Gender Roles in the Primary Classroom, Development Education Centre, Birmingham. (T)

Notes and Addresses

Books followed by (T) are publications which are intended primarily for teachers.

Letterbox Library, 8 Bradbury Street, London N16 8JN, specializes in non-racist, non-sexist and anti-stereotype books. Send for the catalogue.

Videos in the Through the Eyes of Children series, introducing the major world faiths, are available from Chansitor Publications Ltd, St Mary's Works, St Mary's Plain, Norwich NR3 3BH.

CEM (Christian Education Movement), Royal Buildings, Victoria Street, Derby DE1 1GW, publishes a range of poster packs and booklets introducing the major world faiths in addition to the titles listed above.

Commission for Racial Equality, Institute of Race Relations, 247/9 Pentonville Road, London N1 9WG.

Cooperative Education Network, CRS, Friary House, 15 Colston Street, Bristol BS1 5AP.

Development Education Centre, Gillett Centre, Bristol Road, Selly Oak, Birmingham B29 6LE.

Jewish Education Bureau, 8 Westcombe Avenue, Leeds LS8 2BS.

Save the Children Fund, Mary Datchelor House, 17 Grove Lane, London SE5 8RD.

Westhill College RE Centre (Midlands), Weoley Park Road, Selly Oak, Birmingham B29 6LL.

World Wide Fund for Nature, Panda House, Weyside Park, Godalming, Surrey GU7 1XR.

Appendix 2: Extracts from Roman Writings

Publius Cornelius Tacitus (55–120) wrote *Annals* covering most of the period 14–68. In Book XV: 44, Tacitus describes how a great fire occurred in Rome during the reign of the Emperor Nero (37–68). Rumours spread that the fire had been deliberately started on the orders of a Roman official. This was embarrassing for the government, and Tacitus has this to say:

> Consequently ... Nero fastened the guilt and inflicted the most exquisite tortures on a class hated for their abominations, called Christians by the populace. Christus, from whom the name had its origin, suffered the extreme penalty during the reign of Tiberius at the hands of one of our procurators, Pontius Pilatus, and a most mischievous superstition, thus checked for the moment, again broke out, not only in Judea, the first source of the evil, but even in Rome where all things hideous and shameful from every part of the world find their centre and become popular. (From *An Introduction to Tacitus*, by Herbert Benario)

Gaius Plinius Caecilius Secundus, Pliny the Younger (*c*. 62–*c*. 114) was a Roman author and administrator. Many of his letters have survived. Among these are some of his correspondence with the Emperor Trajan (who ruled from 98 to 117), written while Pliny was governor of the Roman province of Bithynia Pontus (North-West Asia Minor, the greater part of modern Turkey), in which he discusses what should be done with the people who called themselves Christians, whom he regarded as instigators of social unrest.

The following extracts from Book X: Letters 96 and 97 give some impression of the treatment Christians could expect in Rome at this period. The letters were written not later than the year 112.

Letter 96: Pliny to Emperor Trajan
It is my custom, sir, to bring before you everything about which I am in doubt. For who can better guide my uncertainty or inform my ignorance? I have never been present at trials of Christians; for that reason, I do not know what the charge usually is and to what extent it is usually punished. I have been in no little uncertainty about whether any distinction should be made between different ages or whether, however young they be, they should be treated no differently from the more mature ones; whether pardon should be granted for repentance or whether it is of no help to the man who has been a Christian at all to have given it up; whether it is the name itself, if it is free from crimes, or the crimes associated with the name which are being punished. Meanwhile, in the case of those who were prosecuted before me on the charge of being Christians, I

followed this procedure. I asked the people themselves whether they were Christians. Those who admitted that they were I asked a second and a third time, warning them of the punishment; those who persisted I ordered to be executed. For I was in no doubt that, whatever it might be that they were admitting to, their stubbornness and unyielding obstinacy certainly ought to be punished. There were others of similar madness whom I have listed as due to be sent on to the city because they were Roman citizens.

Subsequently, through the very course of dealing with the matter, as usually happens, the charge spread widely and more forms of it turned up. An anonymous pamphlet containing the names of many persons was posted up. Those that denied that they were or had been Christians, after they had called upon the gods when I dictated the formula, and after they had made offerings of incense and wine to your statue which I had ordered to be brought in along with the cult-images of the gods for this purpose, and had in addition cursed Christ, none of which acts, it is said, those who are truly Christians can be compelled to perform, I decided should be discharged. Others, named by an informer, said that they were Christians and then denied it; they said that they had in fact been Christians but had given it up, some three years before, some more years earlier than that, and a few even twenty years ago. All these also both paid homage to your statue and to the cult-images of the gods and cursed Christ. Moreover, they maintained that this had been the sum of their guilt or error, that they had been in the habit of gathering together before dawn on a fixed day, and of singing antiphonally a hymn to Christ as if to a god, and of binding themselves by oath, not to some wickedness, but not to commit acts of theft or robbery or adultery, not to break faith, not to refuse to return money placed in their keeping when called upon to do so. When these ceremonies had been completed, they said it had been their custom to disperse and to meet again to take food, but food that was ordinary and harmless; they said that they had given up doing even this after my edict, in which, in accordance with your instructions, I had banned secret societies. (From *Pliny: Correspondence with Trajan from Bithynia*, by Wynne Williams)

Letter 97: Emperor Trajan to Pliny
You followed the procedure which you ought to have followed, my dear Secundus, in examining the cases of those who were being prosecuted before you as Christians. For no rule with a universal application, such as would have, as it were, a fixed form, can be laid down. They should not be sought out; if they are prosecuted and proved to be guilty, they should be punished, provided, however, that the man who denies that he is a Christian and makes this evident by his action, that is by offering prayers to our gods, shall obtain pardon for his repentance, however suspect he may be with regard to the past. However, pamphlets posted up without an author's name ought to have no place in any criminal charge. For they both set the worst precedent and are not in keeping with the spirit of our age. (From *Pliny: Correspondence with Trajan from Bithynia*, by Wynne Williams)

INDEX OF THEMES AND ISSUES

We have listed the main themes and issues encountered in the stories and indicated the pages where these stories may be found. Page numbers in **bold** type show where ideas for exploring these themes and issues are suggested in the Notes. Numbers preceded by 'OT' refer to pages in the companion volume of Old Testament stories.

232

233

234